I0752920

(RE)WRITING WITHOUT BORDERS

Contemporary Intermedial Perspectives on Literature and the Visual Arts

---

Edited by
Brigitte Le Juez,
Nina Shiel,
and Mark Wallace

(RE)WRITING WITHOUT BORDERS

Contemporary Intermedial Perspectives on Literature and the Visual Arts

---

Edited by
Brigitte Le Juez,
Nina Shiel,
and Mark Wallace

COMMON GROUND RESEARCH NETWORKS 2018

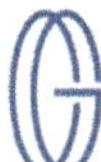

First published in 2018
as part of the New Directions in the Humanities Book Imprint
doi: 10.18848/978-1-61229-993-8/CGP (Full Book)

Common Ground Research Networks
2001 South First Street, Suite 202
University of Illinois Research Park
Champaign, IL
61820

Library of Congress Cataloging-in-Publication Data

Names: Le Juez, Brigitte, 1959- editor. | Shiel, Nina, 1978- editor. | Wallace, Mark, 1983- editor.
Title: (Re)writing without borders : contemporary intermedial perspectives on literature and the visual arts / edited by Brigitte Le Juez, Nina Shiel, and Mark Wallace.
Description: Champaign, IL : Common Ground Research Networks, 2018. | Includes bibliographical references and index.
Identifiers: LCCN 2018022375| ISBN 9781612299938 (pdf) | ISBN 9781612299914 (hardback : alk. paper) | ISBN 9781612299921 (paperback : alk. paper)
Subjects: LCSH: Art and literature. | Motion pictures and literature.
Classification: LCC PN53 .R48 2018 | DDC 700.1/04--dc23
LC record available at https://lccn.loc.gov/2018022375

Cover Photo Credit: Mónica O'Doherty López-Varela
Logo for CompLit InterArt book series Credit: Mónica O'Doherty López-Varela

Table of Contents

Acknowledgements

The editors would like to express their gratitude to the following colleagues for their assistance in the process of preparing this publication: Prof Marina Grishakova (University of Tartu, Estonia), Prof Asuncion Lopez-Varela Azcarate (Complutense University of Madrid, Spain), Dr Bevin Doyle (Dublin City University, Ireland), as well as Phillip Kisubika and Caitlyn D'Aunno (Common Ground Research Networks).

We also wish to thank all those who took part in the European Network for Comparative Literary Studies / Réseau Européen d'Études Littéraires Comparées' 6th Biennial Congress on the theme of "Longing and Belonging", which took place in Dublin and Galway (Ireland) in August 2015. The essays selected for this volume stem from presentations and discussions that took place on that occasion.

Introduction

Brigitte Le Juez, Nina Shiel and Mark Wallace

Cultures produce and exchange meanings. Within them, the same questions are asked about the nature of individual and communal lives. Views are articulated in multifarious ways, explicit as well as implicit, always opened to interpretation and challenge. Among the many possible vehicles for personal, national or global expressions and conversations around cultural matters, be they philosophical, social, political or historical, the arts have always held a pivotal position. Literature and art, in particular, regardless of their sometimes-perceived rivalry, have played complementary roles in the representation—and therefore in our perception—of the world.

(Re)Writing Without Borders: Contemporary Intermedial Perspectives on Literature and the Visual Arts gathers twelve essays all dealing with different aspects pertaining to the relationship between word and image. The breadth of expertise (whether in film studies, adaptation studies, art studies, media studies or comparative literary studies) from an international array of authors (Brazil, Greece, Ireland, Italy, Poland, Slovenia) offers a collective examination of diverse critical approaches that explore how different topics (adaptation and ideology, politics and national cinemas, modernization of traditional genres such as the western, relations between art and digital graphics, ekphrastic narratives, etc.) are expressed through different types of texts and media.

Writing, be it for fiction or the screen, is studied here from different perspectives, including that of transposition. Texts are transformed temporally and culturally, and their references evolve with their rewriting. This is most evidently true when dealing with ancient myths, which can be modernized and subverted in different ways. However, contemporary texts can also be transgressed through intermedial means, thus taking new dimensions.

Cross-artistic encounters are analyzed in this volume with a view to better capture the most up-to-date interaction between literature and the visual arts. This new interface thus adds to existing studies of the collaboration between the written and the visual, raising important questions, such as: what kind of narratives are born of such mergers, or how do they represent and articulate today's reality?

This volume examines different types of discourse, i.e. groups of statements that structure the way(s) a thing is thought and the way action takes place based on that thinking. Thus, adaptation can reveal how a culture moves from tradition toward modernity, for instance. Other examples, presenting innovative topics, deal with the mixture of narrative and non-narrative techniques such as ekphrasis, art catalogue, auto-fiction and historiography.

Writing and rewriting without borders also means examining the transnational, cross-cultural backgrounds of transposition-related source and target texts, in particular the cultural, political and artistic implications contained in the process of appropriation. Such questions bring us to consider reader- and audience-response, especially with new phenomena such as emerging forms of literature on social media.

In order to allow the conceptual model at the heart of this selection of perspectives to develop according to a logical thread, the volume is divided into two equal parts. The first, Screen Adaptation and Comparative Ideology, illustrates Julie Sanders' premise that the adaptive course is "engaged with process, ideology and methodology" and that its role is, contrary to what is regularly argued through notions of fidelity to source texts, remote from "polarized value judgements".[1] Each new text freshly conceived with another in mind is a form of conversation aiming to address original questions that either have remained unanswered or are in need of a contemporary answer. The second, Intermediality and Innovation, shows that new modes of intertextuality, exemplifying the interconnectedness of modern media of communication, also verify the fact, as Tom McCarthy once said, that "writing technologies themselves are imbued with terrifying and sacred dimensions, and become the subject, not just the medium, of the story," adding that they reveal creators as they "always in fact were: networked, distributed, laced with code".[2] The two parts are thus complementary in their demonstration of the continued, inescapable, increasing relation between literature and the visual arts.

SCREEN ADAPTATION AND COMPARATIVE IDEOLOGY

Adaptation study is a growing field, and it is increasingly recognized that adaptations have their own particular features and attractions:

> [T]he existence of adaptations is vital. They cross the boundaries; challenge or reassert our notions of medium specificity and art, interpretation, and evaluation; and refresh our intellectual appetites[.][3]

Adaptations cross the boundaries of media, and challenge scholars to cross disciplinary boundaries and to consider narrative works comparatively rather than in isolation. The activity of adaptation is not confined to any particular time or space. In the Middle Ages, as André Bazin noted, there were only a few themes, and they were

---

[1] Julie Sanders, *Adaptation and Appropriation*, The New Critical Idiom series, London and New York: Routledge, 2016, 24.

[2] Tom McCarthy, "My desktop", *The Guardian*, 24/11/2017. https://www.theguardian.com/books/2011/nov/24/tom-mccarthy-desktop [accessed 27/11/2017].

[3] Sarah Cardwell, "Adaptation Studies Revisited", in *The Literature/Film Reader: Issues of Adaptation*, eds. James M. Welsh and Peter Lev, Lanham, MD: Scarecrow Press, 2007, 51-64 (61).

common to all arts.[4] As for the geographical spread of adaptation, it will be clear from the essays making up this section.

The section focuses particularly on the ideological consequences of adaptation. The constituent essays collectively illustrate the notion that it is through creatively rewriting the narratives of the past that we deal with the most pressing ideological problems of the present. For Stuart Hall, ideology comprises the following:

> [T]he mental frameworks—the languages, the concepts, categories, imagery of thought, and the systems of representation—which different classes and social groups deploy in order to make sense of, figure out and render intelligible the way society works.[5]

Such frameworks are found in their most developed and practically analyzable form in extended narratives, as in those found in literature and on screen. What the essays in this section show is that the use of narratives from the past to illustrate present concerns with the way society works is an authentically cross-cultural phenomenon. Adaptations studied by the authors in this section hail from the UK, Russia, the US and Brazil, and each demonstrates that the present is not understood simply on its own terms. Rather, its problems are worked through by juxtaposition with those of the past, and adaptation provides the canvas upon which ideological comparators work (consciously or unconsciously).

The opening essay in the section, Mark Wallace's "Adaptation, Transtemporality and Ideology: The BBC Series *Oliver Twist* (2007)", proposes that the temporal distance that often separates adaptations from their sources is, potentially, a particularly fruitful factor in the analysis of adaptations. The element of tension or struggle that exists between a source and its temporally distant (or transtemporal) adaptation is exemplified in the 2007 BBC series adaptation of Charles Dickens' *Oliver Twist*, a close comparative reading of which problematizes the assumptions underlying the source, while also detecting the ideological underpinning of the narrative changes wrought in the TV series.

Panayiota Mini's "Going Back to Gorki's Ideas: Donskoi's Film Adaptation of *Mother*" takes a 1906 novel by Gorki and a (hitherto little studied) 1955 film adaptation thereof and provides a detailed reading using an approach informed by historical circumstances. The film presages both technical developments in post-Stalinist cinema and the widescale ideological re-orientation associated with the Soviet Thaw, as the very notion of the subject undergoes a re-evaluation in terms of psychological depth and interpersonal relations. The comparison between the adaptation and the source text brings into relief the ideological climate of immediately post-Stalinist Russia, and its conditioning effect on the narrative is made apparent.

---

[4] André Bazin, "Adaptation, or the Cinema as Digest", in *Film Adaptation*, ed. James Naremore, New Brunswick, NJ: Rutgers University Press, 2000, 19-27 (23).

[5] Stuart Hall, "The Problem of Ideology: Marxism without Guarantees", in *Stuart Hall: Critical Dialogues in Cultural Studies*, eds. David Morley and Kuan-Hsing Chen, London and New York: Routledge, 2005, 24-45 (25-26).

The section then turns to Brazil for two essays mapping ideological variations in adapted narratives in that country. Carlinda Nuñez's "Orpheus in Brazilian Film: Disobedience as Theme and Theoretical Approach" details changing Brazilian responses to the Orpheus myth. Nuñez begins with Vinicius de Moraes' play *Orfeu da Conceição* (1955); and continues with two films adapted from the play: *Orfeu Negro* (dir. Marcel Camus, 1959), and *Orfeu* (dir. Carlos Diegues, 1999). Nuñez employs Gaston Bachelard's notion of creative disobedience (as well as Aby Warburg's concept of the image vehicle) to perform a close comparative reading of the two films, revealing that the first is an obedient adaptation and the second disobedient. Nuñez innovatively reads variations in the ideological framework of the two films as functions of a disobedient thematic.

Maria Cristina Cardoso Ribas contributes "Re-reading Literature in Contemporary Cinema: Intermediality in Machado de Assis' Story 'Father Against Mother' (1906) and Sergio Bianchi's film *How much is it worth or is it per kilo?* (2005)". Machado's oeuvre is a classic of Brazilian literature, though perhaps less known in Anglophone regions. Nevertheless, Ribas' reading illustrates the enduring and renewed relevance of Machado's work. In "Father Against Mother", Machado wrote of racism and poverty in Brazil in the late 19th century, referencing the country's (then very recent) history of slavery. Bianchi writes and directs his film, a loose adaptation of "Father Against Mother", in what the juxtaposition of the two stories reveals are surprisingly similar circumstances. Ribas elucidates how the narrative techniques of Bianchi's provocative film imply parallels between slavery and the conditions of Brazil's contemporary urban poor, with NGOs performing the narrative function Machado gave to slave owners.

Beata Waligorska-Olejniczak's "Quentin Tarantino's *Django Unchained* (2012) and the Afterlife of the Western" reads the eponymous work alongside its various antecedents in literature and film, teasing out *Django*'s complicated relationship to the genre of the Western. Waligorska-Olejniczak shows once again the importance of appropriating the narrative structures of past times to deal with difficult social problems of contemporary times. The western is used by *Django* director Quentin Tarantino as "a kind of historical costume to drape over difficult problems of the contemporary world". Waligorska-Olejniczak shows that humour, hyperbole and violence are among the tools Tarantino uses to discuss racism and socioeconomic inequalities, and that his dialogue on these issues builds on while also subverting that found in his generic precursors.

Colm Kenny's "Belonging and Moral Relations in *Justified*" also deals with the Western genre, using the US TV series *Justified* (2010-15) as the basis of a detailed case study. Kenny turns to the issue of embedded ethics in narrative: an ethic is seen as, once again, being specific to a time and place, and as being implicit in genres such as the Western. The difficulties an ethic can face in crossing a border, physical or generic, is demonstrated by Kenny's reading of the cowboy-hatted protagonist's estrangement in the contemporary setting of *Justified*, the juxtaposition of character and setting serving to raise important questions about justice that echo through the series.

INTERMEDIALITY AND INNOVATION

In the second section, we expand from adaptation towards a wider transpositional, interart experience, via perspectives on how text interacts with various forms of digital media, visual arts, and hybrid genres. In a sense, we never abandon the concept of adaptation. As we progress along this section's essays, starting with adapting Shakespeare's plays for digital artworks and finishing with a discussion of how new media feeds our need to nourish our past, we come to realize that each rewriting and re-imagination, each intertextual or interart influence bears the hallmarks of adaptation. On the one hand, a rewriting appropriates the original work —text, image, or something else—but, on the other hand, it owes its existence to the creative influence of the original. The elements adapted from the original and the new elements together create an innovative work which is free to address its contemporary audience at artistic, societal and political levels, while it is supported by the intertextual context of the original.

Essays in this section emphasize the dialogue between the works that come together in today's interart process. No longer is it assumed that a visual image is simply mute and might need to be given a voice through a pseudo-mystical prosopopoeia. When authors and literary scholars write about a piece of visual art, it is allowed to speak in its own terms, as particularly demonstrated by Narvika Bovcon and Aleš Vaupotič, and by Ana Lúcia Beck, who all travel deep into the creative process behind text and image. In the new media, the image is becoming an integral part of any textual experience, as Claudia Cao and Anna Notaro show in their respective essays, while Nina Shiel explores computer code as a form of writing that contains in itself the images it represents. Massimo Fusillo reminds us that while today's social media in particular mixes genres and creates uncategorizable hybrid texts, we need not look further than the 19th century to find examples of creative works involving techniques of catalogues, art criticism, literary criticism and autobiography—all familiar from today's Facebooks, Instagrams, and Buzzfeeds.

The intermediality present in the dialogue of the respective elements of the interart works discussed here has two consequences which arise from the essays of this section as distinct themes. The first of these is the strong presence of the element of memory, both in its positive and negative guises. To adapt or to rewrite means to recall the original work. A successful adaptation or rewriting stands on its own merits, but a fuller, more satisfactory audience experience requires recollection of the context of the original work and the understanding of how the adapted elements of the original address contemporary concerns. This, according to Cartmell and Whelehan, takes place via three broad categories of adaptation: transposition that relocates source texts and brings the text closer to the audience's personal frame of reference, commentary that assumes the reader-viewer's familiarity and awareness of the source text, and analogue, the stand-alone product that results from this process, so different is it from the original.[6]

---

[6] Deborah Cartmell and Imelda Whelehan, eds. *Adaptations: From Text to Screen, Screen to Text*, London: Routledge, 1999, 24.

On the level of the individual, each essay in this section explores the effects of memory on authors and artists. Similarly, in each essay, we see that memory operates as a powerful creative force. Bovcon and Vaupotič document how artworks are conceived and brought to being in the process of adaptation. In Cao's paper, multi-authored Twitter works fully rely on each author's memory and personal experience. Fusillo and Beck discuss how traumatic memories have spurred on creative process, while Shiel analyzes a poet's longing for kinship with a known figure in the past, and Notaro examines how nostalgia for times past presents itself in social media.

As already implied, the presence of memory is connected to the second theme of these essays: a question of authorship and how the evolving of the intermedial landscape has affected it. From Bovcon and Vaupotič' discussion of their own creations to Shiel's assessment of Eavan Boland's personal voice, Fusillo's analysis of Edmond de Goncourt's autobiographical elements and Beck's exploration of the presence Bourgeois' and Leonilson's personal memories in their artworks, many of the texts discussed in this section bear a strong personal element regarding their authors. At the opposite end of the spectrum, by outlining the effects of the shared nature of social media on rewritings of canonical and personally experienced narratives, Cao's and Notaro's essays reveal a shift away from traditional, strictly defined authorship. As we are increasingly writing without borders, we are led to question where our own borders as authors ought to be drawn.

In the first essay, "Transmedia Adaptation—a Dialogue of Genres and Communication Media", Narvika Bovcon and Aleš Vaupotič show examples of adaptation crossing media boundaries and emphasize the nature of adapted works as original works of art, employing the Bakhtinian idea of dialogism as a ubiquitous intertextuality. They begin by discussing the work of D.W. Griffith using Dickens' novelistic technique in the earliest examples of modern film montage. This example of medium-specific different works and different media coming together in a new cultural medium precedes the artistic inquiry of the second part of the essay, which presents a series of new media art works by the authors which relate to Shakespeare's "King Richard the Third" and the theme of the forest of Arden. The artistic research of the authors shows how artists conceptualize the transition of content from original material to adaptations.

In the second essay, "The Tweetbook as a New Frontier of Literary Retellings", Claudia Cao analyzes Twitter adaptations of literary classics. Such adaptations act as examples of the way the participatory nature of digital media allows its audiences to function as consumers and produces at the same time. Cao's comparison of the relationship of contemporary readership with canonical texts to examples of fandom of popular works remind us that the difference between "high culture" literary rewritings and "low culture" fan fiction is not as big as we may think. Cao discusses the Italian social-reading community TwLetteratura and multi-author rewritings of classics using hashtags, images, parody, pastiches and other techniques to create contemporary reinterpretations.

In the third essay, "Poetry and Code as 'Sister Arts' in Eavan Boland's 'Code'" (2001), Nina Shiel considers Eavan Boland's parallelizing of the arts of writing poetry and the art of writing computer code in a close reading of the poem. She compares Boland's treatment of poetry and code to the Early Modern theory of the Sister Arts of poetry and painting, with aspirational similarities between the art forms as well as a degree of tension resulting from their differences. This essay puts forward the proposition that code occupies a peculiar place between writing and a non-writing art form.

In the fourth essay, "The House as Work of Art: Edmond de Goncourt between Catalogue, Historiography and Autobiography", Massimo Fusillo examines Edmond de Goncourt's *La Maison d'un artiste* in the context of the proposed tension between narration and description in the history and theory of literature. This essay further contextualizes *La Maison,* a hybrid catalogue-like text with elements of ekphrasis, autobiography, historiography and essay, in relation to the proliferation of details found in Gustave Flaubert's *Madame Bovary* and, even more so, in his encyclopedic text *Bouvard et Pécuchet.* Fusillo shows that, through its detailed descriptions of the objects of the house de Goncourt and his brother inhabited, the author uses the text to work out his trauma of his brother's illness and death.

We follow the theme of using art related to significant poetic spaces and objects in order to address a past trauma in the fifth essay, Ana Lúcia Beck's "'*Voilà mon cœur*: it's been to hell and back!' Longing and Belonging in José Leonilson and Louise Bourgeois". Using Gaston Bachelard's concepts of poetics of significant space, Beck develops the discussion on the poetic images of longing and belonging in the textile works of the two visual artists in close comparison with W.B. Yeats' poetic images of longing in his poem "Towards the break of day".

Finally, in the sixth essay, Anna Notaro, in "Total Recall: Longing in the (Post)Digital Age" brings our attention back to digital media by discussing nostalgia in the post-digital world and emerging artistic works that combine multimedia and live performance. This essay closes this section, and this volume, by pointing out that even as new technology blurs borders between readers and authors, the personal and the public and the virtual and the real, we are developing a nostalgia for physical objects that held a significance in the past but are now verging on the border of oblivion, such as vinyl records, print books and even typewriters. Notaro returns to the concept of fetishism, discussed by Fusillo, by observing that such physical objects are imbued with nostalgia for the emotional and sensual.

The past century has seen an increase in the use and in the variety of uses of words in conjunction with visual images. This combination of verbal and visual elements is now evident in a broad range of artistic approaches, as the essays gathered here demonstrate. The forms in which language is presented in visual formats are as numerous (and developing) as the types of artistic genres exploring them. Words and images are thus inseparable due to the fact that they both serve to increase each other's potential for meaning. Whether one strengthens or challenges the other, the combination creates an eloquent and captivating new significance. The various techniques used in analyzing narrative experimentalism displayed here confirm that, whether the visual text is the result of a transposition or not, when literature and the arts meet within any type of creative process, they seek differentiation, questioning former writing norms, in order to present the reader-viewer with perpetually renovated stories.

Part I: Screen Adaptation and Comparative Ideology

CHAPTER 1

Adaptation, Transtemporality, and Ideology: The BBC Series *Oliver Twist* (2007)

Mark Wallace

In *A Theory of Adaptation*, Linda Hutcheon notes that every telling of a story occurs in a "particular time and space in a society", and that this placing has a conditioning effect on the telling.[1] With specific reference to adaptations, Hutcheon calls those retellings which are produced in a place distinct from that in which the story was originally told, transcultural adaptations. Such adaptations, she avers, almost always feature "an accompanying shift in political valence".[2] Hutcheon also acknowledges that a distance in time between source and adaptation can be a significant factor in conditioning the latter. For such an adaptation, she offers no name, but this essay will propose the adjective *transtemporal*. Modifying Hutcheon somewhat, it is suggested that we might divide the transcultural into the transtemporal (source distant in time from production of adaptation) and transspatial (source distant in space from production of adaptation)—though the suggestion is that both terms can be profitably introduced into the field, only the former will be dealt with here. That transtemporal adaptations have a particular interest of their own and invite and reward a particular type of analysis will be the central contention of this essay, and a (necessarily somewhat provisional) approach to elucidating such an analysis through theory and case study will be the central objective. The study texts will be Charles Dickens' *Oliver Twist* (1837-38) and the 2007 BBC television series *Oliver Twist*, directed by Coky Giedroyc and scripted by Sarah Phelps, works produced at a distance of one hundred and seventy years apart. H.G. Wells' novel *The War of the Worlds* (1898) and its 1953 Hollywood film adaptation will also be (more briefly) considered for the light they shed on the ideological implications of adapting transtemporally.

Transtemporality is one of the concepts that can help us bolster Deborah Cartmell and Imelda Whelehan's claim that "studying adaptations produces something new that neither belongs to film nor literature":[3] transtemporality is a necessarily dialectical feature which belongs neither to the film nor the adaptation, but to the relationship

---

[1] Linda Hutcheon, *A Theory of Adaptation*, Abingdon: Routledge, 2013, 144.
[2] *Ibid.*, 145.
[3] Deborah Cartmell and Imelda Whelehan, *Screen Adaptation: Impure Cinema* Basingstoke, Hampshire: Palgrave Macmillan, 2010, 14.

that commonly exists between them. As such, it is a characteristic and perhaps essential element of adaptation study. It also offers a partial response to prevailing worries in adaptation study about throwing out the baby of comparative analysis with the (supposed) bathwater of fidelity.[4] The concept of transtemporality demands an element of comparative analysis, but not for the purpose of declaring that the adaptation is unfaithful or a "betrayal" of its source;[5] rather, transtemporal analysis foregrounds the inter-relation between each text and its particular context, finding in textual difference between source and adaptation a potential locus for extended reflection on the relation of narrative to relevant aspects of socio-political context.

By emphasizing this socio-political context, we acknowledge that transtemporal adaptations tend to bring into focus questions of ideology. This is certainly the conviction of Slavoj Žižek, for whom "The Sad Lesson of Remakes" is that analysis of recent retellings of older narratives reveals "a global ideological regression" amounting to "the destruction of (emancipatory) reason".[6] Žižek's comparative analysis of various retellings of Richard Matheson's *I Am Legend* (1954) plays a significant role in his efforts to map a precipitous decline in potentialities for radical political thought in Western culture. Although Žižek is not an explicit theorist of adaptation *per se*, his work with adaptations and retellings is of relevance to the field. A particularly noteworthy unspoken premise of Žižek's analysis of *I Am Legend* and other adaptations is that narrative is relatively independent of ideology. The same basic narrative can be used as a vehicle for contrasting ideological positions, without the need for any major formal narrative changes.

This position can be supported by empirical analysis of transtemporal adaptations. One such adaptation which illustrates Žižek's point in fairly stark terms is *The War of the Worlds* (1953, dir. Byron Haskin), based on H.G. Wells' 1898 novel of the same name. The character of the curate in Wells' work is foolish, selfish and cowardly, a decided liability in the fight against extra-terrestrial interlopers. Within the terms of the plot of the novel, the curate plays little part: he ultimately neither helps nor hinders the aliens in their quest. He is simply killed by them, as are many other unnamed and uncharacterized persons. The greater narrative focus on the curate as opposed to these other victims of the invasion fulfils not a plot function, but an ideological function: he represents the obsolescence of the priestly class and the death of religion. This is, of course, entirely consistent with Wells' own position.[7] The film

---

[4] One problem with the attack on fidelity in adaptation studies is that often the term is, implicitly or explicitly, defined very broadly; as Casie Hermansson puts it: "Any comparative work—the case-study approach most obviously—can be seen as fidelity criticism in essence, even when evaluative criteria may be entirely absent from the analysis." ("Flogging Fidelity: In Defense of the (Un)Dead Horse", *Adaptation*, 8:2, 2015, 148.) Rather than risk jettisoning this important element of adaptation study, this essay prefers Cartmell and Whelehan's position that the field of adaptation study is shaped by a multiplicity of discourses, some comparative, none of which need to be assigned precedence. (*Screen Adaptation*, 15)

[5] Such language, deemed to be characteristic of adaptation study, has been critiqued by, among others, Robert Stam in "Beyond Fidelity: The Dialogics of Adaptation", in *Film Adaptation*, ed. James Naremore, New Brunswick, NJ: Rutgers University Press, 2000, 54.

[6] Slavoj Žižek, *Living in the End Times*, London: Verso, 2010, 61.

[7] See, for example, the account of various religions in H.G. Wells, *The State of Homo Sapiens*, London: Secker and Warburg, 1939, 127-179.

adaptation retains the basic features of Wells' plot: an alien race begins to lay waste to the Earth, eventually halted by microbial infection. The setting is updated to 1950s America, and an entire ideological repositioning of the text takes place, manifest most of all in the figure of the curate, now given an individual name: Pastor Matthew. Pastor Matthew, like his original, dies at the hands of the aliens and has no substantial role in the working out of the plot. Yet, in his centrality in the community response to the invasion, his thoughtful and humane attitude towards the aliens, and his bravery in approaching them, his ideological function is opposed to Wells' curate: he represents the importance of the Church in community relations and morale, and its success in leavening the inhumanity of the scientific worldview. This characterological innovation and some other altered details mean that no substantial changes at the level of cardinal functions[8] are needed to perform an ideological inversion of Wells' text, demonstrating a considerable independence between plot and ideology.

Though not all adaptations go so far as to invert the ideology of the source in this manner, Thomas Leitch suggests that adaptations in general can be read as "illustrations of the incessant process of rewriting as critical reading".[9] For Leitch, adaptations can be used to encourage an active rather than passive literacy, because they themselves exemplify such an approach. This need not accord with a conscious intention on the behalf of the adapter: "source texts must be rewritten; we cannot help rewriting them."[10] Rewriting in Leitch's sense is to be contrasted with the notion of merely *copying* the text: pure copying is an impossibility, for alongside and intermingled with the replicated elements will be the traces of the text's otherness with regard to the adapter. Any text is somewhat other, so an attempt to reproduce or rewrite it will also record this encounter with otherness. There are several ways of attempting to map or account for the otherness of a text to its reader, but one method is by considering its transtemporality, its emergence from a past that is different from and indifferent to the time of reading, a past which it is not adequate to experience wholly from the vantage point of the present.

Relevant to this approach is Gillian Beer's conception of "arguing with the past". Beer promotes this concept on the grounds that reading in the light of "arguing with the past" protects against a "presentist mode of argument", wherein an "autocratic emphasis on the self and the present" dictates our responses to and judgements of texts.[11] Rather than presentist essentialism, Beer proposes the privileging of complexity and contestation, thus moving away from the provision of specific

---

[8] Cardinal functions are defined by Barthes as the "hinge-points" in a narrative, and as being "consequent to the subsequent development of the narrative". See Roland Barthes, "Introduction to the Structural Analysis of Narrative", *Image Music Text*, trans. Stephen Heath, London: Fontana, 1977, 93-94. The retention of the cardinal functions of a source's narrative equates to what have been described above as the "basic features" of the plot. Barthes' approach has been applied to adaptations in Brian McFarlane, *Novel to Film: An Introduction to the Theory of Adaptation,* Oxford: Clarendon Press, 1996.

[9] Thomas Leitch, *Film Adaptation and its Discontents: From Gone with the Wind to The Passion of the Christ*, Baltimore, MD: Johns Hopkins University Press, 2009, 16.

[10] *Ibid*., 16.

[11] Gillian Beer, *Arguing with the Past: Essays in Narrative from Woolf to Sidney*, London: Routledge, 1989, 1.

resolutions, considering the text, instead, as offering "questions we had not thought of".[12] Such a process can be seen at work in adaptation. Adaptations are suffused with questions its authors may not have thought of, and questions the author of its source may not have thought of, but questions which nonetheless arise in the complex dialectic that arises between source and adaptation, and are embodied in the latter. In engaging with a source work borne of a different situation and aimed at a different audience, some degree of contestation is inevitable, some textual moment in which is embodied the ideological impasse that exists between the source text and its adapting reader, wherein a challenge is presented to the reader's immersion in the text (and to the reader's ingrained presentism), one which can be met in various ways. Some specific challenges and arguments of this type will be analysed in this essay in relation to Charles Dickens' *Oliver Twist* and its adaptation.

The challenge posed by past literature is certainly to a considerable degree one of political valence. The manner in which this challenge is customarily met in adaptations has been criticized by Kamilla Elliott:

> Film adapters build on a hypercorrect historical material realism to usher in a host of anachronistic ideological "corrections" of novels. Quite inconsistently, while adaptations pursue a hyperfidelity to nineteenth-century material culture, they reject and correct Victorian psychology, ethics, and politics. When filmmakers set modern politically correct views against historically correct backdrops, the effect is to authorize these modern ideologies as historically authentic.[13]

Elliott evidently disapproves of the ideological corrections she finds in adaptations of Victorian texts, but it is also the case, as will be seen, that the otherness of Victorian writing makes the straightforward reproduction of Victorian ideology within a complex narrative text an impossibility, going, as it does, against the grain of pervasive contemporary ideologies. These ideologies necessarily speak through adaptations, just as the ideologies of the source continue to speak through the adaptation, perhaps despite the efforts of the adapter. Neither the cultural code dominant within the temporal context of the source nor the ideologies contemporary with the adaptation are ever fully silent, whatever the intentions of the adapter.

If not able to silence it, the adapting screenwriter may decide to challenge the ideology of a source text. It is instructive to consider the adaptation history of *Oliver Twist* in that regard. This is particularly appropriate choice of text because of the long-standing controversy that has surrounded the figure of Fagin, the Jewish "fence" (receiver of stolen goods). Fagin has been frequently considered anti-Semitic since Eliza Davis wrote a letter to the author to that effect in 1863, prompting Dickens to respond, "Fagin, in *Oliver Twist*, is a Jew, because it unfortunately was true of the time to which that story refers, that that class of criminal almost invariably was a

---

[12] *Ibid.*, 6.

[13] Quoted Hutcheon, *Adaptation*, 152.

Jew".[14] This became a particular issue at the time of the release of David Lean's *Oliver Twist* (1948), which, produced in the aftermath of the Holocaust, caused a riot in Berlin and led to the film's US release being held up for three years, before it was passed with substantial cuts to scenes involving Fagin.[15] More recent adaptations have implicitly taken this controversy into account so that "Fagin on screen has seldom subsequently been both very Jewish and very evil".[16] Ron Moody's Fagin in Carol Reed's musical *Oliver!* (1967) was a markedly more benign presence than Alec Guinness' in Lean's film, and perhaps the true hero of the story,[17] while George C. Scott's Fagin in Clive Donner's *Oliver Twist* (1982) has been described as a "sympathetic victim of circumstances".[18] Sometimes, as in the 1997 Disney film directed by Tony Bill, Fagin is neither Jewish nor evil, demonstrating the continuing visibility of the text's anti-Semitism. Conveniently, the text has several other characters (Sikes, Monks) on whom the structural and ideological burden of the villain can fall.

The development of Fagin is a particularly clear-cut case of narrative responding to history and to cultural context, and overriding the source content. In a less extreme form, however, this development is found throughout frequently adapted narratives such as *Oliver Twist*, wherein the otherness of past writing always creates some tensions with dominant tropes, conventions and ideologies of the present. With regard to *Oliver Twist*, this was at its most evident in the 2007 BBC adaptation, directed by Coky Giedroyc and with a screenplay by Sarah Phelps. The latter choice is particularly notable, as she had no background in classical adaptations, but was at the time a scriptwriter on popular UK soap *EastEnders*. Thus a product somewhat different from conventional classical adaptations was envisaged from the start. The series, comprising a 60-minute first episode followed by four 30-minute episodes, did provide a different *Oliver Twist*, "innovative rather than repetitive throughout";[19] that is, one that marks an ideological and characterological distance from its numerous precursors, as will be shown. One form this difference took was that of "arguments with the past", in Gillian Beer's term. In line with this, we will examine the manner in which the pastness of the source text (and, at times, previous adaptations) presents a

---

[14] Stephen Wall, ed., *Charles Dickens: A Critical Anthology*, Harmondsworth: Penguin, 1970, 161. Shortly afterwards, Dickens introduced the far more benevolent Jewish character Riah in *Our Mutual Friend* (1864-65), an ineffective gesture since Riah has had none of the cultural resonance of Fagin.

[15] Juliet John, *Dickens and Mass Culture*, Oxford: Oxford University Press, 2010, 222-223.

[16] John, *Dickens*, 227.

[17] On this point, and the "problem of Fagin" generally, see Christine Geraghty, *Now a Major Motion Picture: Film Adaptations of Literature and Drama*, Lanham: Rowman and Littlefield, 2008, 29-32. Geraghty discusses several adaptations, but not the 2007 BBC serial that is the primary subject of this essay.

[18] Shari Hodges Holt, "'Please, Sir, I Want Some More': Clive Donner's Marxist Adaptation of *Oliver Twist*", *Literature/Film Quarterly*, 38:4, 2010, 259. The Fagin of this adaptation in some ways anticipates Phelps' writing of the character, his victimhood explicitly related to his Jewishness. But Phelps and Giedroyc's comments in the "Behind the Scenes" feature on the DVD show no evidence of familiarity with this precursor (concentrating instead on Lean's and Reed's films, unsurprisingly, with Roman Polanski's 2005 film also getting a mention).

[19] John, *Dickens*, 232.

challenge to contemporary narrativization, and the way these challenges are met in this series.

The medium of the television series is, like film, a screen medium. An adaptation to the screen media provides a means of rendering a narrative not only in words like literature, but in "words, performance, music, sound effects and moving photographic images".[20] Yet, despite these similarities, there is a generic specificity to television adaptations that differs from films. With particular reference to the British tradition of television adaptations of classic novels, Sarah Cardwell identifies the existence of a particular "heritage aesthetic" which includes "greater emphasis on dialogue, and on the slow development of characters and their interrelations".[21] This tradition provides a generic context from which *Oliver Twist* emerges, but, as will be seen, the relation of the series to its generic predecessors is as much one of critique as it is one of influence.

The interests of the adapters of this *Oliver Twist* are neither in fidelity to Dickens' text nor in fidelity to the historical period in which that text (and the adaptation) are set. The dialogue, for example, is never taken from Dickens' novel (with only a few exceptions like the still obligatory "I want some more" [1; 9:24])[22], nor does it consistently attempt to reproduce characteristic nineteenth-century usages. The upper-class characters, like Rose Maylie and Monks, employ identifiably nineteenth-century phraseology, or approximations thereof, but the characters of Fagin's underworld milieu use frequently anachronous slang. Dickens' characters and their ideological relation to the implied author are also up for renegotiation. This is most striking with regard to the character of Fagin. John notes in a brief overview of the series that Fagin is placed as a "victim of discriminatory social circumstances" throughout.[23] This climaxes in the trial scene, in which Fagin (played by Timothy Spall) is sentenced to death by Judge Fang,[24] who further makes him the offer of a reprieve if he will convert to Christianity: "Fall to your knees before this assembly and take Christ as your saviour" (5; 22:15). Fagin refuses and becomes a martyr for the Jewish religion. The exchange is not found in Dickens, and Fagin's principled refusal to forsake his religion contrasts with the greedy opportunism of Dickens' villainous character. The offer made by Fang cannot be explained with reference to nineteenth-century legal practices, either.[25]

---

[20] Stam in *Film Adaptation*, ed. Naremore, 56.

[21] Sarah Cardwell, "Literature on the Small Screen: Television Adaptations", in *Literature on Screen*, eds. Deborah Cartmell and Imelda Whelehan, Cambridge: Cambridge University Press, 2007, 181-196 (184).

[22] Coky Giedroyc, dir., *Oliver Twist*, scr. Sarah Phelps (BBCDVD2572, 2008) [DVD]. Quotes from this series cited in episode; minute:second form.

[23] John, *Dickens*, 233.

[24] Fang has earlier dealt with the case of Oliver's theft from a bookseller (in source and adaptation). His re-introduction to try Fagin is an innovation of this particular adaptation.

[25] Fagin's trial and execution in Dickens' novel does not appear to be wholly consistent with legal practice, either. Nothing he has done would have warranted the death penalty at the time the novel appears to be set (the mid-1830s). See John Sutherland, *Can Jane Eyre Be Happy? More Puzzles in Classic Literature*, Oxford: Oxford University Press, 2000, 52-60.

Rather, Fagin's trial scene constitutes an argument directed against the ideology of the source text from a presentist perspective, from which perspective ideologies of religious tolerance and idealization of the socially or politically marginalized or oppressed provides a basis from which the narrative is re-constructed, said re-construction incorporating a dialectic between source and adaptation.[26] The ideology of Dickens' novel was one of unqualified condemnation of the criminal underclass as represented by Fagin and Sikes,[27] bolstered by the surplus enjoyment generated, particularly, in the depiction of Nancy's murder.[28] As such, the novel attested to Žižek's theory that ideology functions most effectively by the production of a certain "surplus enjoyment" in conjunction with the overt renunciation for the higher cause.[29] Thus Dickens' condemnation of criminality is shot through by a vicarious enjoyment of the acts described.[30] Within the contemporary ideological context, however, Fagin's marginalization gives rise to a new counter-narrative, providing an ideological inversion with regard to the character without having to perform any changes to major plot functions. Textual ideology is expressed here (as in the case of *War of the Worlds*) through character and at the level of discourse, rather than at the level of story.[31]

Fagin's demeanour at his trial in the face of the obscene and sadistic injunctions of the symbolic authority (Fang) demonstrates *par excellence* "the gaze of a perplexed victim" that Slavoj Žižek sees as being the central image of contemporary ideology. The representation of such a gaze neutralizes the threat of the other, but at the same time deprives him/her of the possibility of agency.[32] Such an ascription of victimhood functions to render the other tolerable. Following Žižek's analysis, we can see the contemporary quest for tolerance as the source of the emphasis on the victim-figure, and its imposition on pre-existing characters bearing a relevant identity, whether it be ethnic, religious or other.

Such an ideology can potentially be seen at work at all levels of a text. In Dickens' own text, the demonization of Fagin is begun with physical description, when "a villainous-looking and repulsive face" is attributed to him.[33] In the

---

[26] That the Fagin of this adaptation was conceived consciously against Dickens is confirmed by Sarah Phelps: "The anti-Semitism bothered me hugely, but rather than sweep it under the carpet, rather than make it comedy, I wanted to look at it in its squinty, nasty, horrible little eye." ["Behind the Scenes" feature on *Oliver Twist*, BBCDVD2572, 2008, 17:10.]

[27] As made explicit in the preface to the 1841 edition of the novel: Charles Dickens, *Oliver Twist*, ed. Philip Horne, London: Penguin, 2003, 457.

[28] Dickens' manic investment in readings of the scenes around Nancy's murder is well documented. See Peter Ackroyd, *Dickens*, London: Sinclair-Stevenson, 1990, 1030-32, 1036-42.

[29] See Slavoj Žižek, *The Sublime Object of Ideology*, London: Verso, 2008, 90-92.

[30] For the ambivalence towards criminal violence in Dickens' works, see John Carey, *The Violent Effigy*, London: Faber and Faber, 2008, 11-29.

[31] The story-discourse (or *fabula-sjuzhet*) distinction of narratology differentiates between "what is being told versus the manner in which it is told" (David Herman, "Introduction", *Companion to Narrative*, ed. Herman, Cambridge: Cambridge University Press, 2007, 13). Changes in the latter can provide an ideological inversion without the need to alter the cardinal functions of the former.

[32] Slavoj Žižek, *The Metastases of Enjoyment: Six Essays on Woman and Casuality*, London: Verso, 2001, 211.

[33] Dickens, *Oliver Twist*, 64.

Phelps/Giedroyc[34] adaptation, the work of ideology begins in the casting, with Timothy Spall playing Fagin. Spall is a popular character actor not known for playing villains,[35] and his rotund physique and friendly demeanour[36] contrast with earlier Fagins such as Alec Guinness in the 1948 film and, perhaps most of all, Lon Chaney's rat-like version from 1922. This classical approach could be seen as overdetermined: a product, perhaps, of a general anti-Semitic ideology, and/or a materialization of the source's description of Fagin's physicality.[37] Spall's presence, physically counter to previous avatars, registers a protest against the character's heritage, one that is articulated throughout the series, culminating in his condemnation to death before a jeering mob and then an execution scene, not seen in previous adaptations. If it could be said that Reed's musical turned Fagin from villain to comic hero, the 2007 version makes of him a *tragic* hero,[38] and all, again, without changing the plot in its broad contours. The change is wrought, rather, by casting, and by wholly eschewing Dickens' dialogue, replacing it with dialogue by which Fagin indexes his status as hero and victim.

The character of Sikes is also an important locus of ideological re-orientation. Dickens, again, immediately inscribes Sikes' irredeemable criminality in his appearance by attributing to him "a bulky pair of legs, with large swelling calves; — the kind of legs, which in such costume, always look in an unfinished and incomplete state without a set of fetters to garnish them".[39] The vividness of Dickens' descriptions of Sikes and Fagin has contributed to the iconic status both have attained. Descriptive detail and character interlock, the former operating as an invariable predictor of the latter, encouraging the reader to reach certain judgements about the character before he begins to act. If not heroized to the same degree as Fagin, Sikes is also partially redeemed by Phelps/ Giedroyc.[40] He is no less volatile and violent than his Dickensian predecessor, but he is capable also of tenderness towards Nancy, and is tormented by grief and guilt after the murder. The one most significant change in plot-function involving Sikes in the 2007 series is that he becomes a suicide, rather than being hunted to death by an angry mob. This encapsulates the shift in the

---

[34] Hutcheon considers the director and screenwriter as the most important figures in an adaptation, noting that the director is a sort of "Sun-King" of the film set to whom everybody is answerable, but that the director can only begin his/her work when the screenwriter has done his/hers (Hutcheon, *Adaptation*, 81-85).

[35] His most acclaimed roles, perhaps, are in *Pierrepoint* (2005) and *Mr. Turner* (2013), biopics in which he plays a sensitive hangman and an eccentric painter, respectively. He is also popularly known for his role as the admittedly somewhat villainous Wormtail in several of the *Harry Potter* films.

[36] Spall's Fagin is "slightly cuddly", according to Serena Davies, "An Oliver for our times", *Daily Telegraph,* 15 Dec 2007. http://www.telegraph.co.uk/ culture/tvandradio/3669961/An-Oliver-for-our-times.html [accessed 13 Jan 2016].

[37] "The source" needs to be taken to include George Cruikshank's illustrations, direct influences on, at least, the Fagin in Lean's film (Geraghty, *Motion Picture*, 29).

[38] Again, it should be noted that Donner's film could be said to do a similar thing with Fagin, though the characterological changes in Giedroyc/Phelps are more wide-ranging, as will be discussed.

[39] Dickens, *Oliver Twist*, 98.

[40] Notable in light of Geraghty's observation that post-Lean adaptations "make Fagin a more sympathetic character, particularly in contrast with the unredeemable Bill Sikes" (*Motion Picture*, 29). The 2007 series demonstrates that Sikes is not *fully* unredeemable.

depiction of Sikes from an embodiment of criminal brutality to a human figure—prone to brutality, certainly, but not limited to that feature, and demonstrating a greater emotional range than previous incarnations. He is a confused victim of his own uncontrollable aggression.[41] As Phelps' Nancy puts it: "He ain't a bad man, Oliver. He's just Bill" (2; 23:21). The humanizing shift in character articulated by Nancy is performed less by changing Sikes' actions than by introducing an element of conscience and tenderness into his behaviour at narratively catalysing moments, placing these actions within an expanded characterological context.

One similarity between the Phelps/Giedroyc series and its Dickensian source is that both evince a strong pull towards a melodramatic ethic and aesthetic. As described by Peter Brooks, melodrama identifies a moral occult in the everyday gestures and details of life; in the melodramatic mode, "every gesture, however frivolous or insignificant it may seem, is charged with the conflict between light and darkness."[42] Melodrama for Brooks is a heroic pushing through convention into pure emotion, motivated by the impossible "desire to express all", without repression.[43] Dickens' commitment to this mode, while not constant and absolute, is signalled by his interrogation of Sikes' legs, showing that they reveal an essential criminality, an evil awaiting final expression in the blind violence of the murder of Nancy. Conversely, Rose Maylie is registered as pure and angelic even before her appearance, her voice and her footstep both conveying evidence of a "soft and gentle" nature.[44] Such a detection of a moral occult in every sensory manifestation of an individual character places Dickens firmly in the melodramatic and Manichaean class of writer, an element of his work that all adapters thereof have to contend with in some measure.

Clearly the inscription of victimhood on the characters of Sikes and Fagin in the 2007 series removes them from the realm of the melodramatic villain. Yet, pure Manichaean evil is equally present in the series in embodied form, that of Fang and of Monks. Monks' centrality to this adaptation is notable, as his role—structurally central to Dickens' plot—has been minimized in previous adaptations, and omitted entirely from *Oliver!*[45] This can perhaps be partially linked to the vague and clichéd manner in which Dickens describes his physical appearance, contrasting with the use of novel figurative language in descriptions of Sikes and Fagin. On his first appearance, Monks is described only as "a dark figure emerg[ing] from [...] deep

---

[41] Though space does not permit any substantial discussion here, this is certainly a point at which Phelps' background in the genre of soap could be cited. Geraghty notes that men in UK soaps are often "clumsy and uncomprehending" and "enraged and frustrated", and Sikes certainly fits this trope. Christine Geraghty, *Women and Soap Opera: A Study of Prime Time Soaps*, Cambridge: Polity, 1991, 50-51.

[42] Peter Brooks, *The Melodramatic Imagination: Balzac, Henry James, Melodrama, and the Mode of Excess*, New York: Columbia University Press, 1985, 5.

[43] *Ibid.*, 4.

[44] Dickens, *Oliver Twist*, 233.

[45] One other adaptation has expanded Monks' role conspicuously: the series, scripted by Alan Bleasdale, broadcast by ITV in 1999. This adaptation takes the opposite tack to the 2007 series, presenting Monks as a somewhat sympathetic, if very disturbed, victim of his abusive and domineering mother.

shadow".[46] Monks is a less distinct figure than Fagin or Sikes, and in the diegesis of the novel is barely linked to any other characters, emerging only to set the melodramatic plot of unknown parentage and hidden inheritance in motion. But a further difference between him and the other villains of the novel is that Monks is a representative of the aristocratic class, and, as such, available to fulfil a useful function for the adapters of the 2007 series—as the aristocratic male, he is, according to modern ideology, the paradigmatic *non-victim*.[47] Consistent with the ideological drift of the series, the aristocratic Monks becomes an embodiment of pure, irredeemable evil, attended by physical signifiers of his aristocratic status, notably the jewel-encrusted cane featured in numerous close-ups throughout the series, metonymous with the character and a signifier of the wealth and privilege he exploits for nefarious purposes.

Monks' evil is expressed in his desire to kill Oliver, a desire whose melodramatic colouring is intensified in Phelps' script. Monks' very first lines in the series are: "I want him dead. I want him wiped off the face of the earth" (1; 57:46).[48] Already, Monks' words are explicitly charged with the conflict between light and darkness, his absolute commitment to evil immediately announced, and reinforced throughout the series by the introduction of a sub-plot wherein he tries to force Rose Maylie into marriage with him, informing her that "Someone in your position must learn to endure anything" (3; 24:48). This opens out the general context of Monks' devious machinations: Rose is limited by her social position and her sex, and her vulnerability to Monks' machinations is socially structured. Not only is Monks' evil heightened, but the narrative's themes of female disempowerment, found in the development of the Nancy plotline, are communicated with doubled force in the Rose plot.

Monks' evil is less a personal trait than an embodiment of inequities structural to the diegetic socio-political situation. Thus he attempts to kill Oliver not through personal violence but using the justice system, on the grounds that "It's easy enough to get a pauper boy hung" (2; 3:38); and, similarly, he attempts to gain Rose's assent to marriage not through seductive techniques but by reminding her of her precarious social and economic circumstances. The increased role of Fang in the series serves to confirm Monks' intuitions on the workings of the justice system, as Fang is motivated by overt anti-Semitism and a general sadism. He does indeed sentence Oliver to be hung for a minor offence. Fang makes his judgements with the backing of a jeering mob, representative of the dominant inhumanity and racism of the society, which is supported by political institutions and a self-serving aristocracy, and counterpointed only by the decency of a few individuals—all of whom are in some way victimized or disempowered. This nexus between decency and victimhood is particularly clear in

---

[46] Dickens, *Oliver Twist*, 211.

[47] And thus non-human. Žižek cites Richard Rorty's definition of man as such as the potential victim, as "something that can be hurt" (*Metastases of Enjoyment*, 214), as the representative philosophical statement of this ideological position. Note the closing scenes of this *Oliver Twist*, where Monks, though disinherited and exiled by Brownlow, fails to react with Rortean humanism, maintaining a malignant cheerfulness.

[48] A reversal of the character's attitude in Dickens, where Monks responds with horror at the thought of being involved in the death of Oliver (214).

the case of Rose: she is idealized by Dickens' for her "angel-in-the-house" qualities, but her availability for such treatment here depends on her victimization at the hands of Monks throughout the series.

Finally, the character of Nancy also undergoes considerable change in this series, and this again links unmistakably to dominant contemporary ideological discourse. Dickens TV adaptations have traditionally been the preserve of white actors, but here for the first time the role of Nancy is played by a black actor, Sophie Okonedo.[49] Scriptwriter Sarah Phelps says of this casting choice: "I wanted to have a black or mixed-race Nancy, because I'm sick of watching period drama where every character is white [...]. From the first time you sent a ship across the water, you'd have different peoples in London."[50] Phelps cites historical fidelity as her motivation, but contemporary concerns are also implicated in such a choice: the largely white casts of classic adaptations means that black actors working opportunities are significantly reduced; and, more broadly, the invitation to see an actor's racial identity as not relevant to his or her performance is a strategy which can play "a powerful role in shaping popular perceptions of British identity and heritage".[51] Indeed, a strict attention to details of historical fidelity would tend to suggest less a black Nancy than an Irish Nancy: documentary works such as Engel's *The Condition of the Working Class in England in 1844* (1845) and Mayhew's *London Labour and the London Poor* (1851) register the Irish as a huge presence among the urban working class in England, but none of Dickens' novels features a substantial Irish character. However, this curious gap in Dickens' novels—however historically significant—resonates less with contemporary concerns and debates than the subject of blackness, and thus does not provoke an argument with the source in Phelps' adaptation. The text instead stages an investigation of a more topical problem of socio-politics and of ideology, sidelining both the source and certain legitimate historical issues, and puts forth an argument here conceived not only against Dickens' text but also against previous adaptations, and the genre of the classic adaptation itself. It is similarly the ideological weight that comes with providing a black Nancy that leads to this Nancy being far more unambiguously good than previous avatars, and her relationship with Oliver partaking, in numerous scenes throughout the series, of a maternal intimacy that in Dickens' novel is reserved for the relationship between Oliver and Rose.[52] In Phelps' retelling, it is Nancy rather than Rose who tenderly nurses Oliver after he is wounded during a robbery. Indeed, Nancy physically carries the wounded boy through the streets, providing a Pietà-esque iconography and confirming the sanctification of the character in this version. The ground-breaking casting choice involved here—apparently written into Phelps' script from an early stage—provides the impetus for a

---

[49] See Rachel Carroll, "Black Britain and the Classic Adaptation: Integrated Casting in Television Adaptations of *Oliver Twist* and *Little Dorrit*", *Adaptation*, 8:1, 2015, 16-30.

[50] "Behind the Scenes" feature on *Oliver Twist* DVD, 05:24.

[51] Carroll, "Black Britain", 27.

[52] Dickens' Nancy, far from harbouring maternal sentiments towards Oliver, is positively averse to his presence: "I can't bear to have him about me. The sight of him turns me against myself, and all of you" (*Oliver Twist*, 209).

rewriting of the character, and both rewriting and casting combined provide Phelps' critique both of Dickens and of his previous adapters.

In conclusion, the plot of the 2007 series *Oliver Twist* is broadly that of its source. There is no need to alter the plot at the level of cardinal functions to register an ideological shift. But much of the content of the series is shaped by an evident brooding on the ideological implications of that source ending in a wholesale rejection of various elements, and the irruption of various tendencies and presuppositions unmistakably related to ideologies contemporary with the series itself. These are the ideologies that find most clear and unambiguous expression in the series, rather than those that could have been imbibed from the source. But despite this, the adaptation cannot help but incorporate a certain impasse between Dickensian ideology and contemporary ideologies relating to multiculturalism and the ontology of victimhood. This tension is shown by the series' final scene wherein the incorporation of Oliver into the white, middle-class household comprising Mr Brownlow, Rose Maylie and Mrs Bedwin is completed,[53] Fagin, Sikes and Nancy having been discarded along the way.

If it is posited, then, that one possible way of making a judgement of a transtemporal adaptation is how it reaches a final synthesis in its argument with the past, it is seen that this adaptation does not harmoniously integrate the ideological threads that run through it. Source narrative and contemporary ideological factors are at continual war in the series: the former attain greater expression for the most part, but the final resolution sees the exclusion of all Phelps' presentism and a return of the Dickensian ideological repressed, making the ending less a conclusion than the confirmation of the irresoluble tensions inherent in such an adaptation. In a more general sense, the temporal distance between a source and its adaptation can be mapped out in terms of ideological tensions. It is in the comparative analysis of both relevant texts that the challenge to presentism is brought into relief, and the particular value of adaptations as tools of dialectical thought becomes apparent.

BIBLIOGRAPHY

Ackroyd, Peter, *Dickens*, London: Sinclair-Stevenson, 1990.

Barthes, Roland, *Image Music Text*, trans. Stephen Heath, London: Fontana, 1977.

Beer, Gillian, *Arguing with the Past: Essays in Narrative from Woolf to Sidney*, London: Routledge, 1989.

Brooks, Peter, *The Melodramatic Imagination: Balzac, Henry James, Melodrama, and the Mode of Excess*, New York: Columbia University Press, 1985.

Cardwell, Sarah, "Adaptation Studies Revisited: Purposes, Perspectives and Inspiration", in *The Literature/Film Reader: Issues of Adaptation*, eds. James M. Welsh and Peter Lev, Lanham, MD: Scarecrow Press, 2007, 51-63.

Carey, John, *The Violent Effigy*, London: Faber and Faber, 2008.

---

[53] The final scene takes place with Oliver and Rose playing piano together. The ideological significance of this instrument lies in the facts that it is a very expensive one, and one that requires a great deal of room, thus functioning as a marker of absolute distance between Oliver and the cramped, dingy quarters in which Fagin and his boys lived.

Carroll, Rachel, "Black Britain and the Classic Adaptation: Integrated Casting in Television Adaptations of *Oliver Twist* and *Little Dorrit*", *Adaptation*, 8:1, 2015, 16-30.

Cartmell, Deborah, and Imelda Whelehan, *Screen Adaptation: Impure Cinema*, Basingstoke, Hampshire: Palgrave Macmillan, 2010.

———, eds., *Literature on Screen*, Cambridge: Cambridge University Press, 2007.

Davies, Serena, "An Oliver for our Times", *Daily Telegraph* (15 Dec 2007) http://www.telegraph.co.uk/culture/tvandradio/3669961/An-Oliver-for-our-times.html [accessed 01/02/2018].

Dickens, Charles, *Oliver Twist*, ed. Philip Horne, London: Penguin, 2003.

Donner, Clive, dir., *Oliver Twist*, Cinema Club, 2003 [DVD].

Geraghty, Christine, *Women and Soap Opera: A Study of Prime Time Soaps*, Cambridge: Polity, 1991.

Giedroyc, Coky, dir., *Oliver Twist*, scr. Sarah Phelps, BBCDVD2572, 2008 [DVD].

Haskin, Byron, dir., *The War of the Worlds* [1953], Paramount, 2005 [DVD].

Herman, David, ed., *Companion to Narrative*, Cambridge: Cambridge University Press, 2007.

Hermansson, Casie, "Flogging Fidelity: In Defense of the (Un)Dead Horse", *Adaptation* 8:2, 2015, 147-160.

Holt, Shari Hodges, "'Please, Sir, I Want Some More': Clive Donner's Marxist Adaptation of *Oliver Twist*", *Literature/Film Quarterly*, 38:4, 2010, 254-268.

Hutcheon, Linda, *A Theory of Adaptation*, Abingdon: Routledge, 2013.

John, Juliet, *Dickens and Mass Culture*, Oxford: Oxford University Press, 2010.

Lean, David, dir., *Oliver Twist* [1948], Carlton, 2000 [DVD].

Leitch, Thomas, *Film Adaptation and its Discontents: From Gone with the Wind to The Passion of the Christ*, Baltimore, MD: Johns Hopkins University Press, 2009.

McFarlane, Brian, *Novel to Film: An Introduction to the Theory of Adaptation*, Oxford: Clarendon Press, 1996.

Naremore, James, ed., *Film Adaptation*, New Brunswick, NJ: Rutgers University Press, 2000.

Reed, Carol, dir., *Oliver*! [1967], Sony, 2006 [DVD].

Rye, Renny, dir., *Oliver Twist* [1999], scr. Alan Bleasdale, ITVDVD 3711522163, no date, [DVD].

Sutherland, John, *Can Jane Eyre Be Happy? More Puzzles in Classic Literature*, Oxford: Oxford University Press, 2000.

Wall, Stephen, ed., *Charles Dickens: A Critical Anthology*, Harmondsworth: Penguin, 1970.

Wells, H.G., *The State of Homo Sapiens*, London: Secker and Warburg, 1939.

———, *The War of the Worlds* [1898], ed. Patrick Parrinder, London: Penguin, 2005.

Žižek, Slavoj, *Living in the End Times*, London: Verso, 2010.

———, *The Metastases of Enjoyment: Six Essays on Woman and Casuality*, London: Verso, 2001.

———, *The Sublime Object of Ideology*, London: Verso, 2008.

Žižek, Slavoj, and Glyn Daly, *Conversations with Žižek*, Cambridge: Polity, 2004.

CHAPTER 2

Going Back to Gorki's Ideas: Donskoi's Film Adaptation of *Mother*

Panayiota Mini

In 1955, the Soviet film director Mark Donskoi (1901-1981) shot an adaptation of one of the most famous Russian books worldwide, considered by some the archetypical socialist realist novel, Maxim Gorki's (1868-1936) *Mother* (*Mat'*, 1907/rev. 1922). Released in the Soviet Union in February 1956 and entered into the Cannes Film Festival the following May, *Mother* was not Donskoi's first adaptation of a Gorki work. Between 1938 and 1940 this director had transferred to the screen the Gorki trilogy, consisting of *The Childhood of Maxim Gorki* (*Detstvo Gorkovo*, 1938), *My Apprenticeship* (*V liudiakh*, 1939, al. *Among People* or *Out in the World*), and *My Universities* (*Moi universiteti*, 1940), that earned him his first Stalin Prize and international fame[1] Subsequently, Donskoi secured his reputation with two tragic war films, *The Rainbow* (*Raduga*, 1944, based on a story by the Polish writer Wanda Wasilewska) and *The Unvanquished* (*Nepokorennye*,1945); the bitter-sweet *The Village Teacher* (*Sel'skaia uchitel'nitsa*, 1947); and two adaptations of socialist realist milestones, *How the Steel Was Tempered* (*Kak zakalialas'stal'*, 1942, based on Nikolay Ostrovski's novel), and *Alitet Leaves for the Mountains* (*Alitet ukhodit v gory*, 1949, based on Tikhon Semushkin's novel).

Despite its director's credentials and Gorki's fame, *Mother* failed to gather any awards in Cannes and soon fell into oblivion. Since then, this film has rarely been discussed in scholarly literature. The single detailed analysis of the film in English appears in Evgeny Dobrenko's *Stalinist Cinema and the Production of History*. In a chapter titled "Three Mothers—Pudovkin, Donskoi, Panfilov", Dobrenko compares three adaptations of *Mother*—by Vsevolod Pudovkin (1893-1953) in 1926, Donskoi, and Gleb Panfilov (b. 1934) in 1990—and considers Donskoi's version an artistic flop. By convincingly describing Donskoi's *Mother* as faithful to the book, Dobrenko dismisses the film as "untimely", a relic of Socialist Realism with no contact with its contemporary time, the Soviet Thaw.[2] Dobrenko reaches this conclusion after criticizing Gorki's novel as weak, characterized by "the artificiality of style, the

---

[1] Peter Rollberg, *Historical Dictionary of Russian and Soviet Cinema*, Lanham, MD: Scarecrow Press, 2009, 181-184.
[2] Evgeny Dobrenko, *Stalinist Cinema and the Production of History: Museum of the Revolution*, trans. Sarah Young, Edinburgh: Edinburgh University Press, 2008, 177-182.

unconvincing nature of the speech and behaviour of the characters".[3] "It is significant", Dobrenko remarks, "that precisely this novel ended up being the foundation of socialist realism".[4] For Dobrenko, since Donskoi had remained faithful to Gorki's work, he produced an unsuccessful socialist realist film.[5]

However, a closer look at Donskoi's film leads us to a different conclusion. His adaptation of *Mother* was shaped by the social and cultural climate of the early Thaw. *Mother* alluded to crucial ideologies of its time, while reflecting the transition of Soviet cinema from Socialist Realism to more open forms. Donskoi returned to Gorki's novel to denounce state violence and promote the Thaw principles of freedom of speech and opinion, fearless defense of truth, enlightenment through peaceful means, respect for all social groups as well as the notion of socialism as a modern version of Christian religion. Donskoi often amplified Gorki's ideas by making small, yet telling changes to the novel and occasionally turned to Gorki's first, 1907 version of the novel instead of the final 1922 one.

Examining Donskoi's *Mother* along these lines helps us to reconsider an aesthetic label such as "Socialist Realism", which may have been tenuously and reproachfully applied to an artwork, and to appreciate the history of Soviet cinema of the 1950s as a gradual move away from Socialist Realism. My re-evaluation of aesthetic labels should also include Gorki's work; as we will see, Donskoi did not adapt a typical socialist realist novel, but one that was described as such much later. Moreover, my discussion contributes to illuminating the dialogue between different adaptations of the same work. In remaining faithful to Gorki's spirit, Donskoi indirectly responded to Pudovkin's famous montage film of 1926, which had greatly departed from the novel.[6] As Donskoi said, "Pudovkin's masterpiece" shaped his desire to adapt *Mother*, but his own goal was to bring his work close to Gorki's text.[7] Thus, before examining Donskoi's work, we need to situate Gorki's novel in its historical context and discuss briefly Pudovkin's adaptation.

Gorki's *Mother* focuses on Pelageya Nilovna Vlasova, the mother of a politically sophisticated factory worker, Pavel, and her acquisition of socialist consciousness. At first, Nilovna is a naïve, religious woman, ignorant of the causes of her life's plight. However, as she witnesses the socialists' secret meetings at her home, listens to her son's and other workers' inspiring words, and teaches herself how to read, she gradually gains knowledge. Midway through the novel, Nilovna participates in a May Day demonstration and picks up the red banner when Pavel, who had been leading the demonstration, is arrested. After May Day, the mother moves in with the intellectuals Nikolay Ivanovich and Sophia in the city, traveling from there to villages to distribute

---

[3] *Ibid.*, 170.
[4] *Ibid.*, 172.
[5] A flattering description of Donskoi's *Mother* appears in Rollberg's *Historical Dictionary of Russian and Soviet Cinema* (89, 113), where the film is characterized "underrated", a work of "indubitable merits".
[6] See also Dobrenko's assessment that "much of his [Donskoi's] adaptation is constructed in direct polemic with Pudovkin's film" (*Stalinist Cinema*, 181).
[7] Mark Donskoi, "O sebe i svoem prizvanii", in *Mark Donskoi. Sbornik*, ed. Liudmila Ivanovna Pazhitnova, Moscow: Iskusstvo, 1973, 26-27.

illegal literature. At novel's end, the police beat Nilovna to death when she is caught smuggling copies of the speech that Pavel had delivered during his trial.

Inspired by some actual events of 1902 in Sormovo and indirectly referring to the 1905 revolutionary ferment, Gorki wrote the greater part of *Mother* during his 1906 visit to the United States and first presented the novel in complete form in English, in an American edition of 1907.[8] Around thirty years later, following a wide discussion among higher politicians and established authors, including Stalin and Gorki, the 1934 First Congress of Soviet Writers heralded Socialist Realism as the sole appropriate method for the Soviet arts. Andrei Zhdanov, the method's chief spokesman and a close associate of Stalin, praised the Soviet literature which was "impregnated with enthusiasm and the spirit of heroic deeds" and explained that Socialist Realism meant the depiction of "reality in its revolutionary development. In addition to this, the truthfulness and historical concreteness of the artistic portrayal should be combined with the ideological remolding and education of the working people in the spirit of socialism".[9] Gorki was acclaimed as "the method's pioneer *par excellence*" and *Mother* as well as his play *Enemies* (*Vragi*, 1906) "the earliest examples of Socialist Realism". [10] Subsequently, Soviet criticism painstakingly examined *Mother* as the precursor of Socialist Realism in literature.[11] By the time he wrote *Mother*, Gorki had indeed been associated with a realist school, a group of writers who opposed the experimental methods of the Russian avant-garde and the elusive writing of the so-called mystics.[12] However, Gorki's affinity with that group does not justify discussing *Mother* as a socialist realist work.[13] *Mother* functioned only *a posteriori* as a prototype for Socialist Realism. It provided the later socialist realist novel with a "master plot" due to Gorki's playing out of the consciousness/spontaneity dialectics and the process of consciousness acquisition.[14] The son's class-conscious commitment to Russia's transformation, the mother's initially spontaneous approach to reality, and her gradual appreciation of the socialist cause became narrative situations which the socialist realist novel later appropriated and developed.

In its own context, *Mother* was related to the nascent God Building (*bogostroitel'stvo*) movement and more broadly to the religious and philosophical

---

[8] Barry P. Scherr, *Maxim Gorki*, Boston: Twayne Publishers, 1988, 43; Richard Freeborn, *The Russian Revolutionary Novel: Turgenev to Pasternak*, Cambridge: Cambridge University Press, 1982, 45; S. Kastorskii, "Iz istorii sozdaniia povesti *Mat'*", in M. Gor'kii, *Materialy i issledovaniia*, Moscow: Izdatel'stvo Akademii Nauk SSSR, 1941, 3: 288-358.

[9] Quoted in Nicholas Luker, "Introduction", *From Furmanov to Sholokhov: An Anthology of the Classics of Socialist Realism*, Ann Arbor: Ardis, 1988, 19.

[10] Luker, "Introduction", 23.

[11] See, for example, S. Kastorskii, *"Mat'" M. Gor'kogo: Tvorcheskaia istoriia povesti*, Leningrad: Khudozhestvennaia Literatura, 1940, especially 210-222; O. Semenovskii, *Marksistskaia kritika o Gor'kom: Iz istorii obshchestvenno-literaturnoi bor'by predoktiabr'skogo perioda*, Kichinev: Kartia Moldoveniaske, 1969.

[12] F.M. Borras, *Maxim Gorki. The Writer: An Interpretation*, Oxford: Clarendon Press, 1967, 50-51.

[13] *Ibid.*, 110.

[14] Katerina Clark, *The Soviet Novel: History as Ritual*, Chicago: The University of Chicago Press, 1981, 55-57, 61-62, 65.

inquiries which preoccupied Russian intellectuals after the failure of the 1905-1906 uprisings.[15] The God Building movement acquired its name after *Mother*'s completion.[16] The term was Gorki's own appearing in his 1908 novella *Confession* (*Ispoved'*). Nevertheless, the movement's principles predated *Confession.* A Bolshevist heresy, God Building sought to marry religion and socialism, by conceiving of socialism as a secular religion. Apart from Gorki, the movement boasted such leaders as Alexander Bogdanov and Anatolii Lunacharskii. The latter succinctly presented the movement's core ideas in his book *Religion and Socialism* (1908):

> I dare to say that this philosophy [of Marx] is a *religious philosophy*, that it has its source in the religious quest of the past, engendered by the economic growth of mankind, and that it gives the brightest, most real, most active solution to the "cursed questions" of human self-consciousness, which were resolved in an illusory way by the old religious systems.[17]

For God Builders, official Christian Orthodoxy was condemned for its superficiality and hypocrisy, but the energy generated in people thanks to religious experiences was seen as capable of being converted into the energy required for building socialism. It is precisely this conversion that takes place in the character of Nilovna. Gorki renders her process of consciousness-acquisition as one that substitutes socialist principles for religious beliefs.[18] Nilovna, for example, perceives the gatherings of the socialist workers as gatherings of martyrs. Her consciousness-gaining is revealed as a symbolic resurrection with the picking up of the red banner—an image religiously coded in pre-Gorkian, radical literature.[19] And her son, Pavel, is a Christ-like worker with his calm temperament, thin physique, and almost heavenly asceticism.[20]

Given *Mother*'s strong religious resonance, it is not surprising that "the father of Marxism", Georgi Plekhanov, considered this work, as well as *Confession*, proof of Gorki's lack of knowledge of Marxism.[21] Moreover, although in 1907 Lenin characterized *Mother* a useful book, he also considered the novel flawed. Furthermore, in 1908, Lenin criticized God Builders' initiative of uniting scientific socialism and religion through their establishment of a political-philosophical school

---

[15] Borras, *Maxim Gorki*, 55-56, 112.

[16] The information on God Building draws on: Clark, *The Soviet Novel*, 55; Christopher Read, *Religion, Revolution and the Russian Intelligentsia, 1900-1912: The* Vekhi *Debate and its Intellectual Background*, London: The Macmillan Press, 1979, 77-94; and Irwin Weil, *Gorki: His Literary Development and Influence on Soviet Intellectual Life*, New York: Random House, 1966, 60-61.

[17] Quoted in Read, Religion, Revolution and the Russian Intelligentsia, 84.

[18] For certain stages in Nilovna's consciousness-acquisition process, see Maxim Gorki, *Mother*, New York: The Citadel Press, 1947, 9-19, 99-112, 124-133, 241-248. See also Borras, *Maxim Gorki*, 110-111; Freeborn, *The Russian Revolutionary Novel*, 48-51.

[19] For the flag as a Russian literary motif, see Clark, The Soviet Novel, 49.

[20] Pavel also hangs on his wall a picture of Christ and reads the Bible.

[21] See G.V. Plekhanov, "Predislovie k tret'emu izdaniiu sbornika "Za dvadtsat' let"," in G.V. Plekhanov, *Literatura i estetika*, vol.1, *Teoriia iskusstva i istoriia esteticheskoi mysli*, Moscow: Khudozhestvennaia literatura, 1958, 132.

for workers in Capri. Lenin's disapproval of Gorki's religious inquiries continued at least until 1913. In 1917 and 1918 the tension between the two men intensified when Gorki denounced the Bolshevik methods of consolidating power.[22] After his reconciliation with Lenin, as well as his re-assessment of the Soviet status quo, Gorki presented in 1922 *Mother*'s sixth and last revision, which contained fewer religious references than the first one.[23] However, Gorki's omissions of some lines and, occasionally, paragraphs did not alter the substance of his novel, which remained a work of strong religious connotations replaying the human quest for God.[24]

In addition to its religious rhetoric, the novel puts emphasis on people's enlightenment, since revolutionary consciousness, for Gorki, "is almost synonymous with enlightenment".[25] The novel's heroes acquire consciousness by reading illegal literature and in their turn spread the socialist ideology through books, pamphlets and inspiring speeches. For example, early in his life, Pavel becomes enlightened through books. Later, the workers are arrested because they hide forbidden books. The mother acquires knowledge by absorbing the socialists' ideas and teaching herself how to read, and throughout the second half of the novel becomes an apostle of her son's truth by smuggling illegal publications to villages. Her last revolutionary act that leads to her death is no other than spreading leaflets of her son's speech. Enlightenment, though, does not emanate solely from the conscious working class. Two more groups work for people's education: the revolutionary peasantry, embodied in the passionate Rybin, and the intellectuals, represented by Nikolay Ivanovich and his sister, Sophia.

Regarding its structure, Gorki's *Mother* is characterized by an episodic unfolding in which many scenes bear independent significance, lengthy argumentative passages function as self-sufficient revelations of truth, and some heroes are mentioned only in passing. The novel is divided into two distinct parts, before and after the May Day demonstration; and similar narrative situations—e.g. discussions, secret meetings, and imprisonments—appear in different chapters. The repetitions and long dialogic scenes delay the action and cue the reader to reflect on theoretical issues such as freedom, truth, enlightenment, underground activism, violence and the union of all people, instead of creating mental images.

In 1926 Pudovkin, who completed *Mother* to commemorate the twentieth anniversary of the 1905 revolution, drastically altered Gorki's novel to make it fit into the Bolshevik interpretation of 1905 as a "dress rehearsal" of the 1917 revolution.[26] In collaboration with his scenarist, Natan Zarkhi (1900-1935), Pudovkin deleted the intellectuals' and Rybin's activism, the people's conversions to socialism through

---

[22] For details on the Gorki-Lenin relationship, see Panayiota Mini, "Pudovkin's Cinema of the 1920s", PhD. Dissertation, University of Wisconsin-Madison, 2002, 174, 241-242.

[23] For a revised version of the novel, see Maxim Gorki, *Mother: A Novel*, trans. M. Wettlin, Moscow: Foreign Languages Publishing House, 1950. Here I quote the first version, unless otherwise noted.

[24] See also Freeborn, *The Russian Revolutionary Novel*, 45.

[25] Clark, *The Soviet Novel,* 66.

[26] On Pudovkin's adaptation see Panayiota Mini, "Striving for the Maximum Appeal: Ideology and Propaganda in the Soviet Cinema of the 1920s and 1930s", in *The Routledge Companion to Cinema and Politics*, eds. Yannis Tzioumakis and Claire Molloy, London and New York: Routledge, 2016, 163-166.

reading, and the depiction of socialism as secular religion. He presented the working class as the single factor in changing history and showed the socialists circulating guns, not books as in Gorki's novel. The mother in the 1926 film does not teach herself how to read; and unlike the novel, the film ends with the May Day demonstration, during which the mother picks up the red flag and she and Pavel are killed by the state troops. Apart from these, Pudovkin converted Gorki's loose plot into a tight family drama characterized by conflicts and suspense aiming at eliciting strong emotions in the spectators.

Contrary to Pudovkin's plot, the script that Donskoi co-authored with Nikolai Kovarski (1904-1974) reproduced Gorki's episodic structure. Donskoi also avoided tension and suspense, letting his spectators concentrate on the consciousness-acquisition process and the socialists' theories. The following outline will help us to follow the film's unfolding, core situations, and ideas:

1. Workers leave a factory. At the Vlasovs', the father—a factory worker—gets drunk, behaves crudely to his wife, and dies.

2. After the father's funeral, Pavel acts in an irresponsible manner, similar to his father, but then feels ashamed.

3. Some time later, during a Paschal feast, Pavel appears class-conscious. He explains to his comrade Sasha that he changed thanks to such nice people as Nikolay Ivanovich and herself.

4. At the Vlasovs', Pavel tells his mother about his political activity and the forbidden books that he reads. The mother worries about him and prays.

5. At the Vlasovs', the mother talks with the Ukrainian worker, Andrei. Then, in a secret meeting, the socialists plan a strike, while the mother recalls bitter moments of her life.

6. At the factory, the workers disregard Pavel's call for a strike. The mother listens to Pavel's speech.

7. At the Vlasovs', the police arrest Pavel because of the illegal literature.

8. At the Vlasovs', the intellectual Nikolay and Sasha carry pamphlets and meet Rybin who is going to distribute the literature that Nikolay will give him.

9. At the factory, the mother distributes leaflets so that the police stop suspecting her son.

10. The mother visits Pavel in prison.

11. At the Vlasovs', the Ukrainian worker Andrei encourages the mother to educate herself. She soon gets eyeglasses and starts reading.

12. Pavel is released from prison and thanks his mother.

13. Pavel plans to hold the flag in the May Day demonstration, while the police prepare themselves for an attack. The mother listens to the words of Pavel and Andrei.

14. On May Day, Pavel holds the flag; he and Andrei are arrested, and the mother collects the fallen flag into her hands.

15. The mother cannot complete her prayer.

16. Nikolay and Sophia take the mother to their home. As she is listening to Sophia playing the piano, the mother recalls her past.

17. Dressed as nuns, the mother and Sophia distribute illegal literature in the countryside. Later, the mother alone continues her mission. She meets Rybin who also enlightens the peasants. Rybin is arrested.

18. Although seriously ill, Nikolay works for the cause by composing texts for pamphlets. Sasha announces that Pavel's friend, Nikolay Vyesovshchikov, has escaped from prison.

19. The mother meets Vyesovshchikov.

20. The mother visits Pavel in prison.

21. At Nikolay's, Vyesovshchikov, Sasha and the mother plan Pavel's escape from prison.

22. At Nikolay's, Rybin, who has escaped from prison instead of Pavel, thanks Nikolay for what he has done for the cause. Nikolay dies.

23. During his trial, Pavel delivers a speech where he defends socialism, the Party, and truth, and denounces private property, injustice and intellectual stagnation. He is sentenced to exile.

24. The mother plans to smuggle copies of Pavel's speech.

25. At a railway station, the mother distributes copies of the speech. The police arrest her. A statue of her closes the film.

As the outline shows, most of Donskoi's narrative situations develop the theme of one's consciousness-raising thanks to enlightenment (3, 4, 5, 6, 7, 8, 9, 11, 13, 17, 18, 22, 23, 24, 25).[27] Donskoi depicts the decisive role that Pavel's words and the socialists' discussions have on Nilovna, her efforts to learn how to read, and the heroes' well-organized network of illegal literature reaching the provinces. By reiterating the statement of Gorki's Pavel, the film's Pavel explains that he wants "to study and then teach others". Donskoi's camerawork and small changes to the novel underscore the impact of enlightenment. When Pavel fails to convince the factory workers to go on strike, by altering Gorki's description of the scene Donskoi shows everyone but the mother abandoning Pavel in the factory yard.[28] A conscious camera movement tracks around Pavel until it shows him from his back; in the shot's depth, in front of Pavel, Nilovna stands still, affected by the power of her son's bold speech. Later, Donskoi associates enlightenment with none other than Lenin. At the moment that the mother gives illegal literature to some villagers, Donskoi cuts to a close view of it so the spectator sees *Iskra*, the newspaper which Lenin ran from abroad in the early 1900s.[29]

As the outline also suggests, Donskoi's class-conscious individuals never use violence to promote their ideas or even in self-defense. Their weapons are words, books, and pamphlets. Only the tsarist state and its agents—troops, policemen, and judges—rely on methods of coercion: shootings, beatings, labor camps and exile to Siberia. The film's rejection of violence shines through at the end, where Donskoi borrows some of the mother's last words in the novel and presents Nilovna asserting that the enemies will not be able to extinguish the truth in blood. A phrase of Gorki's Nilovna also constitutes the film's concluding statement, made vigorously by the mother: "The resuscitated soul they will not kill".[30]

Furthermore, Donskoi's adaptation reiterates and even reinforces Gorki's theory that socialism is a substitution for religious faith. After his irresponsible behavior (2), the film's Pavel first appears class-conscious at an outdoor feast near a church, where people celebrate the Orthodox Easter (3). The people kiss and greet one another with the words, "Christ is Risen", "Truly, He is Risen" (Khristos voskrese! Voistinu voskrese!). The mental change in Gorki's Christ-like Pavel is thus paralleled in the film with the Resurrection. In addition to devising an Easter scene, which transfers Pavel's acquisition of consciousness from the novel's winter time to spring, Donskoi introduces the Easter celebration with shots of a thaw, an allusion to Pudovkin's famous thaw images in his own adaptation of *Mother*. At the same time that he borrows Pudovkin's symbolic imagery, Donskoi alters its meaning. Instead of

---

[27] I have briefly discussed some of these ideas in Panayiota Mini, "Mia methodos analisis kinimatografikon diaskevon: To paradeigma tis diaskevis tis *Manas* tou Gorki apo ton Pudovkin kai ton Donskoi", in *Apo ti logotehnia ston kinimatografo*, eds. F. Tabaki-Iona and M.E. Galani, Athens: Aigokeros, 2011, 34-38.

[28] In the novel, the workers do not leave the yard. Gorki describes the scene as follows: "One after the other, workmen approached him [Pavel] praising his speech, but doubting the success of a strike". Afterwards Pavel goes home (Gorki, *Mother*, 72).

[29] A second publication that can be seen is a Russian translation of Szymon Dickstein's highly popular Polish pamphlet *What Do People Live By?* (*Kto z czego zyje?*, 1881).

[30] Gorki, *Mother*, 401.

implying life's rejuvenation due to people's fights and the flow of the uninterrupted revolution, the thaw in Donskoi's *Mother* has religious connotations, suggesting spiritual resurrection. Later, Donskoi reinforces the religious overtones that Rybin's arrest bears in the novel. Gorki depicts Rybin as a sort of prophet. When Rybin passionately addresses the peasants, one listener remarks that "he's speaking the gospel"; and after Rybin is beaten by a policeman, a woman washes his bloody face with water,[31] a detail that Donskoi includes in the film. Moreover, Donskoi's Rybin wears ragged clothes and a cross, and preaches with a church in the background, while bells are ringing.

Donskoi presents socialism as a secular religion even more pronouncedly in the case of Nilovna. In the novel's first chapters, Gorki often describes Nilovna praying before religious icons or crossing herself, motifs that Donskoi also uses in the film's first part. After the May Day scene, Gorki mentions:

> Recollecting that she had not yet said her prayers, she [Nilovna] walked up to the images, and after standing before them for a few seconds, she sat down again. Her heart was empty.[32]

Donskoi elaborates upon this description. Hiding the torn red banner in her bosom, Nilovna stands before an icon of Christ (15). Donskoi cuts to the icon and then to a medium shot of Nilovna, who starts crossing herself but cannot finish. In voice-over, we hear some words that Pavel had earlier told her. Donskoi cuts to a closer view of the icon, as if Christ looks at Nilovna. Back to Nilovna, the camera shows her trying once more to cross herself, with no result. Music starts playing and the woman leaves her home, resolutely shutting the door behind her. Donskoi cuts to the icon, which suddenly plunges into darkness. The words of a conscious socialist (Pavel), Donskoi implies, replace God's Word and convert one's religious faith into socialist belief.

Furthermore, Donskoi restores the importance of the intellectuals in Russia's emancipation which Gorki had suggested, but Pudovkin excised from his film. Donskoi's intellectuals, Nikolay and Sophia, are two of the most memorable characters in *Mother*. At this point, we should bear in mind that in the novel's first version of 1907, Nikolay Ivanovich and Sophia attract a reader's attention through their unselfish and wholehearted commitment to socialism; in the 1922 revision, Nikolay and Sophia still work for the people and support Nilovna, but they have been transformed into figures rather alienated from the people's problems.[33] Not only does Donskoi follow the 1907 version, presenting the intellectuals in an absolutely positive light. He extends Nikolay's role in the film's first half. First, he names Nikolay as one of those who helped Pavel acquire consciousness (3). Second, he devises a meeting between Rybin and Nikolay (8), during which the peasant expresses his distrust for the "gentlemen" (*gospoda*), whom Nikolay represents. Rybin, however, proves

---

[31] *Ibid.*, 291, 295.
[32] *Ibid.*, 197.
[33] For Gorki's revisions compare pp. 242 and 422-424, and 244 and 427-9 of the first and last versions respectively.

wrong. Thus, towards the film's end (18), when Nikolay lies dying in his bed, Rybin thanks him on behalf of the people for everything he has does for them and acknowledges that some *gospoda* will lie, others will betray the cause, and some others will take the people's side. A few moments later, Nikolay is dead, a narrative situation absent in the novel where Nikolay is only arrested. Nikolay's death as well as his work for the cause until his very last moment make him a truly exceptional figure, who sacrifices himself for the people's future.

Nikolay's pamphlets, like all illegal publications and the socialists' sermons in the film, promote first and foremost the diffusion of the truth. The books which Pavel reads are forbidden because, as he explains, they tell the truth about life for the workers. The tsarist state, he later explains, sentences and sends to exile and labor camps those who want to know the truth and pass it on to others. The flag of the May Day demonstration is the flag of truth, reason and freedom. Rybin encourages the peasants to search for the truth. Similar to Gorki's heroes, the film's socialists envisage the triumph of freedom, reason, goodness, justice, and the union of all countries' working people over greed, evil, falsehood, violence and cowardice. Donskoi adds one more ideal, absent from the book: democracy. Nikolay asserts that the Party includes many nice people; looking at them, he says, one hopes that "Russia will become a great democratic country".

Donskoi's Adaptation in Context

Donskoi's adaptation is explained if we consider the political and cultural circumstances in the wake of Stalin's death in 1953. As soon as Stalin died, Soviet culture experienced some openness, the political system started changing and the criticism of Stalin began.[34] This criticism primarily concerned the arbitrary, violent execution of power—the terror, imprisonments, exiles, and murders—and took various forms. For example, right after Stalin's death, the new leadership under Nikita Khrushchev interrogated and executed Lavrenti Beria, the chief of the secret police, who had been in charge of the Gulag, and weakened the secret police by putting it under the direct control of the Party.[35] In addition, the leadership released thousands of persons from imprisonment, mostly Komsomol and Party members who had been arrested in the 1930s.[36] The Soviet Union's destalinization policy was announced by Khrushchev in his "secret speech" at the 20th Congress of the Communist Party on February 25, 1956, where he denounced Stalin's abuse of power:

---

[34] Peter Kenez, *A History of the Soviet Union from the Beginning to the End* (2nd ed), Cambridge: Cambridge University Press, 2009, 190-192.

[35] Dmitri Volkogonov, *The Rise and Fall of the Soviet Empire: Political Leaders from Lenin to Gorbachev*, trans. H. Shukman, London: Harper Collins, 1999, 185-193.

[36] Roy A. Medvedev, "The Stalin Question," in *The Soviet Union Since Stalin*, eds. Stephen F. Cohen, Alexander Rabinowitch and Robert Sharlet, Bloomington: Indiana University Press, 1980, 33; Edward Acton and Tom Stableford, *The Soviet Union: A Documentary History*, vol. 2: *1939-1991*, Exeter: University of Exeter Press, 2007, 305-306.

> Stalin acted not through persuasion, explanation and patient cooperation with people, but by imposing his concepts and demanding absolute submission to his opinion [...]. Stalin originated the concept "enemy of the people". This term automatically rendered it unnecessary that the ideological errors of a man or men engaged in a controversy be proven; this term made possible the usage of the most cruel repression, violating all norms of revolutionary legality, against anyone who in any way disagreed with Stalin, against those who were only suspected of hostile intent, against those who had bad reputations. This concept "enemy of the people", actually eliminated the possibility of any kind of ideological fight or the making of one's view known on this or that issue.[37]

Seen against the 1953-1956 background, Donskoi's *Mother*, released just eleven days before Khrushchev's secret speech,[38] looks like a veiled criticism of Stalin's crude methods and a reaffirmation of the need for ideological fight through peaceful means, including persuasion and reasonable argument. Donskoi's emphasis on truth, the film's most frequently heard ideal, looks like a campaign for a major principle of the Thaw. His references to Pavel's exile in Siberia and Rybin's arrest without a trial, which Gorki mentions but Pudovkin left out, would most likely remind the mid-1950s spectators of arbitrary punishments inflicted by Stalin and his secret police. Donskoi's addition of "democracy" to Gorki's concepts concerns a notion which came to the fore in the Thaw—although the term "democracy" was primarily used in relation to the Party structure and the factories' organization. The call for the union of all countries' workers into a big family in the film is consistent with the Soviet Union's turn to internationalism and cultural exchanges with the West that marked the post-1954 period.[39] And the film's insistence on people's spiritual awaking and courageous declaration of truth seems like an idealized metaphor for life under the Thaw. It is noteworthy that in reviewing Donskoi's *Mother* in 1956, Zoia Vladimirova welcomed the director's return to Gorki's notion of enlightenment, which had not appeared in Pudovkin's film, and paid particular attention to Nilovna's concluding phrase ("The resuscitated soul they will not kill"), which became the title of the critic's review.[40]

Donskoi's emphasis on the undermining of religion through enlightenment also bears topical significance. After a short period of religious persecution—from July to November 1954—the new leadership adopted a more tolerant stance that lasted until 1957. Specifically, in November 1954 Khrushchev signed a resolution that

---

[37] Quoted in *A Documentary History of Communism in Russia*: *From Lenin to Gorbachev*, ed. Robert V. Daniels, Hanover and London: University Press of New England, 1993, 255.

[38] The film was released on February 14; Khrushchev delivered his speech on February 25.

[39] Eleonor Gilburd, "The Revival of Soviet Internationalism in the Mid to Late 1950s", in *The Thaw: Soviet Society and Culture during the 1950s and 1960s*, eds. Denis Kozlov and Eleonory Gilburd, Toronto, Buffalo, London: Toronto University Press, 2013, 362-401.

[40] Zoia Vladimirova, "Dushchu voskresshchuiu ne ub'iut!", in *Mark Donskoi. Sbornik*, ed. Liudmila Ivanovna Pazhitnova, Moscow: Iskusstvo, 1973, 124-129. In her generally positive review, Vladimirova also pinpointed some weaknesses, such as lack of humor, neutral language, one-dimensional characters and some sentimentality.

emphasized intensifying the ideological fight against religion but condemning "administrative interference with religious organizations". Two years later the first publication of the Bible since 1917 was allowed.[41]

The social climate of the mid-1950s also helps us to understand Donskoi's favorable depiction of the intellectuals.[42] Both the artistic and the scientific intelligentsia acquired a prominent role during the Thaw. As soon as Stalin died, the artistic intelligentsia became a leader in the criticism of the old system and its cultural falseness, and Khrushchev strove to integrate experts of the scientific intelligentsia into the state's decision-making process, even if they were not Party members.[43] It is also significant that Donskoi retains a major hero of the novel, whom Pudovkin had removed, the Ukrainian Andrei. Not only was the film produced by Kiev Studios of Ukraine, the birthplace of Donskoi, but Ukraine was also the birthplace of Khrushchev, who had been First Secretary of the Ukrainian Communist party and later kept underlining the significance of Ukraine for Soviet economy and recalling with enthusiasm his early political experiences there.[44] In addition, in 1954 the tricentennial of Ukraine's union with Russia was celebrated, on the occasion of which Khrushchev transferred Crimea to Ukraine as a gift.

Donskoi's film was shaped not only by political events but also by developments in Soviet cinema. No doubt, to a large extent *Mother* conforms to socialist realist methods. It adopts a traditional style, helping the spectator to follow the plot easily. Moreover, it observes three major tenets of Socialist Realism, *patrinost'* ("Party-ness": allegiance to the Party spirit), *narodnost'* ("people-ness", meaning art's reflection of the life and culture of ordinary people), and *klassovost'*, ("class-ness": the depiction of the class ideology of the masses).[45] Donskoi found all three of these tenets in Gorki's novel and reinforced *narodnost'* by including folk songs and idyllic depictions of the Russian countryside.

At the same time that it follows typical socialist realist practices, *Mother* gives evidence of the spirit of renewal that appeared in Soviet cinema around 1954, when some filmmakers turned their backs on the standardized superheroes of earlier years and enriched Soviet film production with new themes related to everyday life, interpersonal relations and human psychology.[46] Following the path that had been blazed by such films as Ivan Pyryev's *The Test of Fidelity* (al. *Devotion*, *Ispytanie Vernosti*, 1954) and Iosif Kheifits's *A Big Family* (*Bol'shaia semia*, 1954, nominated

---

[41] Julie Ann Behling, "David's Quest to Outmaneuver Goliath - Clandestine Christians in the USSR, 1953-1985", *Electronic Theses, Treatises and Dissertations*, 2004. Paper 1209, 13-14.

[42] As Oksana Bulgakowa has observed for the Thaw cinema in general, "For the first time, members of the intelligentsia appeared on the screen not as negative characters" ("Cine-Weathers: Soviet Thaw Cinema in the International Context", in *The Thaw: Soviet Society and Culture during the 1950s and 1960s*, eds. Denis Kozlov and Eleonory Gilburd, Toronto, Buffalo, London: Toronto University Press, 2013, 467).

[43] Richard Stites, *Russian Popular Culture: Entertainment and Society since 1900*, Cambridge: Cambridge University Press, 1992, 123-124; and George W. Breslauer, "Khrushchev Reconsidered", in *The Soviet Union Since Stalin*, eds. Stephen F. Cohen, Alexander Rabinowitch and Robert Sharlet, Bloomington: Indiana University Press, 1980, 53-54, respectively.

[44] Volkogonov, *The Rise and Fall of the Soviet Empire*, 184, 196-198.

[45] Luker, "Introduction", 20-21

[46] Neya Zorkaya, *The Illustrated History of Soviet Cinema*, New York: Hippocrene Books, 1991, 197-8.

for the Golden Palm at the 1955 Cannes Film Festival), Donskoi gives depth to his characters. He reveals Andrei's and Sasha's sensitive traits and depicts the worries of Nilovna and other parents for their children. In two artistic flashbacks, he illustrates the mother's memories[47] which are mentioned in the novel. He often self-consciously moves his camera towards the heroes as if trying to penetrate their inner worlds and render their emotions. Furthermore, he depicts Nilovna in the May Day scene in a less heroic manner than Gorki. While Gorki's Nilovna picks up the flag from the ground, leans against the flagpole and boldly addresses the people, Donskoi's heroine simply takes the flag, brings it to her chest and leaves, greatly distancing herself from Pudovkin's character as well. Pudovkin had ended his adaptation with the mother heroically picking up the banner on May Day. Donskoi's *Mother* is a film about simple people, not heroes.

Donskoi's adaptation was shaped by the cultural and social-political developments of its time. As I have suggested here, Donskoi went back to Gorki in an attempt not to perpetuate ideas prevalent under Stalin but to evoke links between the contemporary Soviet Union and a pre-Stalinist era, when socialism meant justice, freedom, open defense of truth, and spiritual resurrection. That Donskoi's *Mother* fell into oblivion does not make this film "untimely". We can attribute its limited popularity to other factors. First, Donskoi's work could hardly compete with the worldwide fame and experimental vigor of Pudovkin's silent adaptation. Second, it appeared at a transitional period for Soviet cinema, when, as Zorkaya has argued, "the old and the new were intricately linked in the films".[48] In addition, after 1956, innovation and "thaw" in Soviet cinema were increasingly associated in the West with anti-war films (e.g. Mikhail Kalatozov's *The Cranes are Flying/Letyat zhuravli*, 1957), Sergei Bondarchuk's *Destiny of a Man/Sud'ba Cheloveka*, 1959), Grigori Chukhrai's *Ballad of a Soldier/Ballada o soldate*, 1959),[49] not with family dramas of the old. Whatever the reasons of *Mother*'s short-lived fame, the film bespeaks the climate of the mid-1950s in Soviet Russia, inviting us to revise aesthetic characterizations and observe the nuances of change in film history.

BIBLIOGRAPHY

Acton, Edward and Tom Stableford, *The Soviet Union: A Documentary History*, vol. 2: *1939-1991*, Exeter: University of Exeter Press, 2007.

Behling, Julie Ann, "David's Quest to Outmaneuver Goliath - Clandestine Christians in the USSR, 1953-1985", *Electronic Theses, Treatises and Dissertations*, 2004. Paper 1209.

Borras, F.M., *Maxim Gorki. The Writer: An Interpretation*, Oxford: Clarendon Press, 1967.

Breslauer, George W., "Khrushchev Reconsidered", in *The Soviet Union Since Stalin*, eds. Stephen F. Cohen, Alexander Rabinowitch and Robert Sharlet, Bloomington: Indiana University Press, 1980, 50-70.

[47] For similar examples in other Thaw films see Bulgakowa, "Cine-Weathers", 461.

[48] Zorkaya, *The Illustrated History of Soviet Cinema*, 201.

[49] Stites, *Russia Popular Culture*, 139-142. Denise J. Youngblood, *Russian War Films: On the Cinema Front, 1914-2005*, Lawrence: University Press of Kansas, 2007, 117-118.

Bulgakowa, Oksana, "Cine-Weathers: Soviet Thaw Cinema in the International Context", in *The Thaw: Soviet Society and Culture during the 1950s and 1960s*, eds. Denis Kozlov and Eleonory Gilburd, Toronto, Buffalo, London: Toronto University Press, 2013, 436-481.

Clark, Katerina, *The Soviet Novel: History as Ritual*, Chicago: The University of Chicago Press, 1981.

Daniels, Robert V., ed., *A Documentary History of Communism in Russia: From Lenin to Gorbachev*, Hanover and London: University Press of New England, 1993.

Dobrenko, Evgeny, *Stalinist Cinema and the Production of History: Museum of the Revolution*, trans. Sarah Young, Edinburgh: Edinburgh University Press, 2008.

Donskoi, Mark, "O sebe i svoem prizvanii", in *Mark Donskoi. Sbornik*, ed. Liudmila Ivanovna Pazhitnova, Moscow: Iskusstvo, 1973, 26-27.

Freeborn, Richard, *The Russian Revolutionary Novel: Turgenev to Pasternak*, Cambridge: Cambridge University Press, 1982.

Gilburd, Eleonor, "The Revival of Soviet Internationalism in the Mid to Late 1950s", in *The Thaw: Soviet Society and Culture during the 1950s and 1960s*, eds. Denis Kozlov and Eleonory Gilburd, Toronto, Buffalo, London: Toronto University Press, 2013, 362-401.

Gorki, Maxim, *Mother: A Novel*, trans. M. Wettlin, Moscow: Foreign Languages Publishing House, 1950.

———, *Mother*, New York: The Citadel Press, 1947.

Kastorskii, S., "Iz istorii sozdaniia povesti *Mat'*", in M. Gor'kii,_*Materialy i issledovaniia*, Moscow: Izdatel'stvo Akademii Nauk SSSR, 1941, 3: 288-358.

———, *"Mat'" M. Gor'kogo: Tvorcheskaia istoriia povesti*, Leningrad: Khudozhestvennaia Literatura, 1940.

Kenez, Peter, *A History of the Soviet Union from the Beginning to the End* (2nd ed), Cambridge: Cambridge University Press, 2009.

Luker, Nicholas, "Introduction", *From Furmanov to Sholokhov: An Anthology of the Classics of Socialist Realism*, Ann Arbor: Ardis, 1988, 11-38.

Medvedev, Roy A., "The Stalin Question", in *The Soviet Union Since Stalin*, eds. Stephen F. Cohen, Alexander Rabinowitch and Robert Sharlet, Bloomington: Indiana University Press, 1980, 32-49.

Mini, Panayiota, "Pudovkin's Cinema of the 1920s", Ph.D. Dissertation, University of Wisconsin-Madison, 2002.

———, "Mia methodos analisis kinimatografikon diaskevon: To paradeigma tis diaskevis tis *Manas* tou Gorki apo ton Pudovkin kai ton Donskoi", in *Apo ti logotehnia ston kinimatografo*, eds. F.Tabaki-Iona and M.E. Galani, Athens: Aigokeros, 2011, 19-42.

———, "Striving for the Maximum Appeal: Ideology and Propaganda in the Soviet Cinema of the 1920s and 1930s", in: *The Routledge Companion to Cinema and Politics*, eds. Yannis Tzioumakis and Claire Molloy, London and New York: Routledge, 2016, 161-174.

Plekhanov, G.V., "Predislovie k tret'emu izdaniiu sbornika "Za dvadtsat' let"", in G.V. Plekhanov, *Literatura i estetika*, vol.1,_*Teoriia iskusstva i istoriia esteticheskoi mysli*, Moscow: Khudozhestvennaia literatura, 1958, 123-132.

Read, Christopher, *Religion, Revolution and the Russian Intelligentsia, 1900-1912: The* Vekhi *Debate and its Intellectual Background*, London: The Macmillan Press, 1979.

Rollberg, Peter, *Historical Dictionary of Russian and Soviet Cinema*, Lanham, MD: Scarecrow Press, 2009.

Scherr, Barry P., *Maxim Gorki*, Boston: Twayne Publishers, 1988.

Semenovskii, O., *Marksistskaia kritika o Gor'kom: Iz istorii obshchestvenno-literaturnoi bor'by predoktiabr'skogo perioda*, Kichinev: Kartia Moldoveniaske, 1969.

Stites, Richard, *Russian Popular Culture: Entertainment and Society since 1900*, Cambridge: Cambridge University Press, 1992.

Vladimirova, Zoia, "Dushchu voskresshchuiu ne ub'iut!", in *Mark Donskoi. Sbornik*, ed. Liudmila Ivanovna Pazhitnova, Moscow: Iskusstvo, 1973, 124-129.

Volkogonov, Dmitri, *The Rise and Fall of the Soviet Empire: Political Leaders from Lenin to Gorbachev*, trans. H. Shukman, London: Harper Collins, 1999.

Weil, Irwin, *Gorki: His Literary Development and Influence on Soviet Intellectual Life*, New York: Random House, 1966.

Youngblood, Denise J., *Russian War Films: On the Cinema Front, 1914-2005*, Lawrence: University Press of Kansas, 2007.

Zorkaya, Neya, *The Illustrated History of Soviet Cinema*, New York: Hippocrene Books, 1991.

CHAPTER 3

Orpheus in Brazilian Film: Disobedience as Theme and Theoretical Approach

Carlinda Fragale Pate Nuñez

Orpheus makes two appearances in Brazilian film: *Orfeu Negro* (*Black Orpheus*, 1959), directed by Marcel Camus, and *Orfeu* (1999), by Carlos Diegues. Both take as their springboard the play *Orfeu da Conceição* (*Orpheus of the Conception*, 1955) by Vinicius de Moraes. The first film, although based on the dramatist's script, adopts domesticated procedures (among others, the idealized visual rhetoric and the stereotypical *modus* of presenting Brazilians as remaining *bons sauvages* in the tropics, exemplarily represented by the exotic behavior of local people, the *cariocas*). Such a work will be referred to as an "obedient" adaptation in this essay. The second one preserves the basic idea of portraying the protagonist in one of Rio's slums as a black songwriter, but differs in everything else: plot, mythical references, socio-cultural dynamics and aesthetic procedures. This is a "disobedient" adaptation (a "cultural appropriation"),[1] mainly in terms of its extreme aestheticism, but also in the way it transgresses the darkness of the Greek myth that prevails in the thematic lineage. The notions of obedience and disobedience with regard to adaptations will be further explored later in this essay.

Unlike the existing studies dealing with the Brazilian Orphic triad (play and films), this essay examines the Orphic images that turn up in the triad, along with the multifaceted process that takes place therein: the assimilation into Brazilian culture of what Aby Warburg (1866-1929) has named the *Bilderfahrzeuge* ("image vehicles") circuit.[2] It will be shown that it is through such "image vehicles" that themes such as that of disobedience are reformulated.

---

1 Julie Sanders, *Adaptation and Appropriation*, London: Routledge, 2006, 81.

2 In the 1907 essay "Peasants at Work in Burgundian Tapestries" (Aby Warburg, *The Renewal of Pagan Antiquity. Contributions to the Cultural History of the European Renaissance*. Los Angeles: Getty Research Institute for the History of Art and the Humanities, 1999, 315-323), Warburg offered a completely new interpretation of the uses of tapestries by earlier generations. Instead of "aristocratic fossil[s] in a show collection", he describes tapestries as "democratic features", since the weavers could repeat the designs as often as they were demanded to. Besides that, he considered tapestries as the most efficient "mobile image vehicle" (*bewegliches Bildvehikel*): as removable and usually displaced pieces, they served as powerful artefacts of linkage between private and public spaces, old and new contexts, present and ancient times. So, tapestry became the first image vehicle conceived by Warburg.

Along with other uncommon and innovative terms coined by Warburg, these image vehicles are linked to his research on the "afterlife of Antiquity" (*Nachleben der Antike*) in the Renaissance and later. In the famous *Mnemosyne Atlas* (2001), Warburg employed as organizational criterion a list of image vehicles made of motifs of remote provenance, embodied in cultural signs and artistic forms, which became visible with the "migration of images" (*Bildwanderung*) in space and time. As vehicles, such images put in motion the "posthumous life" of pagan culture in a two-fold way: they transport feelings, knowledge, beliefs, emotionally intensified gestures (*Pathosformeln*), and at the same time they disseminate stylistic and structural frameworks, eventually including propagandistic content. This line of reverse continuity to the ancient and even to the archaic retrieves meaningful elements and events, deposited over eons and now fully inscribed in human memory. In short, the Warburgian image vehicles, due to the immediate transmission of their contents and emotions, start a creative process in the human brain, which produces new thoughts.

Connections between Warburgian investigation and adaptation and appropriation studies are many, but we shall underline two of them. First, myths are known as the most adaptable forms of narrative, and Warburg relied on old mythology to provide the fundamentals for his history of human culture and organize his *Mnemosyne Atlas* of images.[3] Second, thanks to their brevity and economy, myths lend themselves to continuous retellings, easily adjust to different media and communicate efficiently through their inherent pathos and symbolism. Warburgian research set out to detect and demonstrate the strategies and processes myths commonly rely on in their negotiations with history.[4]

The rebirth of Orpheus in post-classical adaptations in Brazil depends mainly on the proficiency of artists in handling the image vehicles related to the Orphic myth, as will be discussed below. This essay thus belongs with the Warburg school of mythographic scholarship, whilst also being informed by Gaston Bachelard's epistemology of complexity, as set out in *The New Scientific Spirit* (*Le nouvel esprit scientifique,* 1934) and in *The Philosophy of No* (*La philosophie du non,* 1940).[5]

Bachelard and Disobedience

Following Bachelard, it is reasonable to consider that the remaking of artistic texts, in addition to representing courageous acts of creative intelligence, is not at all innocent. Adaptations may arise from an acquiescent and affirmative arrangement of the reference work or from the incitement to move forward to issues suggested (or neglected) by the source text. But they may also disprove the source work, indeed counteract it, albeit making use of the narrative thread, the structural organization or

---

[3] This work was unfinished at the time of his death in 1929.

[4] See https://www.goethe.de/en/kul/bku/20867100.html [accessed 30/12/2017].

[5] Gaston Bachelard, *The New Scientific Spirit*, trans. A. Goldhammer, Boston: Beacon Press, 1985; *The Philosophy of No*: *A Philosophy of the New Scientific Mind*, trans. G. C. Waterston. Orion Press, New York, 1968.

the supporting elements for the new plot. From this perspective, adaptation is a special case of disobedience.

Bachelard is compelling on this subject. According to him,

> To disobey in order to take action is the creator's motto. The history of human progress consists of a series of Promethean acts. But in the very fabric of an individual life, the autonomy won is made up of a series of small Promethean disobediences, astute, well-associated disobedience, patiently pursued. Disobedience can even be subtle enough to avoid punishment. All that remains is an equivocal guilt, a diffuse guilt. There is a sense, we believe, in studying the dynamism of disobedience which animates all knowledge.[6]

That is to say, the metaphor of (dis)obedience can be useful in adaptation studies because—beyond the usual metaphor of fidelity and/or infidelity[7] in relation to the source text—disobedience projects the adapted version onto a sea of complexities that both helps to discern extra-aesthetic merits involved in the artistic equation under study, and to detect compliant versions of the same theme.

Here, disobedience is metaphorically employed upon issues that endure the tests of time, geographic displacement and a change in medium. But not only that. Some aspects of disobedience should be noted, without excluding further possibilities:

1. The disobedient thematic involves a certain representational eclecticism, thanks to a micropolitics that interferes with the remodelling of the plot. It explains variations in the ideological framework.

2. Disobedient subjects are agents of significant changes, either from the diegetic point of view, or from the degree of criticality they reach. They contribute to the manifestation of somewhat activist subjectivities. We

---

6 In the original: "Désobéir pour agir est la devise du créateur. L'histoire des hommes en ses progrès est une suite d'actes prométhéens. Mais, dans le tissu même d'une vie individuelle, l'autonomie conquise est faite d'une série de menues désobéissances prométhéen nés, de désobéissances adroites, bien associées, patiemment poursuivies. La désobéissance peut même être assez subtile pour éviter la punition. Il n'en reste qu'une culpabilité équivoque, une culpabilité diffuse. Il y a un sens, croyons-nous, à étudier le dynamisme de désobéissance qui anime tout savoir." Gaston Bachelard, *Fragments d'une poétique du feu*, Copy-text editing, foreword and notes by Suzanne Bachelard, Paris: Presses Universitaires de France, 1988, 107. Our translation.

7 This quarrel about (in)fidelity in literary adaptations is wide. Although this is not the main focus here, it is impossible to avoid touching on this issue, somewhat related to disobedience. See Robert Stam, "Beyond Fidelity: The Dialogics of Adaptation", in *Film Adaptation*, ed. James Naremore, New Brunswick, NJ: Rutgers University Press, 2000. 38-53; David L. Kranz and Nancy C. Mellerski, eds., *In/Fidelity: Essays on Film Adaptation*. Newcastle: Cambridge Scholars, 2008; Kamilla Elliott, *Rethinking the Novel/Film Debate*. UK: Cambridge University Press, 2003; Deborah Cartmell and Imelda Whelehan eds., *Adaptation: From Text to Screen, Screen to Text,* New York: Routledge, 1993; Andrew Dudley, "The Well-Worn Muse: Adaptation in film History and Theory", in *Narrative Strategies: Original Essays in Film and Prose Fiction*, eds. Syndy M. Conger and Janice R. Welsch, Illinois: Western Illinois University, 1980, 12-13.

can even think of activist themes associated with platforms of social change. Disobedient subjects "take sides", attempt to intervene, and believe that things might be otherwise (whereas obedient subjects remain captives of their sharp scholasticism and conservatism).

3. Disobedient themes reinvent pre-existent versions, recycling literary forms. They might be simple in terms of signification, but are generally rich in their ramifications ("spread factor").

4. They are neither defined in one single theory, nor approached by one single discipline; they challenge standard epistemologies.

5. Moreover, in order to compare two things, you need an organizing principle by which they can be brought together in a meaningful way.[8] Disobedience is such a principle, a *tertium quid*[9] ("some third thing") by which the comparison is more likely to go beyond the mere correlation of works, and by which the adaptation points to whatever the work adds—whether obediently or disobediently—to thematology, intertextual studies and intermedial approaches.

Myths—potential stories of disobedience—are the most adaptive materials for anything. They have always been used as a support for extraordinary ideas. Perhaps an emblematic figure here is Orpheus himself. The hero, disobedient *par excellence*, shapes the gesture that must be repeated by critics if they wish to capture the overcoding in the adapted work: to gaze in opposite directions, to look back in order to change the future, to move from the bottom up and vice-versa, to evaluate that which is near and that which is distant, to attune art criticism to other aspects of culture.

The recurrence of the theme of disobedience is not fortuitous. On the contrary, each adaptation offers brand new strategies for well-known formulations; each improves universal, popular and local traditions. The remanufacture of a theme instigates a new way of thinking about aesthetic value itself, and about the objective of the remodelling; it exposes the political dimension of art. To disobey, in this sense, is healthy even from a theoretical point of view: disobedient art objects demand a complex epistemology of art, capable of mapping out the particular space of inter-appropriations and multiple interstitialities—*metakosmia,* [10] the cosmic *vacuum*

---

8 An explicit statement of this need is to be found in Plato's *Timaeus*: "It is impossible that two things only should be joined together without a third. There must be some bond in between both to bring them together" (*Tim*, 31b-c). Simultaneously, the third contains both and acts as an organizing device that enables a comparison.

9 The Latin expression translates the Greek *tríton ti*.

10 The empty space between cosmic bodies; extra-cosmic hiatuses understood as an undetermined cosmos that cannot know itself, but that sets limits. Analogically, we identify meta-cosmic spaces and interstitial figures apprehended in them from witty correlations (the "able", or "creative", "disobediences" Bachelard [1988] refers to).

wherein different forms of knowledge and abilities stand collectively, informally and empirically. It is within this interstitial space that the spark of Promethean deeds shines, the dynamics of creative disobedience whence the adaptations spring.

In short, disobedient themes correspond to unconventional approaches, characterized by the commanding multiplicity in the adapted work. Bachelard's reference to Prometheus, an icon of the paradoxical relationship between authority and rebellion, knowledge and power, pleasure and torture, human love and divine revenge, is justifiable. Titanic thinking is viscerally connected to disobedience and to the imagery of defiance, to the desire of seeing beyond that which shows itself.[11]

Brazilian Adaptations of the Orpheus Myth

Orpheus was never a protagonist in Ancient Greek theatre.[12] Conversely, twentieth-century Brazilian theatre and cinema afforded him a privileged place in renowned and successful masterpieces. *Orfeu da Conceição* (1955),[13] by Vinicius de Moraes (1913-1980), announces in its title an adaptation of the Greek myth with Brazilian citizenship, considering the family name given to the protagonist. Conceição is a very common name in Brazil, and bears the marks of syncretism (pagan/Christian) and multiculturalism (Brazilian/foreigner). The playwright conceived his "carioca tragedy" in 1942, according to the chronology offered at the end of the play: the idea was born in Niterói, 1942; developed in Los Angeles, 1948; improved in Rio in 1953; and reached its final version for publication in Paris, 1955.

The play inverts the traditional referencing, for the divine musician of Thrace is only evoked by the sublime samba player of the carioca slum; Greek gods are embodied in black actors, carnivalizing the traditional paradigm: it is not the Greek Pantheon that is the object of the homage, but the black. The adaptation of the myth to the universe of blacks precedes both the African movement that celebrates being black, and Jean-Paul Sartre's renowned preface[14] to the anthology of black and Malagasy poetry edited in 1948 by Senegalese poet and politician Léopold Sédar Senghor, whose title was the same used in the movie version of the play, directed by Marcel Camus in 1959.

---

[11] It is not by chance that our disobedient figure here is Orpheus who, like Prometheus, denies incomprehensible laws (fate); who, as a divine singer, won Eurydice, but who, in disrespecting Hades' sovereign will, lost her.

[12] According to Rachel Aélion (*Euripide, Héritier d'Eschyle* [*Euripides, Heir of Aeschylus*]. Paris: Les Belles Lettres, 1983, I, 255), Aeschylus staged the death of Orpheus in *Bassarids* (alternative designation for the Maenads), of which only fragments are extant. There are only six references to Orpheus in the remaining repertoire of Athenian tragedy (*Ag.*, 1617; *Alc.*, 328; *Bac.*, 556; Cicl. 642; *Hip.*, 936; *Res.* 915), and even fewer in comedy (apart from *Frogs*, 1006). Sophocles does not mention him.

[13] Vinicius de Moraes. *Orfeu da Conceição: Uma Tragédia Carioca*, 2nd. ed., Rio de Janeiro: Dois Amigos, 1967.

[14] Jean-Paul Sartre [1948], "Orphée noir", in *Anthologie de la Nouvelle Poésie Nègre et Magache de la Langue Française* [*Anthology of the new Negro and Malagasy Poetry of the French Language*], ed. L.S. Senghor, Paris: Quadrige/Presses Universitaires de France, 1998.

In a testimonial, Vinicius de Moraes declared himself to have been "impregnated with the spirit of that ethnic group" since 1942,[15] reproducing the atmosphere of those days, a time when ethnography experienced a great push[16] and many interpretations of Brazil were discussed; a time when the left supported the African cause worldwide. In Brazil, contrary to this trend, shortly after the "Estado Novo" period (New State, 1937-1945), i.e., Getúlio Vargas' dictatorship, African exotericism was prohibited.

The inspiration for the play came in a conversation with a North-American writer hosted by Moraes, whom he took to "*favelas* (slums), *macumbas* (black witchcraft), clubs and black parties in Rio". Both men concluded that:

> [A]ll of those celebrations and festivities [...] had something to do with Greece; as if the black carioca [native of Rio] were a Greek in ganga [i.e. African clothes]—a Greek still lacking the culture and the Apollonian cult of beauty, but nevertheless marked by the Dionysian feel for life.[17]

Another event, not long afterwards, prompted the early writing process. As Moraes read the myth of Orpheus, in a hilltop house on the shore, he heard:

> [S]omewhere in the hill, black residents started an infernal drumming, and the rough rhythm of their instruments—the cuíca [a Brazilian friction drum], the tambourine, the surdo [bass drum]—reached me in a nostalgic way, all at the same time, with yet farther echoes of Orpheus' weeping.[18]

The use of "infernal" and "rough" to designate the sounds produced by the black people calls our attention, providing contrast to the "magic and nostalgic atmosphere in which Orpheus surrounds himself". Granted, the friction and bass drums produce very peculiar sounds—the friction drum sounds like a snore; the bass drum produces grave tones, albeit not scary or rude—but the testimonial underscores a bipolarity that can be found in the play *Orfeu da Conceição*. An Apollonian Orpheus plays the guitar; his space is the slum, where he consummates an idealized love for Eurydice up above, in the kingdom of order. The samba bandsmen players, right in the fullness of Carnival, play the friction drum and the bass drum in the violent atmosphere of the city and in a club called "*Maiorais do Inferno*" (The Best Ones in Hell), a Dionysian

---

[15] Maria Claudete de Souza Oliveira, *Presenças de Orfeu*, São Paulo: Universidade de São Paulo, 2006, 106.

[16] Roger Bastide, Robert Aubreton and Lévi-Strauss, for instance, went to Brazil. The latter taught at the University of São Paulo from 1934 to 1939, when he collected data on Brazilian indigenous tribes to be used in *Elementary Structures of Kinship*, published in 1949. Years later, he reported the field experience among the Brazilian Indians in *Tristes Tropiques* (Paris: Librairie Plon, 1955).

[17] Vinicius de Moraes, "Radar da Batucada" (presentation text of *Orfeu da Conceição*), in *Vinicius de Moraes Teatro em Versos*, ed. Carlos Augusto Calil, São Paulo: Companhia das Letras, 2008, 47. Our translation.

[18] *Ibid.*, 47-48.

space of disorder.[19] The slum has been pacified thanks to the musical culture of strings (European); in the club, whose door is kept by a bouncer called Cerberus, Carnival seethes to the rhythm of the musical culture of drums (African).

In other words, the dramaturgical text slips in a discourse that enjoyed ample circulation in Brazilian intellectual circles of the time: a discourse which represented African-Brazilian cultural elements as stigmatized by backwardness, and connoted with the danger of disturbing the social harmony, whereas elements of European origin were represented as "civilizing".

The poet-playwright's interpretation of Brazil confirms the contradictions of the period. The play was acclaimed 13 years after its conception, in a different political-ideological context (now democratic and progressive) but the social contradictions were still there.

Moraes created surprising correspondences (some of them unacceptable nowadays) between nuclear aspects of the myth of Orpheus and Brazilian cultural features, taking up "image vehicles" from the Classic heritage as *tertium quids*. Let us consider some details:

- The Incantatory music: In *Orfeu da Conceição*, the magic power of black art (which Sartre exulted in his well-known preface) still brings a mythic fecundity, in process of reaching an Apollonian state, which reveals an evolutionary vision that will be frustrated, however, because Orpheus' samba outlives him. Moraes' play is a musical drama that finds in its soundtrack a meta-text in charge of producing meanings in other spheres, mainly in the history of Brazilian movies and cultural politics.

- The Hero's double genealogy: The Greek Orpheus is quite divine due to his familiar ties with Apollo, and quite human due to his mysterious religion. Orpheus, the son of King Oeagrus of Thrace, was educated by Dactyls, magi of Phrygia. Something similar happens to Orfeu da Conceição, admired as a white man amidst the black, as a black man amidst the white, in the multiethnic context of Brazil. Christian and Afro-Brazilian deities protect him. The confluence of so many opposing elements promotes an overcoding upon the figure of Orpheus: theologian, poet, musician and magician. The Brazilian Orpheus is mestizo, multi-ethnic, syncretic and multicultural. Various forms of knowledge, in Ancient Greece and in Brazil today, enrich Orpheus' artistic attributes.

- The Mystery Feature of Orphean Poetry: The invention of the hexameter is attributed to Orpheus, as well as the co-authorship of Eleusinian Mysteries, which connects Orpheus to the emergence of *philomythia*, the

[19] Victor Hugo A. Pereira, "A Lira e os Infernos da Exclusão—Orfeu no Brasil", in *Estudos da Linguagem através de Textos*, III Congresso Nacional de Linguística e Filologia, Rio de Janeiro: CiFeFIL, 2000, v. 1, 95.

philosophical mythology adopted as a base for Orphean eschatology and for Ancient Pythagorean study centers. Orfeu da Conceição has powerful words; everybody hears him, even the dead.

- *Katabasis* and *Anabasis*: Both heroes, the Greek and the Brazilian, undertook the most difficult of journeys. This are the ultimate experience of the mythic hero—the arduous and prohibited descent to the Underworld followed by the fearful, but successful, ascent and reintegration into the world of the living.

- The Ideology of Defiance: Influenced by an exclusivist viewpoint, Orpheus first loved all women; then, he preferred Eurydice, the harmony of Orphean lyre. Orpheus is alone among the champions of *nóstos* ("return") literature to have broken the taboo of directions, daring to "look back". Upon losing Eurydice, he despised all women and became the first pederast. Then he embarked on the most feared journey: *katabasis* ("descent"), followed by *anabasis* ("ascent"), the journey, undertaken by heroes and all souls, into/ from the Underworld.[20]

In fact, Carnival is a manifestation of Orphism-Dionysism in the tropics. The Carnivalesque rites—parades, masquerades, costumes—reflect critically on aspects of reality and on forms of social interaction within the system: the ineffectiveness of legal instruments in the regulation of daily life, the disparity between excess and lack, the social deadlock between things remaining as they are and changing.[21]

The adaptation of the Orpheus theme occurs through the image vehicles of the mythical tradition. As indicated in the table below, the fundamental traits of the Orphean myth are preserved—in inverse ratio—through an altered transfiguration. At a deeper level, adaptations of the Orpheus theme cover up, as the myth itself, some shades: what at first glance is taken to be a new arrangement of a plot is, in fact, a process of transcultural articulation emphasizing selected elements.

Elements of Transcultural Articulation

"IMAGE VEHICLES"	GREEK MYTH	BRAZILIAN CULTURE
Incantatory music	Orpheus - The inventor of the lyre and the hexameter; associated to a hearing culture and an acoustic mimesis	Samba / guitar

[20] According to the Orphic-Dionysian eschatology, the human soul migrates through different bodies in successive reincarnations (gr. *metempsykhosis*) until it has reached full purification.

[21] Roberto Da Matta, Carnavais, Malandros e Heróis: Para uma Sociologia do Dilema Brasileiro, Rio de Janeiro: Rocco, 1997.

Dance	The duplicity of the hero	Olympic genealogy / popular genealogy Paved streets / slum Elite / people Hero / lawbreakers
Mysterious feature	Orphean poetry *Metempsykhosis*	*Macumba*, occultism, magic thinking, night
Ideology of defiance	Breaking taboos	Enthusiasm and ecstasy
Exclusive look	"Looking back"	Carnival
Katabasis / Anabasis	Searching for Eurydice Return Death under the wrath of Bacchae	Desecration of sacred spaces / entering forbidden spaces
Eschatological landscape	Journey into the Underworld	World of criminality

In fact, each of these articulatory elements taken from the ancient legend anchors a group of image vehicles. The mobile images travel in time and space, and reappear, adapted, in historic figurations of art.

The transposition of the legendary narrative to the slum in which the action of Moraes' play takes place involves combining the mystic saga with a romantic plot, introducing jealousy as a motivation for Eurydice's death—the jealousy of an ignored suitor who stabs her under the influence of a magic spell cast by Mira, one of Orpheus' vengeful ex-girlfriends.[22] However, the text is not limited to the conflict between characters, instead prioritizing "a panel of relationships that strongly indicates features that may be attributed to a specific culture, instead of individual psychological characteristics".[23]

Eurydice and Mira confront each other in the sphere of cultural representations: Eurydice embodies the principle of order that Orpheus exerts amidst the chaos of the slum, apart from being a Christian and a virgin (and that is how she intends to remain until they marry). In contrast, Mira practices *macumba* rituals; she is eroticized, actively connected to Carnival—that is, she represents disorder. Eurydice is the opposite of all women in the slum, including Orpheus' mother,[24] who announces the categorical imperative of love relationships in a slum: "Wedding in the slums is wooing"—that is, a wedding dispenses with civil formalization and divine blessings. Based on this unwritten law, the relationship with Mira should prevail. The play anticipates the motive that provokes the divergences between Eurydice and Mira, and forms a base for the tragic error, the *hamartía*, committed by the hero who breaks the slum's social code.

---

[22] Et. lt. *mira*, "surprising", "wonderful", worthy to be admired. Hence fr. *miroir* a. eng. *mirror*.

[23] V. H. Pereira, "A Lira e os Infernos da Exclusão—Orfeu no Brasil", 95.

[24] Another alteration made in the Greek legend: in the play, Orpheus' mother is called Clio (the muse of History).

Mira evokes the Black Lady, who invades Orpheus' dreams. In the oneiric fight, Orpheus wins. The argument with the Lady of Death consummates the hero's *hýbris*:

> Orpheus controls the slum! Orpheus is life.
> [...], the slum is Orpheus,
> [...] Nothing in the slum
> exists without Orpheus and his guitar![25]

Eurydice's death, at the end of Act I, compels Orpheus to descend from the slum towards the Carnival club *Maiorais do Inferno* ("The Best Ones in Hell"), located in the city. The clash of opposing forces takes place downtown, far from the favela (slum). Old mythical figures emerge at this point of the plot, embodied in hybrid characters: identified as typically Greek by their names and function in the scene, and as authentically cariocas by the social places that they occupy. In Act II, Cerberus, the bouncer, does not allow Orpheus to enter, but melts when he hears the guitar tunes. Orpheus wants to know where Eurydice is, no longer the representation of his lyre's harmony, but of love. Pluto is the club's president, and Proserpina is his queen. Mira is the chief of the Bacchae. They all rage against Orpheus. Music and tragedy underline the actions. In the scene, The Moon is an icon for death. The catastrophe takes place in Act III: under Mira's command, Orpheus' previous lovers tear him into pieces using a razor. The double murder caused by jealousy is perfectly integrated into the tragic economy.

The poetic transposition into Marcel Camus' film *Orfeu Negro* modifies the dramatic text, beginning with the prominence conceded to the city of Rio and to the utopian favela. The film explores Rio's fascinating landscape. It poetically explores black Brazilian music, but from a totally different perspective to that of the theatrical play, which emphasizes "the old black world",[26] its religious, acoustic, sensual values. The master of incantations that Moraes brought to the stage is reduced to a caricature in Camus' film, full of commonplaces and exoticism.

Eurydice is stunned when she reaches the city by boat (in the source version, she came by bus, an arduous journey of three days). She has been plagued by a man who wants to kill her; no one knows why. The carnival masquerade that dominates downtown is an environment conducive for him to chase her. The initial scene is of mythological inspiration, no doubt: the beloved came from the water to traverse streets in overcrowded trams, crossing the modern metropolis, the capital of Brazil at the time.

Despite the dualities depicted (black and white people, workers and pedestrians just hanging out, archaic reminiscences and the modernity of some buildings), Eurydice is only safe on the hill, where fraternity, musicality, and carnival prevail throughout the year, a utopian place, the "high" part of the city that sublimates the "low" into evanescence and purity.

---

[25] Moraes, *Orfeu da Conceição*, 42. Our translation.
[26] Sartre, "Orphée noir", xvii.

The carnival club "The Best Ones in Hell" from the tragic drama becomes the street block "United of Babylon" in *Orfeu Negro*, a strategic change through which the film, as a documentary, reports the modernization of the carnival itself, as commercial and luxurious spectacle. The filmmaker is fascinated by spontaneous scenes of street Carnival, revealing rites of socialization and the myth of social and racial brotherhood. The enchantment of the camera abruptly meets the violent side of the double-faced city, in the chase that ends with Eurydice's accidental death by electrocution.

The *katabasis* of Orpheus is the keynote of the film. It happens in three stages: He first goes to a public office, to find the name of Eurydice in the city's death records; then he visits a *macumba* shrine (guarded by Cerberus), and finally the morgue. The visit to the religious ritual is almost a downright ethnographic documentary exploring primitivism and the strangeness of African-Brazilian cults. When Orpheus sings, Eurydice talks to him, embodied in an old woman. Orpheus gazes back and does not see his lover in the body through which she speaks. The last step on the way to hell is the visit to the Institute of Forensic Medicine, whence he rescues Eurydice's body.

This version domesticates the contradictions present in the theatrical plot and draws an enchanting visual rhetoric, which explores the physical and human landscapes of Rio de Janeiro, with its hills, lush beaches and splendid human figures. These facts make *Orfeu Negro* an "obedient" adaptation of the dramatic text. The contradictions of carnivalized society and of the real condition of life in the favelas of Rio de Janeiro are "tamed," "under control".

THE BIRTH OF POP-ROCK ORPHEUS

The plot changed dramatically in Diegues' *Orfeu* (1999). Carnival moved to the foreground, signalling the renewed myth's positivity, even activism, in light of reality (in opposition to Camus) and consistent with an updated approach. This adaptation features several innovations with regard to the ancient myth and the previous versions. In the following selection of some striking features of this remake, a radical departure from the romantic Orpheus is apparent, without banishing the contradiction of the hero, who remains "politically correct", although disobedient.

The film emphasizes the changes in Rio's slums and the exchange between the culture of the hillside shantytown and that of the "globalized" world. Brazilian slums have changed considerably in recent decades.[27] Diegues takes advantage of the well-known theme to correct Camus' idealized version and to reinterpret Moraes' theatrical play.

The more recent *Orfeu* depicts a fictional slum in a realistic, contemporary way, as these areas have changed a lot since the 1990s: marked by the fight for affirmation

---

[27] Until the 1950s, the slums were represented as a romanticized place. In the following 20 years, they experienced an enormous increase in population density, due to internal migratory waves of the poor, the growth of poverty and urban swelling.

as well as by an open war between official forces and the criminal agents; by the inhabitants' pride in having been born there and their shame for its being a headquarters for drug dealers. Not only has consumerism emerged there, but also social improvement and professionalization projects. Today inhabitants of favelas make and export "fashion from the slum"—handicrafts, music, and Carnival itself.

The character of Diegues' Orpheus embodies the idea that upward mobility can be attained only through modernization and keeping pace with an ever-faster changing world. The new Orpheus is representative of this new social context in the drama. He has achieved citizen status and respectability thanks to education and modern technology such as his cell phone and the laptop he uses to compose his music. Under these conditions, the term "slum" itself no longer corresponds to the image its inhabitants have of the place where they live. It is more appropriate to use the word "community". This is no longer a black ghetto, nor the mythical and nostalgic cradle of a lost paradise. The social profile of the population in Rio's community is the soul of the more recent adaptation of the Orphic myth.

The film underlines the contrast between backwardness and poverty in the slum and Orpheus' new attitude: full consciousness of the conflict-filled heritage that empowers him. Focusing on the culture of exclusion and violence rather than of racial prejudice, Diegues creates an aesthetic contrast between poverty and technology: he juxtaposes images of trash on the streets with scenes of amazing creative energy, and shows us the contrasting powers of music and crime. The paradoxical reality of the slum sparks a chain of images, which represent metaphorical oppositions such as the darkness of the hard life and the brightness of Carnival, guilt and innocence, love and hate, life and death.

Diegues portrays a positive vision of the community. He shows in detail the spectacular life in the community, and uses a Carnival parade as a compelling *exemplum* of it. The fictional samba school, Unidos da Carioca, presents an experimental composition, one in which the traditional soft samba, a precursor of the "bossa nova" style, is mixed with features of pop music and rap. In the course of the film, rap is seen as a new phase in the development of samba. This is suggested in the lyrics to the theme-song of the samba school in the parade, lyrics which recount the history of samba. On the one hand, rap is seen as disrespectful and a breaking away from "authentic" samba while, on the other hand, it also recalls and pays tribute to the tradition.

This samba (composed by Caetano Veloso), along with other parts of the soundtrack, functions as a musical commentary on the plot. While Orpheus dances and sings in the parade, Eurydice is killed. The precise moment of the shot is mimetically represented by the beats of the samba-rap. The gentleness of the film's samba-theme creates a dialogue with the parade's samba-plot, musically depicting the dichotomies mentioned above.

Another interesting feature of this adaptation is the visual commentary on the plot. In the opening of the film, we see a clip, which evokes another film—one by Nelson Pereira dos Santos, *Rio, 40 Graus* (*Rio, 100 Degrees*), released in 1955, a realistic portrayal of Rio's slum life in the 1950s, used primarily to show the creativity of its population.

Diegues' film is concerned with topography and scenery, as much as the earlier ones were, but the human landscape captures, in flashes, the complex social dynamics of the place where diversity prevails and conflicts are always about to explode. The inhabitants come from many different parts of the country and belong to diverse religious denominations, forming a multiethnic whole—all these issues are brought into play in scenes that update the myth.

In Diegues' adaptation, aside from the Orphic imagery, some aspects of the Dionysian myth generate specific symbols: the fires that abound in the film are sometimes shots from police weapons, sometimes fireworks announcing the arrival of drugs or the beginning of a new samba parade. The rhythmic beat of the film delineates both the samba and the police raids in the slum. The exuberance of the samba dancers invading the samba parade catwalk is analogous to that of the police invading the community. The social regeneration of the population of the slum also relates to Dionysian resurrections.

Diegues uses the interweaving of life and death, tragedy and music, to codify other schematic networks present in the work. The musical network interweaves Caetano Veloso, Tom Jobim, Vinicius de Moraes, Luis Bonfá, Michael Jackson, and Fernanda Abreu, as well as anonymous composers of traditional songs well known throughout the world. There is, in addition, the cinematic network: this comprises the 1930s Carnival films of Carmen Miranda; films produced by the company Atlántida - *Rio 40 Graus*, *Rio Zona Norte* (Nelson Pereira dos Santos, 1955); and Cocteau's trilogy *Le sang d'un poète* (1930), *Orphée* (1939) and *Le Testament d'Orphée* (1960); with references to actors, famous scenes, producers, etc.

The aesthetic realism assumes full visibility in the counterpoint between the three protagonists: Orpheus, Eurydice and Lucinho, the Aristaeus, the apiarist in the Greek tale. While Orpheus is centered, educated, and comfortable in his surroundings, Eurydice is completely disoriented in the slum, which to her is a labyrinth. Because of her unclear ethnic origins, her lover calls her "Little Indian". For Carnival, she appears dressed in clouds, as a Dryad, a nymph: her element is water - the humidity of the rainforest. At the same time, Eurydice is a symbolic synthesis of the three races from which the Brazilian people emanate.

Lucinho, who grew up with Orpheus, is his counterpart. The king of music and the drug dealer king are presented as opposites: the black one and his music win and dictate behavior; while the other, the white one, is an outlaw and a frustrated man, though not because of social or racial oppression. In the film, explanations—whether paternalistic, conciliatory, or even recriminatory—are not found to justify the existence of criminals in the slums. Lucinho is resentful of Orpheus' superior musical talent. But the film goes further than this vestige of the past. Lucinho may be in love with Eurydice, but he is more interested in Orpheus, for whom he feels a homosexual passion, made clear by their kiss on the mouth at the moment that Orpheus kills him.

Examples of metamorphoses abound in the film: Orpheus' mother was a "macumbeira" (something between a witch doctor and a voodoo practioner), but she repressed her "faith"; his father transformed himself from drum master to pastor of an Evangelical church. Lucinho is the childhood friend who became a drug dealer.

To conquer Eurydice, Orpheus defies Lucinho: he is given until Ash Wednesday to leave the community. The musician transgresses social norms three times: first, when he defies Lucinho; second, when he includes rap in the samba and subjects the samba school to disqualification; and third, when he appropriates Lucinho's coveted love, Eurydice. For all this, Lucinho kills her. The *katabasis* of Orpheus occurs when he dives off a cliff where drug dealers dump the bodies of their victims.

A Last but not Final Glance

The enchanting music, the duality of the hero, disobedience, metamorphosis, *katabasis* and *anabasis* are indispensable image vehicles from which the theme of the Disobedient Singer has generated adaptations, which are themselves obedient and disobedient. Vinicius de Moraes' theatrical version and Carlos Diegues' film are disobedient adaptations, in the sense that they shape the conflicting aspects of the Orphic ambience. Marcel Camus' version is obedient because it tames and romanticizes the whole context around the samba singer.

In short, *Orfeu da Conceição* is an anti-realistic version; *Orfeu Negro*, an idealistic adaptation of the theater play, and Diegues' *Orfeu* corrects, in a realistic way, both works. Moraes enacts some basic contradictions in Brazilian society; Camus dissolves them, while Diegues rejects them. The post-modern Orpheus is the most authentic renewal of the myth, because the hero's drama corresponds to the greatest tragedy of Rio itself (heaven and hell, arts and crime, life and death are in each corner).

The idea of rebelliousness that Orpheus triggers thus endures vigorously in its post-modern and contemporary incarnations, in the fields of poetry, criticism and cultural history of societies, representing, in art, the disobedience inherent in myths in general, and Orpheus in particular.

Bibliography

Aélion, Rachel, *Euripides, Heir of Aeschylus*, v. I. Paris: Les Belles Lettres, 1983.

Bachelard, Gaston, *Fragments d'une poétique du feu*, Copy-text editing, foreword and notes by Suzanne Bachelard, Paris: Presses Universitaires de France, 1988.

———, *The New Scientific Spirit*, transl. A. Goldhammer, Boston: Beacon Press, 1985.

———, *The Philosophy of No: A Philosophy of the New Scientific Mind*, transl. G.C. Waterston, Orion Press: New York, 1968.

Botelho, André, "Passado e Futuro das Interpretações do País", *Tempo Social*, 22:1, 2010, 47-66.

Cartmell, Deborah and Imelda Whelehan, eds., *Adaptation: From Text to Screen, Screen to Text*, New York: Routledge, 1993.

Da Matta, Roberto, *Carnavais, Malandros e Heróis: Para uma sociologia do dilema brasileiro*, Rio de Janeiro, Rocco, 1997.

Dudley, Andrew, "The Well-Worn Muse: Adaptation in Film History and Theory", in. *Narrative Strategies: Original Essays in Film and Prose Fiction*, eds., Syndy M. Conger and Janice R Welsch, Illinois: Western Illinois University, 1980, 12-13.

Elliott, Kamilla, *Rethinking the Novel/Film Debate*, Cambridge: Cambridge University Press, 2003.

Kranz, David L. and Nancy C Mellerski, eds., *In/Fidelity: Essays on Film Adaptation*, Newcastle: Cambridge Scholars, 2008.

Moraes, Vinicius de, *Orfeu da Conceição: A Carioca tragedy*, 2nd. ed., Rio de Janeiro: Dois Amigos, 1967.

Moraes, Vinicius de, "Drumming Radar" ("Radar da Batucada", presentation text of "Orfeu da Conceição"), in *Vinicius de Moraes Lyric Theatre*, ed. Carlos Augusto Calil, São Paulo: Companhia das Letras, 2008.

Nuñez, Carlinda F.P., "La Visión y la Lira Míticas de Orfeo", in *El ver y el oír en el mundo clásico*, eds. Antonio Arbea et al., Santiago: Universidad Metropolitana de Ciencias de la Educación, 1995, 185-192.

———, "Paisagens Ficcionais: Metamorfoses de Orfeu", in *Cenas do Discurso: Deslocamentos e Transformações*, ed. Fátima Cristina da Rocha, Rio de Janeiro: 7letras, 2006, 29-46.

Oliveira, Maria Claudete de Souza, *Presenças de Orfeu*, São Paulo: University of São Pauslo, 2006.

Paranhos, Luiz Tosta, *Orfeu da Conceição: Tragédia Carioca*, Rio de Janeiro: José Olympio, 1980.

Pereira, Victor Hugo A., "A Lira e os Infernos da Exclusão—Orfeu no Brasil", in *Estudos da Linguagem através de Textos*, III Congresso Nacional de Linguística e Filologia, Rio de Janeiro: CiFeFIL, 2000.

Sanders, Julie, *Adaptation and Appropriation*, London: Routledge, 2006.

Sartre, Jean-Paul [1948], "Orphée Noir", in *Anthologie de la Nouvelle Poésie Nègre et Magache de la Langue Française*, ed. L.S. Senghor, Paris: Quadrige/Presses Universitaires de France, 1998.

Stam, Robert, "Beyond Fidelity: The Dialogics of Adaptation", in *Film Adaptation*, ed. James Naremore, New Brunswick, NJ: Rutgers University Press, 2000, 38-53.

———, *Tropical Multiculturalism: A Comparative History of Race in Brazilian Cinema*, Lurham/London: Duke University Press, 1997.

Warburg, Aby, *The Renewal of Pagan Antiquity: Contributions to the Cultural History of the European Renaissance*, Los Angeles: Getty Research Institute for the History of Art and the Humanities, 1999.

FILMOGRAPHY

Orfeu, dir. Carlos Diegues, scr. Carlos Diegues, Paulo Lins, Hermano Vianna, Hamílton Vaz Pereira, João Emanuel Carneiro, 1999.

Orfeu Negro, dir. Mancel Camus, scr. Jacques Viot, 1960.

CHAPTER 4

Re-reading Literature in Contemporary Cinema: Intermediality in Machado de Assis's story "Father Against Mother" (1906) and Sergio Bianchi's film *How Much is it worth or is it per Kilo?* (2005)

Maria Cristina Cardoso Ribas

This essay is aimed at analyzing the dialogical relationship between Machado de Assis's short story "Pai contra mãe" ("Father Against Mother", 1906) and Sergio Bianchi's film *Quanto Vale ou é por Quilo* (*How much is it worth or is it per kilo?*, 2005) using the theory of intermediality and focusing on literature, cinema and the process of mutual illumination that takes place when a work of literature is adapted to cinema.[1]

The term "intermedia" was introduced by Dick Higgins in his pioneering work *Horizons*: *The Poetics and Theory of Intermedia* (1984) to refer to specific works in which the materials of several forms are conceptually fused instead of being merely juxtaposed. The present essay employs an analysis of Bianchi's film to examine the conceptual fusion that can inform narrative adaptations, and the socio-political elements that enter into such a work.

Certain principles underlie the conception of intermediality used in the present essay. First, the intermedial approach calls for reformulating procedures and viewpoints, insofar as it implies crossing the borders that originally separate media. Second, the term media here is taken to denote both the technical means of production and the instruments of transmission. Third, the materiality of a medium — that which enables and sustains the transmitted media configuration — is consequently considered as an item that interferes in the transposition.

By definition, intermediality involves the intersystemic relations that put forth contemporary cultural productions and therefore include all media interactions. For a closer look at the presence of Machado's short story in Bianchi's film, we focus on a subcategory of intermediality: namely, media transposition, which turns more

[1] All quotes from "Father Against Mother" taken from Machado de Assis, *The Alienist and Other Stories of Nineteenth-Century* Brazil, edited and translated by John Charles Chasteen, Indianapolis: Hackett Publishing Company, 2013, 61-73.

specifically to the literary text's migration to cinema.[2] Understood by critics as a privileged *topos* of comparison between a novel or short story and its filmic adaptation, in addition to taking the meaning of adaptation to another level of loyalty to the original text, media transposition can also imply a broader concept of media.

Media transposition incorporates previous artistic productions to the digital era, it considers the different conventions among the media at play, it perceives the effects of meaning in subversions to the form and content of the verbal text, and it also appreciates both the mobility of the narrative and the stability of every media context involved in the process. Such a process will be considered in this essay in the context of a comparative analysis of Machado's story "Father Against Mother" and Bianchi's film *How much is it worth or is it per kilo?*, loosely inspired by Assis' text.

Machado de Assis and Sergio Bianchi: Slavery and Exploitation of Human Poverty in Brazil

Machado de Assis (1839-1908) was a Brazilian writer who for decades produced a steady stream of fiction, poetry and literary criticism for Rio de Janeiro periodicals as well as popular columns about daily life in the city. His novels employ a special kind of humour to describe patriarchal society, and particularly the Brazilian elite—slavery was abolished in 1888, but the elite became increasingly racist at the close of the nineteenth century.

Sergio Bianchi (1945-) is a controversial Brazilian filmmaker, writer and director, known in Europe for his film *Chronically Unfeasible* (*Cronicamente Inviável*, 2000) nominated for the International Film Festival Rotterdam (2006).

In *How much is it worth or is it per kilo?*[3] Bianchi made a free adaptation of "Father Against Mother". Bianchi highlights the historical debate where Machado had focussed on questions about human beings. Machado emphasized the human condition, the corruption of social life being a result of the basic human predicament. Characters drift in a universe that is indifferent to our fate and to our pathetic efforts to erect all-encompassing and typically phallogocentric systems that seek to make our fate appear other than it really is.

It is important to consider that an adaptation such as *How much?* moves between multiple time frames and becomes a sort of barometer of the discursive tendencies in circulation. This re-creation of Machado's story unmasks and illuminates facets not only of the literary work's theme and plot, but also of its context and ideology.

By mutual illumination, both narratives—literary and filmic—direct our attention to a theoretical question: instead of judging the film for its loyalty to the literary source, we intend to consider the dialogue between Bianchi's film and Machado's short story as a process of medial transposition with its own possibilities. As

---

[2] Irina O. Rajewsky, "Uma Perspectiva Literária Sobre a Intermidialidade", in *Intermidialidade e Estudos Interartes: Desafios da Arte Contemporânea*, Thaïs F. Nogueira Diniz, Belo Horizonte: Universidade Federal de Minas Gerais, 2012, 15-45.

[3] Bianchi directed the film and co-wrote the screenplay with Newton Canito and Sergio Benaim.

mentioned, this discussion focuses on the transformation of a given media product (a text, a film) into another medium. It is a kind of migration. This process creates a dynamic and "impure" hybridization in which one text illuminates the other, thus producing new meanings.

In the literary narrative, Machado de Assis takes for his protagonist a slave catcher named Candido—a name that ironically implies kindness and purity. Candido has become a slave catcher because it is the only job he can get. At the opening of the story, his wife Clara has just given birth and her aunt has threatened to have their newborn son taken away. They have insufficient financial resources to support a family. Candido and his wife, Clara, a seamstress, are threatened with the loss of their newborn son, whom they may have to leave in the "foundling's wheel".[4] To earn money Candido undertakes the task of capturing Arminda, an escaped slave who is also pregnant.

In his film, Bianchi focuses on another kind of slavery by making a transposition from nineteenth-century Rio de Janeiro to São Paulo in contemporary times. (In fact, the opening of the film covers three time settings: the "Slavery and its contradictions" narrative refers to the eighteenth century; the material from the story "Father Against Mother", the nineteenth century; and the episode of the NGOs, which forms the bulk of the film, to the present.)

Characters in "Father Against Mother" and *How much?*

MAIN CHARACTERS	SHORT STORY	FILM The actors play the same characters in different times and their names have specific meanings in Portuguese—an ironic supplemental meaning to their activities.
Cândido Neves: Candy, to friends and family; from the Latin "Candidus", it means white and pure.	Slave catcher	**Candinho** (informal name and from an affective point of view): street cleaner; bounty hunter.
Clara das Neves: Clara means clear, light, pure.	Slave catcher's wife	Young woman from the periphery who wants to be a media success.
Arminda: Teutonic name; it means the one who arms herself to fight against the social system.	Runaway woman slave	Black community leader.

[4] The foundling's wheel: where nuns would find the infant and care for it as an orphan; it was a revolving crib set in the wall of a church or convent, allowing an abandoned baby to be left anonymously and safely. They were common from the twelfth to the nineteenth century in Europe.

The title of the film, *How much is it worth or is it per kilo?* impels the viewer to move to the market street where merchants peddle products screaming, trying to override the noise of the crowd, to sell their goods at the best price and as soon as possible. However, the value of the goods also depends on the customer's need to buy them. In its intersecting stories, the film is not about objects, but about people of different times, turned into merchandise.

Machado's text was written after the abolition of slavery, but improvidence and debt are on the prowl in this story about life among the poor people in nineteenth-century Rio de Janeiro. With a voice heavy with sarcasm and cynicism, the narrator in "Father Against Mother" offers a short and cool introduction on the historical and social reality of Brazilian slavery from a singular point of view.

The opening words of the story are reproduced in the early part of *How much?*, narrated by Milton Gonçalves, a black actor famous in Brazil:

> Half a century ago, slaves ran away frequently. There were a lot of slaves, back then, and not all of them liked slavery. They were occasionally beaten, and not all of them liked to be beaten. (62)

In this scene of the film, the narrator's cynicism disappears and only suffering remains. We hear the distant sound of atabaques and see the character Arminda, tortured with the iron collar and metallic mask. This dark scene in nineteenth-century Rio de Janeiro is followed by one taking place in a contemporary setting, when Arminda is sleeping on a chair during a happy barbecue in the slums. Despite the festive atmosphere, Arminda seems to be having a nightmare—something like a strange memory of her ancestors or some tragic premonition. She is a clever woman, a black leader in the local community, troubled by the existence of exploitation under a mask of charity and welfarism.

In Machado's short story, the character Arminda is a fugitive mulatto woman whom the slave catcher Candido meets by chance. She is a symbol of maternity and of resistance to the degradation caused by the socio-political system. In both narratives—literary and filmic—she cannot beat the system and her newborn son dies in the moment of birth.

The universe that Machado's characters inhabit is a serene and logical one: individuals walk around with their heads enclosed inside instruments of torture, others run away and then there are those who capture fugitives. Everything maintains a social order that requires grotesqueness and even cruelty. Human beings seem to lack any sense of responsibility and are indeed actors in a tragic comedy whose meaning escapes them. The introduction to Machado's short story seems to say: if the slaves run away, there should be someone responsible for capturing and returning them to maintain the equilibrium of the social system—something like an auto-regulated system:

> Now, catching escaped slaves was then a common occupation, useful, if not exactly noble, and, because it enforced the law and the sanctity of property, it had a second-hand sort of respectability. No one studied slave catching or

> took it up merely as a pastime, however [...] such were the motivations of the valiant men who imposed order on disorder in midcentury Rio de Janeiro. (63)

As mentioned, the detached yet ironical tone is typical of the prologues in Machado's writings which present the institution of African slavery as a normative part of the social order, as simply a matter of "racial commonsense". As a master's voice, the narrator composes a description that reveals the indifference, irony and detachment of the Brazilian elite's mentality.

In this narrative, the reader is surprised by the ironic discourse when referring to the instruments of punishment. Machado knows his strategy is risky because people usually understand the narrator's voice as the author's point of view, thus potentially erroneously concluding that Machado is being light-hearted about slavery.

One effect of the Machadian narrator's voice is to expose social disguises. His narratives show us that the discourse and the declared intention of the characters are different from what they do. The action denies the intention and there is a gap between words and deeds. In this space, schemes and conspiracies are plotted in order to maintain the status quo, frustrating the reader's expectation that things will change for the better.

In the central story of Bianchi's film, the slave trade gives way to the operation of government and private companies through an NGO that apparently wants to contribute to the development of a needy community through the implementation of the project "Computing in the Periphery." However, Arminda, who works on the project, discovers that the computers donated for the project are old and have been purchased at an inflated price, the money going to a dummy company to be distributed among the NGO leaders, politicians and the oligarchy. Arminda reports to the press on the embezzlement of public funds and, in retaliation, the NGO hires Candinho, a young unemployed man with a pregnant wife and dreams of upward mobility, to kill her. The final outcome is presented twice, offering two possibilities for resolution: in the first, Candinho simply shoots Arminda; in the second Arminda speaks to Candinho, suggesting to him that they go outside the law to fight corruption and greed together, but the film cuts before his response can be established.

The opening sequence of the film is presented as if it were a documentary. The director shows us how power relations induce people to seek trading strategies, reversing ethical and moral values. In the second sequence, a scenario in pastel shades has nothing but slaves in an empty room, with a spotlight on them, as if they were part of an exhibition. The circular movement of the camera alludes to people visiting a museum. The camera pans slowly around the slaves, each of whom is being subjected to an instrument of torture. There is a voice-over: the language is referential, as if it belonged to a documentary or a museum guide. The image moves from one slave to the next, accompanied by a narrator whose words are taken from Machado's story. The narrator "rescues" the original text to show us, step by step, the types of instruments used to punish slaves in order to correct them and bring benefits to all of us. At this point, both narratives—literary and filmic—seem to caricature a scientific and pedagogic discourse:

> Like other social institutions, slavery brought with it a number of activities and artifacts associated with a particular activity of interest to our story. A sort of iron collar is one; an iron chain attached to the ankle, another; and, third, a metallic mask. The mask eliminates the vice of drunkenness among slaves by covering their mouths. It had only three openings—two for the eyes and one to breathe through—and it was fastened with a lock behind the head. Without the vice of drunkenness, slaves lost the temptation to steal [...]. So the mask eliminated not one vice, but two, and guaranteed both sobriety and honesty. (62)

The Machadian narrator—not the implied author Machado *in person*—takes readers inside this brutal unquestioned reality. The narrator's function seems to be to explain objectively the tragic context from the perspective of a detached and ironic observer. This narrator seems cynical about the possibility of positive change and gives a dispassionately detailed description of the slave's punishment. This *modus operandi* is risky and functions as an aggressive stance against the narrator's voice itself, suggesting to the naïve reader that Machado approved of slavery and oppression. The discursive strategy is a trap. The reader needs to be aware of this in order to capture implicit meanings.

In Bianchi's film, the narrator's voice employs the same dubious discursive strategy as the literary text. The reader is accused, flattered and disdained at the same time by the Machadian narrator—a literary procedure inherited from Modern European poets from the nineteenth century.

THE MISCARRIAGE

The central sequence of Machado's short story involves the capture of Arminda by Candido Neves, the slave catcher. As Candido prepares to leave his son at the foundling's wheel, he sees Arminda walking alone in the street. So, he enters the apothecary's shop and asks the proprietor to take care of his son for a while. He rushes out, follows Arminda and suddenly his powerful hands grab her by the arms. When Arminda is captured by Candido, ironically in a street called Our Lady of Perpetual Help, the slave's master gives him one hundred thousand réis for her capture. Arminda is pregnant and she protests, crying and shouting out loud. She wants her son to be born free.[5]

Candido, unmoved, says: "It's your own fault. Who told you to run away pregnant?" And when she falls into the open doorway, she has a tragic miscarriage in front of the two men (and, as it were, in front of us, the astonished readers). The narrator says: "Her half-formed fetus emerged lifeless into this world, amid the groans of its mother and the exasperation of her owner" (73).

---

[5] It alludes to The Law of Free Birth (1871) in Brazil, also known as Rio Branco Law, intended to provide freedom to all newborn children of slaves. Slaveholders of the children's parents were to provide care for the children until the age of 21, or turn them over to the state in return for monetary compensation.

After that, Candido dashes back to the apothecary. He recovers his son safely and the narrator briefly describes the paradoxical feeling of the slave catcher:

> The father grabbed his son no less furiously than he had grabbed the runaway slave shortly before, though this was a different sort of fury, of course—the fury of love. (73)

At the end of the story, the narrator continues to describe Candido's reaction. He feels neither shame nor guilt because he has simply obeyed the laws of the contemporary social order. The short story ends with a focus on the slave catcher: "Unconcerned about the miscarriage, Candido Neves cried real tears as he kissed his little son. Not all children are meant to make it, said his beating heart" (73). This sentence in Portuguese is "Nem todas as crianças *vingam*"; we could understand the verb *vingar* as literally "to revenge"; it is also surviving/resisting/germinating. The Portuguese word 'vingar' has a double meaning which adds a harsh note to the end of the story: social injustice as fatality.

Bianchi's film opens with imagery evoking the eighteenth and nineteenth centuries, and particularly the situation of slaves in those times, but when the setting is relocated to the present, the director focuses on charitable organizations. The development of the story suggests that the pseudo-benevolence of these groups, ostensibly meant to improve social conditions, in fact does the opposite: they form a money-making industry. In the film, the actors and characters are the same in both historical settings. Sergio Bianchi asks: is there any difference between slavery and the continuous exploitation of misery? What is all of this worth?[6]

The filmmaker was inspired by the people and the ordinary lives he sees around him,[7] so his point of view is aligned with the people's perspective. It becomes clear at the moment when the audience sees, in the film, their own "failing mirrors": that is, when the scenes reflect back what they don't want to see. Thus, Bianchi reveals the hidden underside of organized philanthropy in Brazil, related to its essentially corporate nature and the corruption that is endemic to business negotiation. According to Sérgio Bianchi, Machado's short story implied that things were always a kind of negotiation".[8]

The basis of the business conducted by Stiner Enterprises[9] is the exchange of money for the relief of bad conscience regarding social inequalities. Giving is an instrument of power. Overexposure to human beings in degrading conditions of life

---

[6] Black Screen Film Festival 2007. http://www.pidgin.org.uk/ff2007/Screening.htm [accessed 23/03/2017].

[7] Eduardo Benaim, Newton Cannito and Sergio Bianchi, *Quanto Vale ou é por Quilo*? *Roteiro do filme de Sergio Bianchi*, São Paulo: Imprensa Oficial, 2008.

[8] Marcelo Soler, *Quanto Vale um cineaste brasileiro? Sergio Bianchi em Palavras, Imagens e Provocações,* São Paulo: Garçoni, 2005, 77.

[9] Stiner Enterprises is the company name created by the screen-makers in order to represent a new form of unfree labor in the social interventions practiced by many NGOs in contemporary Brazil.

allows feelings and emotions to vent. We feel disgust, amazement, compassion, affection, happiness, and finally, relief.

Bianchi's film juxtaposes past and present, slavery and non-governmental social intervention in order to propose continuity between ostensibly disparate forms of engaging human beings with labor. In juxtaposing slavery and non-governmental work, Bianchi invites us to look back at Brazilian history to better understand the dilemmas we experience today. Of course, the contexts are different, but for him, even though the historical setting isn't the same, the social contradictions are being repeated in Brazil. As Bianchi emphasizes in many interviews, his film is about "modern slavery".[10] He's talking about the pseudo-benevolence of the charitable organizations that are meant to improve social conditions.

When the Brazilian government finally abolished slavery in 1888, it came with no concessions. Many people had not saved enough money to live in freedom. People had to live with other forms of relationships between individuals that came close to slavery, blurring the limits between "free" and "unfree." Similarly, in a globalized labor system in which exchanges take place between charity and poverty, the economic or psychosocial debt that often goes along with non-governmental social intervention risks leading only to one more form of unfree labor, as Bianchi suggests in his film. If the nineteenth-century poor had nothing to offer other than their bodies and the labour they might engage in, now the poor can offer nothing but their own poverty… so that non-governmental jobs may be created. Therefore, the film denounces NGOs and their funding resources from both government and private enterprises.

As mentioned above, Sergio Bianchi begins his film as if it were a documentary—he presents a sequence adapted from an event in the National Archives: an eighteenth-century account of a woman, a freed slave, Joana Maria da Conceição, who accumulated funds to buy slaves to work on her property. She goes to the house of one of the thieves in order to get her slave back and also to prosecute the man for disturbing the peace. Once again, there is a gap between words and deeds, and the historical scene shows us an ironic event: according to the National Archives, the freed slave, Joana, acts as a slave-holder. Enveloped in social contradictions, she is herself the property of several black brothers.

In the following scene, something strange happens. Joanna and her slaves pose for a photo. When everyone is in position, we hear the sound of a hammer as if it were the end of a trial, followed by the sound ("click") of the camera. Curiously, the scene is set a century before the advent of photography and, on first viewing, it may seem nonsensical.

---

[10] Interview with Sergio Bianchi by Ana Aranha and Cléber Eduardo. Retrieved from http://revistaepoca.globo.com/Epoca/0,6993,EPT961935-1655,00.html [accessed 17/11/2016].

Stills from *How much is it worth or is it per kilo?* (2005):

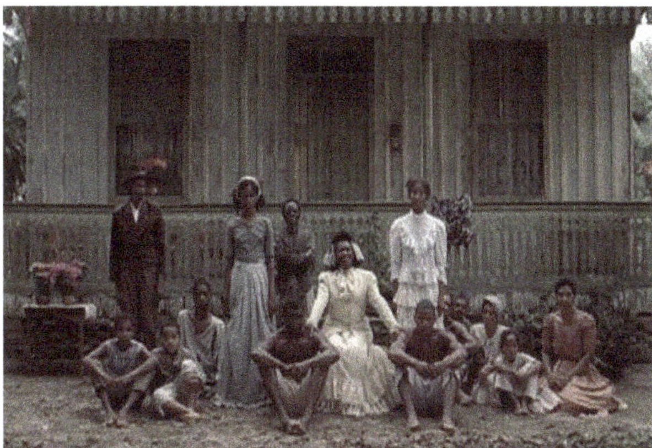

1. Scene from the eighteenth century: a free black woman with her slaves.

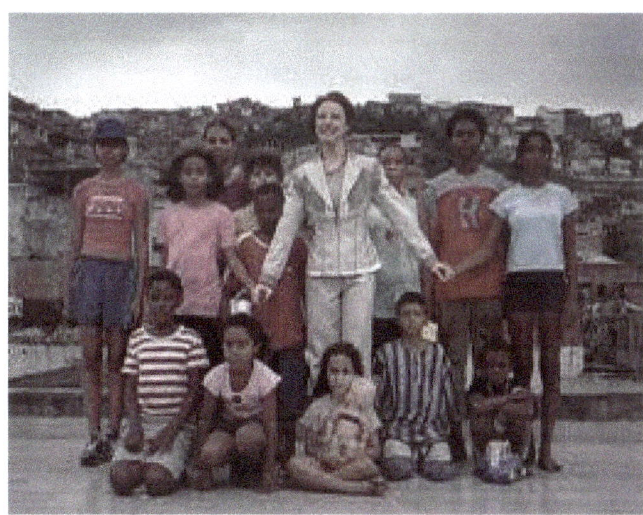

2. Scene from twenty first-century Brazil: a white woman poses as benefactor to the children of the slums.[11]

As Joana and her family pose in fine clothes for a group picture—a quite grotesque situation in an aesthetic and social sense—the narrator's voice cites a document from

[11] These images are taken from, respectively: http://cinefilosconvergentes.blogspot.ie/2012/12/quanto-vale-ou-e-por-quilo-2005.html [accessed 19/03/2017]; and http://posbarao.com.br/blog-da-pos/quanto-vale-ou-e-por-quilo-jose-bianchi-filme-reflete-sobre-as-organizacoes-nao-governamentais-no-brasil/ [accessed 17/03/2017].

the National Archive,[12] which records this moment in history as if it were a documentary. Therefore, the scene of a picture in the eighteenth century—before the invention of photography—is not a mistake but alludes to the rupture of verisimilitude in the filmic narrative. This rupture suggests that the film is not a mere copy of a referent, but a composition freely inspired by a literary text. The second photo—a very similar picture but now with the slums for a background—is made with the poor children and their 'benefactor', Ms. Marta Figueiredo.

As in the photo from the eighteenth century, the poor are well dressed and willing to create a happy image. This image suggests the continuation of social contradictions as well as the maintenance of social disguises in contemporary times. At the same time, both pictures suggest social hypocrisy, a set of lucrative interests and what Bianchi calls the permanence of slavery. It is important to remember that the film, unlike Machado's short story, has two endings that discompose the spectators. In the first one, the denouement flows from the literary narrative, through a painful experience which made characters and spectators lose their hope in social systems and human beings; the second one inverts the situation. The outcome breaks the rules of morality, disrupts the reader's expectations, and deconstructs, with humour, the dichotomy of the plot. This ending bears some similarities to a satirical comedy, with allegorical characters and comical incidents.

We do not consider Bianchi's film an adaptation in a narrow sense, but as an intertextual work, a creative product inspired by Machado's short tale. This is an open interpretation of the term adaptation, one that is more consistent with the sense of intermediality as media transposition. What we have here is a process of intermedial transformation. From this perspective, complete originality is neither possible nor desirable. We should not speak in terms of a hierarchy either, but of a creative dialogue between a literary text and its re-reading.

Even though we observe two diverse media, with their different contexts and materials, this combination does not promote total integration, nor a complete signification, or any hierarchy between the constitutive arts, but an interarts dynamic reading process by which one supplements the other by potentially producing new meanings.

History, irony, portraits and pictures interlink to build a comparison between the oppression caused by slavery and that found in contemporary society. Bianchi's goal is to critique the marketing consultants and non-government organizations that profit from the oppression of the lower classes as slave owners reaped returns from their human property. He draws a comparison between the times of slavery and the pseudo-benevolence of some charitable groups set up to deal with poverty in Brazil. Some contemporary private business has led to a race to the bottom, where standards of living are constantly being reduced. Labor, for example, gets cheaper and cheaper, which benefits the multinational companies, but not the workers themselves. It is interesting to note that while globalization has led to the opening up of borders for

[12] The chronicles were compiled by Nireu Oliveira Cavalcanti from documents belonging to the National Archives in Rio de Janeiro, covering the years between 1700 and 1810, entitled "Slavery and its contradictions", and published in the book *Chronicles of Historical Colonial Rio* (2004).

increased trade, the same is not true for people. Yet, people all over the world seem to be losing their national identity due to the current model of globalization. The introduction of "flexibility", while good for businesses, can hurt workers.

The short story "Father Against Mother", beyond the issue of Candido's responsibilities, explores the thesis that someone must be responsible for capturing slaves who run away. Actually, the protagonist slave catcher is himself a slave in a world that has failed to instil in him the value of ethical work, a world that has compelled him to pit his own enslavement against the life of a newborn son. Mine or yours—that's the question. What's your choice? Is there another alternative? Regarding Arminda's tragedy, she's the hero—or the victim—who fights against the system. The miscarriage alludes to the impossibility of maintaining even the seed of resistance. Machado's short story confronts our own social hypocrisies and human feelings. He deconstructs dichotomic thoughts and inserts his "dear reader" into the social disguises and human soul.

The final question is: who are the father and the mother of the short story's title? The common-sense conclusion says Candido is the father and Arminda is the mother; but if we developed this idea, we can also see the father as a metaphor for the nation, inside a historical and social system; the mother is therefore perhaps the human being, the feelings, and the possibility of running away from this father, the patriarch or coercive system. Her son, the fruit of this fight (Father Against Mother) and also the fruit of the fury of love, enters this world without life: "Not all children are meant to make it."

As a son or a nation, there is no possibility of being born and living free in a nest of slavery or inside a corrupted and greedy organization—even with the best intentions. In different spaces and times—the past of Machado's short story and the present of Bianchi's film—the writers talk about human failures and social contradictions. Considering their contexts, we recognize that both narratives are vigorous and suggest the importance of being attentive to the time we live in.

Bibliography

Machado de Assis, Joaquim Maria, *The Alienist and Other Stories of Nineteenth-Century Brazil*, ed. and trans. John Charles Chasteen, Indianapolis: Hackett Publishing Company, 2013, 61-73.

Azeredo, Genilda, and Arturo Gouveia, eds., *Estudos Comparados: Análises de Narrativas Literárias e Fílmicas*, João Pessoa: Editora Universitária/Universidade Federal de Paraíba, 2012.

Bazin, André, "Por um Cinema Impuro: Defesa da Adaptação", in *O Cinema: Ensaios*, São Paulo: Brasiliense, 2012, 82-104.

Benaim, Eduardo, Newton Cannito and Sergio Bianchi, *Quanto Vale ou é por Quilo? Roteiro do Filme de Sergio Bianchi*, São Paulo: Imprensa Oficial, 2008.

Clüver, Claus, "Introductions to the Intermedial Field: Intermediality and Interarts Studies", in *Changing Borders: Contemporary Positions in Intermediality*, eds. Jens Arvidson et al., Lund: Intermedia Studies Press, 2007.

Gaudreault, André, and Philippe Marion, "Transescritura e Midiática Narrativa: Questões de Intermidialidade", in *Intermidialidade e Estudos interartes: Desafios da Arte Contemporânea*, Thaïs F. Nogueira Diniz, ed., Belo Horizonte: Universidade Federal de Minas Gerais, 2012, 107-128.

Higgins, Dick, *Horizons: The Poetics and Theory of the Intermedia*, Carbondalle and Edwardsville, IL: Southern Illinois University Press, 1984.

How much is it worth or is it per kilo? [Quanto Vale ou é por Quilo?], dir. Sérgio Bianchi, Rio de Janeiro: Agravo Produções Cinematográficas/ Riofilme, 2005.

Hutcheon, Linda, *A Theory of Adaptation*, New York and London: Routledge, 2006.

Rajewsky, Irina O., "Uma Perspectiva Literária Sobre a Intermidialidade", in *Intermidialidade e Estudos Interartes: Desafios da Arte Contemporânea*, Thaïs F. Nogueira Diniz, Belo Horizonte: Universidade Federal de Minas Gerais, 2012, 15-45.

———, "Intermediality, Intertextuality, and Remediation: A Literary Perspective on Intermediality" *Intermédialités*, 6, 2005, 43-64.

Ribas, Maria Cristina Cardoso, "Literatura e(m) Cinema: Breve Passeio Teórico Pelos Bosques da Adaptação", *ALCEU*, 14:28 (2014), 117-128.

Stam, Robert, "Teoria e Prática da Adaptação: da Fidelidade à Intertextualidade" *Ilha do Desterro*, 51 (2006), 19-53.

Soler, Marcelo, ed., *Quanto Vale um Cineasta Brasileiro? Sérgio Bianchi em Palavras, Imagens e Provocações*, São Paulo: Garçoni, 2005.

CHAPTER 5

Quentin Tarantino's *Django Unchained* (2012) and the Afterlife of the Western

Beata Waligorska-Olejniczak

Django Unchained (2012) is a typical Tarantino movie, in which pop aesthetics meets with serious historical and social issues. It can be perceived as both historical fantasy and a cultural text focused first of all on the history of cinema. [1] The aim of this study is to look at the controversial American director's Western from the point of view of its generic filmic and literary intertexts. Taking into account the poetics of Tarantino's films (signature shots, suspense, ultraviolence, characteristic method of montage) I consider *Django Unchained* as a work of art in which the tradition of the Western serves as a kind of matrix to create the *afterlife* of a text to satisfy contemporary audiences. I will argue that Tarantino treats the Western as a kind of historical costume to drape over difficult problems of the contemporary world. He does this with the eclectic use of elements of kitsch, hyperbole, a theatralization of gesticulation, and a patchwork of cultural traditions, which allows him to juggle at once with the sacred and the profane.

The problem of Westward expansion has been one of the central myths shaping American identity, both in terms of individual and national experience. The Wild West has always been seen, on the one hand, as the antithesis of the civilized East and, on the other, as the product of its romantic imagination, associated with a new and better life in a vast unknown space. Life at the frontier was perceived as the opportunity of gaining an independent and self-sufficient existence, although exposed to danger. The strip of land separating the West from the East was the area of particularly tense conflicts, where the white population lost their influence and power to the wild world of nature and the indigenous inhabitants of America. In spite of the fact that, at the end of the nineteenth century, the whole area of the United States was already settled and the frontier formally ceased to exist on the map of the country, the idea, or we should say the metaphor of the frontier, is still present in the literature and culture of the United States. However, it does not always refer to the physical space separating the East from the West of the USA. It is worth recalling that one of the first scholars to turn their attention to the role of the frontier in the American

[1] Glenda R. Carpio, "'I like the way you die, Boy': Fantasy's Role in *Django Unchained*", *Transition*, 112, 2013, 1.

consciousness was Frederick J. Turner.[2] Turner, during his speech in front of the Chicago World Congress of Historians in 1893, emphasized the fact that the frontier, due to the clash of civilization and nature, was the area where the nation was continuously being reborn. The process shaped the American character, described by Turner as one distinguished by its individualism, materialism and resistance to civil government, which can be considered the basis of the democratic system. As time went by, this thought was further developed by other authors who recognized violence as an inseparable element of the dynamic existence of the frontier, many times ascribing mythical meaning to it (e.g. Richard Slotkin in his famous book *Regeneration Through Violence: The Mythology of the American Frontier 1600-1860*).

In the second half of the nineteenth century, *dime novels* became a very specific form of narration about the difficulties of life in the Wild West. This popular type of pulp fiction, which was read mainly by immigrants with a rather poor command of English, could be characterized by its very simple language and uncomplicated plots, which usually reached their climax in a final shooting restoring order in the community. These texts, which were set in beautiful, typically American landscapes, used to function as a kind of short history lesson for incomers and sometimes were even considered as a synonym for American culture.[3] They had significant influence on the structure of classical Westerns, whose main conflict was based on the battle between good and evil. In this context, it is worth noticing that *The Virginian* (1902), made by Owen Wister, is considered to be the first Western novel, whereas the twelve-minute film *The Great Train Robbery* (1903) by Edwin S. Porter is recognized as the first Western movie. A special place in the history of the Western, which is still treated as one of the most distinctive genres of American literature, belongs to the works of James Fenimore Cooper, the author of—among other works—*The Last of the Mohicans* (1826). Cooper's historical novel, with its repetitive dramas of conflicting emotions, and its majestically presented death and struggle with wild nature, constituted a specific attempt at telling the history of the Wild West and the frontier, in which one can even find associations with and references to ancient mythology. William T. Pilkington and Don Graham are of the opinion that each Western is, to some extent, dependent on myths, and they can fully accept and derive from these myths or can be perceived as their total negation.[4] Westerns are often read as the realizations of various kinds of myths, i.e. cosmogonic, anthropogenic, genealogical etc.

Many literary Westerns, inspired by the memoirs of pioneers and settlers, have distinctive features which nowadays we commonly associate with film Westerns: the idealization of heroes, picturesque descriptions of nature, their melodramatic quality

[2] Frederick J. Turner, *The Significance of the Frontier in American History*, Eastford: Martino Fine Books, 2014, 1-32.
[3] Agata Preis-Smith, Marek Paryż, eds, *Amerykański Western Literacki w XX Wieku: Między Historią, Fantazją i Ideologią,* Warszawa: Czuły Barbarzyńca Press, 2013, 7.
[4] William T. Pilkington, Don Graham, eds, *Western Movies*, Albuquerque: University of New Mexico Press, 1979, 74.

and sentimentalism, replacing historical facts and realism with the convention of the spectacle, etc. It is also worth remembering that the invention of film and television gave Western literature a kind of afterlife due to its transformation into "visual literature", which protected the genre from becoming a marginal literary phenomenon or just an insignificant folk curiosity. Several thousand books were turned into films and very often we tend to forget their original literary inspiration. Examples of famous film adaptations are, among others, *The Covered Wagon* (1923) by James Cruze, *The Vanishing American* (1925) by George Seitz, *The Virginian* (1929) by Victor Fleming, *Billy Kid* (1930) by King Vidor, *My Darling Clementine* (1946) by John Ford, *The Man Who Shot Liberty Valence* (1962) by John Ford or *Little Big Man* (1970) by Arthur Penn.

For many years, Western directors did not aspire to become high art creators, and the majority of films were based on third-rate literature, although it often happened that after reaching the movies the perception of a given literary work dramatically changed. Czesław Michalski noticed that when film Westerns had first appeared in Europe after the First World War, they had been praised for their absorbing narrative flow, dynamic action and—most of all—anti-literary quality.[5] Ironically enough, it turned out that this anti-literary quality was mostly attributed to the adaptations of literary works such as, for example, *Riders of the Purple Sage* (1918), based on the novel by Zane Grey (*Riders of the Purple Sage*, 1912). Over time we also notice attempts at a demythologization of Wild West history. The appearance of alternative myths, e.g. showing the moral or ethnic complexity of the conquest and, consequently, more thoroughly explaining the history of America, was very often connected with writing more ambitious novels and stories as far as literary criteria are concerned. In this context one can mention the works of Cormac McCarthy, Annie Proulx's *Brokeback Mountain* (1997), or Thomas Eidson's *The Last Ride* (1995).

The film Western itself has also changed over the years. The first films presenting the Wild West strongly emphasized melodramatic motifs such as pathos, emotional intensification, moral polarization and sensationalism. Then came an increasing tendency to mix and juxtapose in the Western distinctive elements from different film and literature genres. Thus, we encounter the poetics of gangster movies in *Gun Smoke* (1931) by Edward Sloman; the conventions of the musical, comedy or even horror, e.g. *Billy the Kid vs. Dracula* (1966) by William Beaudine; and science fiction in *Timerider* (1983) by William Dear. It could be said that contemporary Westerns absorbed, first of all, the elements of sadism and sex, and nowadays—under the influence of West European tendencies—almost every film sequence is full of irony, cruelty and terror instead of romance.[6] Apart from that, the Western has its local European variations, very often based on transformations of classic Hollywood forms. Special attention should be given in this respect to the German series *Winnetou*, based on Karl May's novels, or the Italian Spaghetti Westerns, which were

---

[5] Czesław Michalski, *Western i Jego Bohaterowie*, Warszawa: Wydawnictwa Artystyczne i Filmowe,1972, 15.

[6] Philip French, *Westerns. Aspects of a Movie Genre and Westerns Revisited*, Manchester: Carcanet Press, 2005.

also called macaroni, pizza, pasta or paella Westerns. As is commonly known, the Spaghetti Westerns were made by Sergio Corbucci, who in 1966 created Django, the Western anti-hero, and together with Sergio Leone determined the further direction of the genre's development.[7] It seems that the new version of the Western, created by Quentin Tarantino, was meant to display references to this genre tradition. It did a lot to refresh and enliven the Western through the use of signature Tarantino's strategies, known from his previous works.

Tarantino's *Django Unchained* was perceived and evaluated in many different ways. It was called a morality play hidden under the surface of a pastiche, a Gothic Western reviving Corbucci's style, a work of art full of Western clichés, in which deconstruction goes hand in hand with fetishization, or a childish fantasy about a world governed by justice and fairness.[8] The genre form of Tarantino's film, whose matrix is undoubtedly built up by elements of various kinds of Westerns, reminds the viewer of the origins of the genre, which from its very beginning constituted a folk spectacle for the masses, where everything was to be simple, unambiguous and easy to understand for everybody, in particular for the multi-lingual and multicultural society of immigrants or lower-class citizens. The warm reception of *Django* by its viewers allows us to make the assumption that contemporary culture, which is mainly focused on *en masse* production and often described by sceptics as permanently carnivalized or even pornographized, accepts this kind of stylization, treating it as an adequate and suitable method for the times.

From this point of view Tarantino is a kind of rewriter, taking advantage of the existing matrix of the Western in order to build up a new variant with the use of his symbolic language, i.e. his recognizable style associated with his famous *signature shots* (for example, the shot made from the inside of a trunk), black screens functioning as pauses, rapid changes of film sets, and characteristically fast camera movements.[9] Maintaining a balance between parody and pastiche, the director seems to be driven by the idea that the Western is first of all a kind of costume, allowing him to tackle difficult or socially and politically inconvenient problems such as the brutality of American slavery or racism. Besides, Tarantino believes that pop aesthetics has more potential to get at topics than "highbrow" forms.[10] Glenda R. Carpio points out that Tarantino's "combination of 'fun' (form) and heaviness […] shuttles viewers between the comic and horrific, which lets them at the same time enjoy the revenge fantasy and witness slavery's violence".[11] Visually attractive code which is easy to understand helps to turn the Western into a modern show, a performance between a morality play and a masquerade, based on striking scenes and special effects. The hybrid nature of Tarantino's work makes us also aware of the fact

---

[7] Howard Hughes, Spaghetti Westerns, Harpenden: Kamera Books, 2010, 20-21.

[8] See for example James E. Ford, "Close-Up: Fugitivity and the Filmic Imagination. Blackness and Legend", *Black Camera*, 7:1, 2015, 199-217.

[9] Dana Polan, *Pulp Fiction*, London: British Film Institute, 2000, 55. See also Beata Waligorska-Olejniczak, *"Sacrum" w Drodze "Moskwa-Pietuszki" Wieniedikta Jerofiejewa i "Pulp Fiction" Quentina Tarantino w Kluczu Montażowego Czytania*, Poznań: Wydawnictwo Naukowe UAM, 2013.

[10] Glenda R. Carpio, "'I like the way you die, Boy'", 1-12.

[11] *Ibid.*, 2.

that plot—as in the case of the translation of a literary text—easily travels in the world, whereas the individual style of an original work can be changed or even lost in the process of translation or transformation into a different language or system of signs. The Western variant which was created by Tarantino is an amalgam of various traditions, and its form is the result of the fusion of the canon and the specific style of the director, which as the film critic Chris Vognar notes "is more about movies than anything else".[12] The director himself comments on his strategies:

> I am taking a story of a slave narrative and blowing it up to folkloric proportions… worthy of high opera. So I could have a little fun with it. One of the things I do is when the bad guys shoot people the bullets usually don't blow people apart. They make little holes and they kill them and wound them, but they don't rip them apart. When Django shoots someone, he blows them in half.[13]

Examining *Django Unchained* from the point of view of the intertextual dialogue with the tradition of the Western allows us to argue with the opinions of naysayers that the postmodern cinema of Quentin Tarantino follows the "anything goes" strategy, i.e. the freedom to do anything if you are famous enough.[14] The director's first Western can be treated, in accordance with the assessment of European film critics, as the newest version of the Spaghetti Western, inspired by contemporary viewers' increasing demand for the screen macabre.[15] The genre created by Italian film-makers in actual fact does not have much in common with its classic American original, whose main character was in most cases an unscrupulous man fighting for justice and order, one who usually respected only his own code of conduct. In Spaghetti Westerns, the distinctive division between the good and the evil disappears. Generally speaking, everybody is badly behaved, kills for fun, gives up love and friendship for money, and shows a liking for sadistic behavior, such as chopping off arms and legs, poking out eyes or burning people alive.[16] This passion for the visualization of cruelty and

---

[12] Chris Vognar, "He Can't Say That, Can He?: Black, White and Shades of Gray in the Films of Tarantino", *Transition*, 112, 2013, 23-31.

[13] Glenda R. Carpio, "'I like the way you die, Boy'", 1.

[14] Damon Wise, "Resist the temptation to ridicule this: Interview with Quentin Tarantino", *The Guardian*, May 4, 2007. http://www.theguardian.com/film/2007/may/04/quentin tarantino [accessed 13/07/2015].

[15] See for example Chris Tookey, "Funny, Gruesome and Brilliant in parts, *Django Unchained* is Tarantino's Best—and Maddest—since *Pulp Fiction*", *Daily Mail*, January 17, 2013. http://www.dailymail.co.uk/tvshowbiz/article-2264232/Django-Unchained [accessed 10/01/2014]; Alan Scherstuhl, "*Django Unchained*: The Most Moving Scene Quentin Tarantino Has Yet Filmed", *LA Weekly*, April 18, 2013. http://www.laweekly.com/2013-04-18/film-tv/django-unchained-best-scene [accessed 10/01/2014]; David Denby, "*Django Unchained*: Put-On, Revenge, and the Aesthetics of Trash", January 22, 2013. http://www.newyorker.com/online/blogs/culture/ 2013/01/django-unchained-reviewed [accessed 11.01.2014]; David Sexton, "*Django Unchained*—Review", *Evening Standard*, January 18, 2013. http://www.standard.co.uk/goingout/film/django-unchained--review-8457022.html [accessed 10/04/2014].

[16] See for example Christopher Frayling, *Spaghetti Western: Cowboys and Europeans from Karl May to Sergio Leone*, London-New York: I. B. Tauris, 2012.

violence is probably the strongest argument allowing us to consider *Django Unchained* as the new embodiment of the Spaghetti-Western tradition.

It is also worth mentioning that the directors of Spaghetti Westerns fulfilled their passion for violence at the expense of the authentic problems of the Wild West, which cannot be said about Tarantino who does not neglect traditionally American issues such as the conflict between the white population and other ethnic groups. However, he approaches them with his own specific dark humor, taking advantage of hyperbole, absurd juxtapositions of incompatible elements or the introduction of eccentric behavior. Using fast movements of the camera, he undoubtedly refers to and develops the recognizable filming style of the Italian filmmakers, emphasizing sometimes their low level of filming abilities.

One of the main social and political issues in *Django Unchained* is slavery and the status of Afro-Americans in the USA. It could be said that Tarantino faces these problems in an explicit and firm way, giving black actor Jamie Foxx the lead role of a cowboy. In doing so he remains faithful to the historical facts as in reality there was quite a number of cowboys of non-Caucasian race, although hardly any dark-skinned cowboys have appeared in Westerns.[17] In *Django Unchained* it seems that the role of the inferior homogenous group belongs to the white community, which—except for Doctor Schultz—constitutes a gang of weak, naïve, badly educated and physically less fit human beings, in spite of their social status and material possessions. Tarantino himself, playing the role of the obese and rather bovine mine worker with a fake Australian accent, seems to laugh in the face of white culture, based mostly on the unstable power captured from the colonized, which can be suddenly lost, as shown in the picture of the dynamite explosion in the film. In this scene, Django easily catches white miners off-guard because he recognizes the fact that power is always imposed by violence, terror and control of the weaker. Johannes Fehrle makes a similar point:

> After Foxx has blown up Tarantino in a cameo as an Australian mine employee, mounted his horse, and ordered (not asked) the other black prisoners to throw him the dynamite that is conveniently stored in the prison wagon, the camera slowly moves in on the face of the man who has just passed Django the dynamite. The camera distance is reduced from a medium shot to a close up, and we see him slowly beginning to smile as he watches Django return to Candyland while we hear John Legend's "Who Did That to You" playing. This is the central scene which opens up the possibility of reading Django as the avenger of all those subjugated to the system of slavery. This is particularly true when we recognize the man as the former

[17] It is hard to give precise statistics concerning the number of dark-skinned cowboys. I would like to thank Johannes Fehrle for his comments during the European Network for Comparative Literary Studies congress in Dublin (2015), which inspired the discussion about this issue. See his article: "Django Unchained and the Neo-Blaxploitation Western", Iperstoria. Testi Letterature Linguaggi, 2, 2013. http://www.iperstoria.it/joomla/15-saggi/90-fehrle [accessed 30/09/2016].

> slave who was earlier castigated by Django-as-slaver for spitting on the ground to show his disgust with Django's supposed identity.[18]

The finale of this scene shows not only solidarity between Django and the slave but can also be understood as a kind of juxtaposition of two groups: passive whites and active blacks. The close-up of the emotionally engaged slave's face is a confirmation of the reversal of the roles the director assigns to those groups. Consequently, Afro-Americans gain the status of the highly-individualized community, whereas the group of whites who are subjected to Django's tricks loses its dominant position.

Death inflicted by Django is always justified, because it is performed in the name of self-defense or vengeance. The white—again with the exception of Schultz—are violent without any reasons, usually because they have whims or a sudden need to act cruelly. Taking advantage of the director's right to lie or compromise old myths, which became a natural part of all Westerns, Tarantino comes up with his own made-up stories and events: the motif of Mandingo fighting (which was not really practiced by slaves), dynamite being used in the Civil War era, or the shock reaction of the whites on seeing a black person riding a horse.[19] Being historically inaccurate seems to constitute another Tarantinian device by which he exposes the vanity and narrow thinking of the whites living in their closed white ghettos. It could also be seen as a kind of manipulation used to produce an effect of artificiality and exaggeration, built up through the use of different clichés connected with the aesthetics of the genre.

The exemplification of this type of solution can be found in the introduction of elements of kitsch, folklore, patchworks, or even the replacement of the sacred reality with the profane (and the other way round), already present in the director's previous films.[20] The giant tooth sitting on a spring on the roof of the cart, in which doctor Schulz keeps cash and later on puts some dynamite; a German legend about Broomhilda and Siegfried which serves as a romantic metaphor and inspiration for *Django*; the cutting of the skull of a Negro in a well-furnished dining-room around mealtime; or the eye-catching inadequacy of the clothes of the former slave and his companion are elements of intentional stylization which can be associated with Bakhtinian carnivalesque aesthetics. Fehrle calls it "the pimp aesthetics"[21], whereas Carpio writes:

> His blue suit was inspired by Thomas Gainsborough's 1770 painting "The Blue Boy" [...] Casting Django in his blue suit nods to the practice in the history of art of ennobling purportedly "primitive" people by dressing and

---

[18] *Ibid.*

[19] Scott R. Nelson, "Django Untangled: The Legend of the Bad Black Man", *The Chronicle of Higher Education*, January 11, 2013. http://chronicle.com/article/Django-Untangled-the-Legend/136643/ [accessed 15/04/2016].

[20] The elements of kitsch and patchwork of various tradition are present in such films as *Pulp Fiction* (e.g. the pawn shop scene), *Inglourious Basterds* (e.g. the Holocaust mixed with the tradition of American Indian warriors), *Kill Bill* based on the recycling of the Far East philosophy and the tradition of martial arts.

[21] Johannes Fehrle, "*Django Unchained*".

> framing them after the fashion of noblemen—a title to which Big Daddy, in his fine suite and big plantation aspires. And yet, in his blue suit Django makes ironic both Big Daddy's aspirations and the civility and the commodity culture that Gainsborough's painting came to represent. Blue Boy he ain't.[22]

These features give the impression that the outside world is an absurd reality, full of contrasts and dissonances. The use of different kinds of hyperbole serves to achieve comic effects, which are often incompatible with the atmosphere of the situation shown on the screen. The final scene of the slaughter of Candy's entourage exemplifies this. In this respect, one should pay attention to the theatralization of the death of Candy's sister, who falls to the floor in a very dramatic pose and is rapidly removed from the scene as if she were a rag doll. In this final sequence of the film, tension and cruelty meets Tarantino's dark humor, which is noticeable in all the theatralized shootings, whose "trademark" is always blood pouring out like a water fountain.

Each time, the red fluid gushes out as if from a punctured plastic bag, intestines are blown into the air, and the ground is covered with dead bodies resembling mannequins rather than people who were torn by emotions and competing feelings just a few seconds earlier. Besides, this artistic solution of the American director is synchronized in *Django Unchained* with the audio-visual effect of excessive spitting, which leads us to the conclusion that the film is full of hyperbolized visions of physical and material aspects of the body. A spectator taking part in such aesthetic and emotional experiments is usually not only shocked or surprised: the strategy of suspense used by the director evokes also a kind of unhealthy curiosity, as well as a specific type of admiration for the sophisticated visual form, harmony of colors or perfectly harmonized visual and audial montage. This assumption can be confirmed by the famous shots of the cotton field marked with blood. The symbolism and aesthetic beauty of the vision make the viewer not only perceive it as a part of a plot but also read it as a synecdoche, a metaphorical sign telling the (hi)story of America. As a result, an aesthetic detail becomes the subject of experiment, it is utilized by the director in order to achieve the effect of turpism, i.e. the replacement of the visually attractive form with its opposite, allowing viewers to build an emotional distance to the screen violence, reminiscent in some respects of the artistic techniques used by Peter Greenaway in his collage-oriented cinema.[23]

The signs of the encoded director's vision can also be found by the engaged spectator on the level of montage. It is worth turning our attention to the opening and

---

[22] Glenda R. Carpio, "'I like the way you die, Boy'", 6.

[23] Turpism can be understood as the literary strategy of introducing the elements of ugliness (death, illness, the images of degraded body etc.) in order to shock the recipient. It was particularly popular in the Polish poetry after 1956 as it was treated as a kind of generation protest against the social and political situation. The aim of the strategy was to help to affirm and accept all aspects of reality. Elements of turpism could be found in Greenaway's films such as *The Draughtsman's Contract* (1982), *The Belly of an Architect* (1987), *The Cook, the Thief, His Wife and Her Lover* (1989), in which the director exposed protagonists' physiology or the materiality of decaying objects.

closing sequences of the film, which can be perceived as compatible and recurring shots. *Django Unchained* finishes—in some respects typically—with a shoot-out, in which evil is defeated whilst the just man rides away crowned in glory. The untypical element here is, however, the fact that victory belongs to the black, which rarely happens in film Westerns, and the anticipation of such an end is announced in the first scene of the film, in which the role of the villain is given to the white, whilst the group of black slaves are treated almost as equal partners in the incident (for example, the trusting Schultz gives one of the slaves a weapon to hold and allows them to make a decision concerning their future fate, at the same time giving necessary information regarding their geographical position). As a result, both scenes remain in a close dialogic relationship, and seen together they could be interpreted as a kind of framework drawn by the director in order to expose and emphasize one of the main ideas of the film, i.e. a reversal of the roles of the victim and the butcher (not only on the level of the plot).

One can assume that it is the continuation of the shock therapy started by Tarantino in *Inglourious Basterds*, his method of dealing with trauma. In both films, we notice the accumulation of elements which are planned to surprise a viewer to such a degree that his or her only reaction seems to be cathartic laughter, the experience leading to some kind of new awakening, an opening to new opportunities of perceiving reality. One can add that this rapid turn of events in the aforementioned initial scene of the film is introduced by Tarantino with the use of one of his favorite montage devices: the sudden replacement of the close-up of one object with the close-up of another one, usually of a completely different symbolic meaning. The shot of the lighting up of a lamp, which in most cases is associated with the peace and quiet of the cosy house, is rapidly replaced by the sound of an explosion and its visual consequences, which brings to mind the beginning of *Pulp Fiction* and its way of setting the plot in motion. In both cases the action starts properly after a heated exchange between the conflicting parties, which finds its equivalent in the dynamic music opening both films.

Apart from this, *Django Unchained* can be treated as Tarantino's polemic against the cultural patterns of presenting women, in particular the visual clichés known from Westerns. Being more a Tarantinian film than a Hollywood film *Django* presents a black character who is disconnected from the black collective and who is deeply concerned about the fate of his wife, who—although she remains marginal—is shown as "human" and "aware of her self-worth".[24] At the same time, Tarantino pays tribute to the directors of *buddy movies*. The friendship of Django and Schultz in its very nature looks paradoxical and improbable, as does the character of the Doctor himself, epitomizing the Western formula of a good-evil man, a gentleman bandit with a reputation for style and sophistication. It is much more difficult to match the role of Hildi with the catalogue of female characters known from Westerns. She functions not only as an inspiration for dramatic events but also takes an active part in them through her repeated attempts to escape. In spite of the fact that each time she is

---

[24] Johannes Fehrle, "Django Unchained".

severely punished for her actions, she demonstrates perseverance in continuing to try. (A more typical Western role of a passive and not very intelligent woman is assigned to Candy's sister.) Hildi does not accept her fate, though she is not a strong and fully independent *cowgirl* shown in the 1930s, perceived as a kind of cowboy's rival, who is doomed to live alone because she is too strong to share life with a man. For Hildi, life is a school of hard knocks and her attempts to run away are a way of desperate protest as only love seems to be worth fighting for.

To some extent, Hildi resembles one of the first representations of female mythology in Westerns: the battle-hardened wife of a pioneer, his faithful companion and *spiritus movens*. Tarantino in this respect demonstrates the tendency to idealize the heroine as in Hildi we can also see the most sincere and real emotional reactions (for example when she loses consciousness while recognizing Django in Doctor Schultz's room) as well as a part of black-black relationship based on mutual love, which is very rare in Westerns. Bearing this in mind, one should consider the circumstances of the women's deaths in *Django Unchained*. The death of Candy's sister strikes the viewer with its artificiality; she dies bloodlessly and—as mentioned above—in a very theatrical pose. The characteristic woman with a covered face working on a plantation also dies bloodlessly, as if behind the scene. The viewer is aware of the fact that she must have died in the final shooting; however, the visual evidence is not presented on the screen.

Considering other myths and role models typically associated with Westerns, among which we could place the character of a sheriff rarely dying in the gunfights, one could come to the conclusion that Tarantino treats the genre with warm irony (Linda Hutcheon), or he even concocts a genre of his own, inspired by the cinematographic tradition. In accordance with the moralizing standards of Westerns, justice must always win the fight against evil. In *Django Unchained*, the messengers of justice are the former slave and a foreign doctor. This fact is emphasized in the scene of the bounty hunters' conversation with the sheriff, which ends with the surprising or even shocking punchline, undermining the reputation of the institution represented by the man with a tin star. The stylization of the dialogue with the sheriff, which finds its rhythm also in the absurd discussion of the riders, dressed up in uncomfortable masks *à la* Ku Klux Klan, resembles Tarantino's "poker", isomorphic dialogues, commonly known not only from *Pulp Fiction*, but also from *Reservoir Dogs*, *Inglourious Basterds* or *The Hateful Eight* (2015) to name just a few examples.

For the spectator of Tarantino's films, those *signature talks* are always the signal of a slowing down of the pace in order to achieve some dramatic effect; they help to build up the Tarantinian variant of *suspense*, based on the "awakening" of the viewer with a rapid turn of events after a seemingly peaceful sequence. In this respect, *Django Unchained* does not surprise the audience with its use of dialogue solutions. Another Western motif recurs in the treatment of Schultz's horse Fritz, the animal treated with respect and affection, introduced in William S. Hart's Westerns and sometimes even having the ability to speak. Furthermore, the director of *Kill Bill* is faithful to classic cinema in his romantic views of enchanting beauty, presenting wild American nature as a means for his protagonists to escape from the everyday hell of slavery and injustice. Tarantino's film method recalls in this respect the cinema of

D.W. Griffith, the founder of modern film techniques, who widely used open air shots, through which he emphasized the differences between cinema and theatre strategies.

The shots of nature untouched by civilization seem to be also the expression of man's longing for freedom, which has always been a desire associated with the American mentality, an indisputable value constituting a kind of genetic matrix that other notions and aspirations are built on. The visualization of this basic American dream in *Django* is the scene of the protagonist's gallop after his liberation from the mine workers, in particular the close-up of one of the slave's faces following the runaway. The eyes of the former companion, who a few minutes earlier had spat with contempt at the sight of Django, express admiration, solidarity and faith in his success. This shot could even be recognized as symptomatic of the American mentality and read as a metaphor of the hope and optimism of the whole nation streaked with a lack of fulfillment and yearning for freedom. The shots presenting the scene of Django's surrender in Candy's mansion could be interpreted as a kind of commentary confirming this interpretation. In spite of the hopeless situation, the hero surrenders in a blaze of glory, his visibly emphasized straight posture as well as the pace of the slowed down shots creating the atmosphere of majesty, causing the viewer to perceive him not as a loser but rather with the impression that by accident the roles of victims and butchers are temporarily exchanged.

The exchangeability of the functions mentioned above is especially visible in the montage approach, which emphasizes and helps to achieve the effect of an exaltation of the acts of violence. As an example, we could mention the scene of the crushing of the Brittle brothers by Django, in which the shots of the delivered blows are synchronized with the rhythm of rap music. Consequently, the viewer may treat the whole sequence as a surreal and engrossing spectacle. The effect of visual attractiveness and artificiality in the sequence is also built up by the introduction of the bright, very colorful, opera-style outfit of Django. On the other hand, however, the act of vengeance of the former slave is shown as an almost exact replica of the earlier scene of violence inflicted by the current victim. The Old Testament mentality of "an eye for an eye, a tooth for a tooth", which gets in this visualization a real dimension, could be perceived as a critical commentary on Christian religious practices, which allowed and justified violence in the past. Such an assumption is confirmed by the fact of "Big John" Brittle's reciting the Bible at the very moment of inflicting violence upon the defenseless victim. Parallel technique can be found also in *Pulp Fiction* in the shots of Jules quoting passages of the book of Ezekiel, which is interpreted by most critics in terms of the caricature of a preacher.[25]

The repetition of particularly graphic scenes of human beings being torn apart by hungry dogs, which was inspired by Schultz's listening to live Beethoven music, shows that in Tarantino's Western, sacred values meet *ultraviolence*, that is to say the lowest level of degradation and mindlessly inflicted terror. As a result, we can see that

---

[25] Todd F. Davis, Kenneth Womack, "Shepherding the Weak: the Ethics of Redemption in Quentin Tarantino's *Pulp Fiction*", *Literature Film Quarterly*, 26 (1), 1998, 61.

the scenes in the American director's variant of the Western do not contain many close-ups of actual rapes or other forms of brutality known from the Italian versions of the story about the Wild West. Tarantino's focuses mainly on showing violence as a kind of spectacular performance, full of dynamic changes and clashes of incompatible elements to keep the viewer in a state of continuous tension.

Summing up, it could be said that the Tarantinian version of the Western is full of intertextual and intercultural allusions. The genre, which was born on American ground, has its many international modifications and equivalents, among which one can mention the German *ersatz-western*, the Soviet *eastern* and other more or less successful attempts at adapting the classical form of the genre on the Old Continent. Being definitely inspired by the Italian tradition of the Spaghetti Western, *Django Unchained* openly keeps the history of the genre at a distance to build up a modern and visually attractive fantasy, deeply ingrained in the American way of thinking and the process of the Disneyfication of everyday life in the New World. Redressing the crime of slavery in pop aesthetics and balancing between comedy and hyperbolic violence Tarantino simultaneously engages us in a make-believe game and reminds us of the necessity of facing difficult American problems, for example the disparities between socioeconomic groups or (reverse) racism. Considering the work of Quentin Tarantino in the context of other Westerns reveals the direction of the continuing development of this genre showing at the same time that using typical Tarantinian strategies can make it very appealing to both young and old contemporary audiences.

BIBLIOGRAPHY

Carpio, Glenda R., "'I like the way you die, Boy': Fantasy's Role in *Django Unchained*", *Transition*, 112, 2013, 1-12.

Davis, Todd F. and Womack, Kenneth, "Shepherding the Weak: the Ethics of Redemption in Quentin Tarantino's *Pulp Fiction*", *Literature Film Quarterly*, 26 (1), 1998.

Denby, David, "*Django Unchained*: Put-On, Revenge, and the Aesthetics of Trash", *The New Yorker*, January 22, 2013. http://www.newyorker.com/culture/ culture-desk/django-unchained-put-on-revenge-and-the-aesthetics-of-trash [accessed 01/02/2018].

Fehrle, Johannes, "*Django Unchained* and the Neo-Blaxploitation Western", *Iperstoria: Testi Letterature Linguaggi*, 2, 2013. http://www.iperstoria.it/joomla/15-saggi/90-fehrle [accessed 01/02/2018].

Ford, James E., "Close-Up: Fugitivity and the Filmic Imagination. Blackness and Legend", *Black Camera*, 7:1, 2015, 199-217.

Frayling, Christopher, *Spaghetti Western: Cowboys and Europeans from Karl May to Sergio Leone*, London-New York: I. B. Tauris, 2012.

French, Philip, *Westerns: Aspects of a Movie Genre and Westerns Revisited*, Manchester: Carcanet Press, 2005.

Hughes, Howard, *Spaghetti Westerns*, Harpenden: Kamera Books, 2010.

Hutcheon, Linda, *Irony's Edge: The Theory and Politics of Irony*, London and New York: Routledge, 1994.

Michalski, Czesław, *Western i Jego Bohaterowie*, Warszawa: Wydawnictwa Artystyczne i Filmowe, 1972.

Nelson, Scott R., "*Django Untangled*: The Legend of the Bad Black Man", *The Chronicle of Higher Education*, January 11, 2013. http://chronicle.com/article/Django-Untangled-the-Legend/ 136643/ [accessed 01/02/2018].

Pilkington, William T., Graham, Don, eds, *Western Movies*, Albuquerque: University of New Mexico Press, 1979.

Polan, Dana, *Pulp Fiction*, London: British Film Institute, 2000.

Preis-Smith, Agata and Paryż, Marek, eds, *Amerykański Western Literacki w XX Wieku: Między Historią, Fantazją i Ideologią*, Warszawa: Czuły Barbarzyńca Press, 2013.

Samuels, Allison, "Quentin Tarantino on *Django Unchained* and the Problem with 'Roots'", *Newsweek*, October 12, 2012. http://europe.newsweek.com/quentin-tarantino-django-unchained-and-problem-roots-63453?rm=eu [accessed 01/02/2018].

Scherstuhl, Alan, "*Django Unchained*: The Most Moving Scene Quentin Tarantino Has Yet Filmed", *LA Weekly*, April 18, 2013. http://www.laweekly.com/ 2013-04-18/film-tv/django-unchained-best-scene [accessed 10/01/2018].

Sexton, David, "*Django Unchained*—review", *Evening Standard*, January 18, 2013. http://www.standard.co.uk/goingout/film/django-unchained--review-8457022.html [accessed 10/01/2018].

Slotkin, Richard, *Regeneration Through Violence: The Mythology of the American Frontier 1600-1860*, Oklahoma: The University of Oklahoma Press, 1973.

Tookey, Chris, "Funny, Gruesome and Brilliant in Parts, *Django Unchained* is Tarantino's Best—and Maddest—since *Pulp Fiction*", *Daily Mail*, January 17, 2013.

Turner, Frederick J., *The Significance of the Frontier in American History*, Eastford: Martino Fine Books, 2014.

Vognar, Chris, "He Can't Say That, Can He?: Black, White and Shades of Gray in the Films of Tarantino", *Transition*, 112, 2013.

Waligorska-Olejniczak, Beata, *"Sacrum" w Drodze: "Moskwa-Pietuszki" Wieniedikta Jerofiejewa i "Pulp Fiction" Quentina Tarantino w Kluczu Montażowego Czytania*, Poznań: Wydawnictwo Naukowe UAM, 2013.

Wise, Damon, "Resist the Temptation to Ridicule this: Interview with Quentin Tarantino", *The Guardian*, May 4, 2007. http://www.theguardian.com/film/ 2007/may/04/quentintarantino [accessed 01/02/2018].

CHAPTER 6

Belonging and Moral Relations in *Justified*

Colm Kenny

In a dialogue on justice, Socrates speaks of "an ancient quarrel between poetry and philosophy".[1] That commentary has cast a long shadow over relations between literature and morality. Fiction and philosophy explore some common concerns, such as knowledge, truth and politics, but differently. Ethics, again, is seen to offer a mutual ground for literary criticism and moral philosophy. Comparative literary criticism studies literary texts and other forms of literary expression, such as film and television. It offers a hospitable meeting place where interdisciplinary dialogue can begin, resume or continue.[2] Belonging offers a valuable focus for exploring relations between narrative fiction and moral philosophy.

The American Western and crime fiction are two genres across literary media with worldwide popularity that present readers and viewers with scenes, themes and issues of moral significance. The genres are connected: the hard-boiled detective is seen as a descendant of the cowboy.[3] The American Western explores frontier and conflict where justice is frequently addressed through the shootout. Crime fiction explores relations between crime, investigators and criminals, and often raises questions of justice through pursuits of, and in confrontations with criminals. Both genres have featured prominently in explorations of what America, being an American and moral authority might mean. *Justified*, the neo-Western crime drama produced by Graham Yost (2010-2015), based on Elmore Leonard's short story "Fire in the Hole",[4] repeatedly provides occasions, through action, character and dialogue, for viewers to respond to matters of morality and justice. It presents claims of belonging—to place, time, groups, and of personal effects—as a notion that can exert a force on the moral formation and ethical development of characters.

Frontiers and shootouts can be considered chronotopes of the American Western. At the frontier and in the shootout the impression of space is stressed or compressed

---

[1] Plato, *Republic*, trans. C.D.C. Reeve, Indianapolis: Hackett Publishing Company, 2004, 311.

[2] Brigitte Le Juez, "Positive Uncertainty and the Ethos of Comparative Literature", *CLCWeb: Comparative Literature and Culture*, 15:7, December 2013, Article 2.
http://docs.lib.purdue.edu/cgi/viewcontent.cgi?article=2376&context=clcweb

[3] John Scaggs, *Crime Fiction*, Abingdon: Routledge, 2005.

[4] Elmore Leonard, "Fire in the Hole" in Elmore Leonard *Fire in the Hole*, New York, NY: William Morrow, 2012, 57-112. Short story first published in 2001.

by time tending towards some limit point of generic and ethical significance, commonly at a thoroughfare around noon. They bring some underlying assumptions in the Western myth into view, including: (i) conceptions of space, frontier or boundary, marking divisions of occupation, possession, protection, and the quest and contest for authority;[5] (ii) the Westerner's rugged individualism, imbued with a sense of autonomy, self-reliance, an acceptance of rough justice and a belief in an ability to settle one's own problems; (iii) exceptionalism, a belief in the uniqueness of personal and collective experience and identity, a sense of being incomparable, as author(s) and subject(s) of different laws and forces; and (iv) the legitimacy of violence as a response to threat and as a form of justice, "swift, sure and reflexive action through the barrel of a gun".[6]

Frederick Jackson Turner held that the American (figured mostly in terms of the male) is forged by encounter with the frontier, and that those values associated with the myth are projected onto the person rather than projected by the person.[7] The Western myth underwrites the pioneer's and the cowboy's claim to a free space where they can be seen as the first sowers and readers of symbolic values, and first to systematize them in moral code. The Western hero is traditionally imperfect: his speech can be rough and often there is some criminal element in his past. He has an intimate sense of his own end, which increases the moral significance of his acts of protection and sacrifice, often made for love or justice.

People are, at least partially, shaped by encounters with space. They are educated in and by the transformation of space to place by virtue of the attachment of values. Belonging can be conceived as a network of relations, such as between places, collectives and objects. Belongings are inscribed with values. A sense of belonging, or its refusal, exerts an influence on identity, including its moral dimension. Stakes to belonging can be made through an appeal to precedence, affection, filiation, affiliation and hospitality. Shootouts can be considered as culminations of narrative and dialogical attempts to resolve rival claims to place and property and to establish forms of authority.

Justified and the stories and novels it draws on contribute to informal education in genre and ethics. Genre can work like ethics and particular genres like moral systems and codes: genres can be considered normative systems for practices of production, classification, reception, and evaluation. Recognizing and working with genres is a form of education for readers and writers.[8] Watching Westerns and crime drama is part of an education in the forms, codes and conventions of those genres, their modes of making and transmitting sense and meaning, and how they could or should be received and decoded. *Justified* makes use and contributes to the

---

[5] Martin Shuster, "'Boyd and I Dug Coal Together': Norms, Persons and Being Justified", *MLN*, 127:5, December 2012, 1040-58.
[6] Richard W. Slatta, "Making and Unmaking Myths of the American Frontier", *European Journal of American Culture*, 29:2, July 2010, 81-92 (85).
[7] Frederick Jackson Turner, *The Significance of the Frontier in American History*, American Historical Association, 1894, https://www.historians.org/about-aha-and-membership/aha-history-and-archives/archives/the-significance-of-the-frontier-in-american-history [accessed 20 July 2015].
[8] John Frow, *Genre*, Abingdon: Routledge, 2006.

development of conventions of Western and crime fiction genres, such as the moral coding of character, place and object through use of light, color, sound, language, focalization and time.

The words "ethics" and "morality" are often used interchangeably in general conversation. In technical use, there is some distinction between them. Morality is the practical expression of the precepts, principles, values or virtues set out in a common code.[9] The term ethics often means moral philosophy, that is, the study of morality, a theoretical exercise involving "systematizing, defending, and recommending concepts of right and wrong behavior".[10] However, for Socrates and Aristotle ethics concerns the practical and theoretical pursuit of questions of how one ought to live, what one needs to know in order to live well, what one ought to do or what kind of person one should be. There can be some blurring at the borders of morality and ethics.

The field of inquiry involving narrative fiction and moral philosophy appears to have resisted the imposition or development of a unified theory or practice. Lawrence Buell has described it as pluriform and cacophonous.[11] He suggests that, perhaps, this is as it should be: a prescriptive method with specific rules for application, and criteria for evaluation, determined in advance of reading the text, might not be ethical. It might not be sensitive to relevant literary and ethical features, and could have undesirable consequences. Studies of ethics, literature and the relations between them presented in a highly-specialized language might give the impression that they are matters of academic concern and irrelevant, inaccessible or too difficult for many. Nevertheless, some narrative fictions insist on providing stimuli for readers to react to moral themes and issues.

There are tensions between theory and practice in ethics as in literary studies. Some theories may be so broad that they neglect relevant local particulars; some practices may be so specific that they may not be meaningfully generalized. *Phronesis*, the kind of wisdom that comes from and develops with reflective experience and practice, which is sensitive to particulars and relevant differences in situations, is a concept that can connect theory and practice in ethics and literary study. As Aristotle conceives it, *phronesis* is a form of moral reasoning and judgement.[12] In this analysis, reasoning does not mean a purely rationalistic application of grammars of logic, but an articulation of memory, feeling, imagination and thought. For Hans Robert Jauss, the creation and development of the meaning of a text is located in the relationship between the reader and the text. Meaning is informed by personal and historical contexts, and by the experiences and memories of readers. Meanings and significance are sustained by chains of receptions, altered by previous receptions and influence future receptions and projections. For Jauss, the

---

[9] Bernard Gert and Joshua Gert, "The Definition of Morality", in Edward N. Zalta, ed, *The Stanford Encyclopedia of Philosophy*, 2015, Fall 2015 Edition, https://plato.stanford.edu/entries/morality-definition/ [accessed 02/02/2018].

[10] James Fieser, "Ethics", in James Fieser and Bradley Dowden, eds, *Internet Encyclopedia of Philosophy*, 2015, http:// www.iep.utm.edu/ethics/#H4 [accessed 02/02/2018].

[11] Lawrence Buell, "Introduction: In Pursuit of Ethics", *PMLA*, 114:1, January 1999, 7-19.

[12] Aristotle, *Nicomachean Ethics*, trans. Terence Irwin, Indianapolis: Hackett Publishing Company, 1999.

anticipatory dimension of expectation allows for the creativity of the literary experience to affect the reader's perception of and reflection on the everyday.[13] When readers react to moral notes sounded in texts, those reactions can enter into further chains of perceptions, receptions, reflections and projections.

Moral issues and interests may develop through cumulative effects of language, imagery, character and other textual features. The reader may then consider the memories, experiences and imaginings stirred, comparing his or her thoughts, feelings, expectations and judgements with those met in the text. When a sensitive and receptive reader attends to texts in such a manner, there are conditions and opportunities for moral awareness, perception, discernment and deliberation to develop.[14] Television series which run over a number of seasons—like *Justified*—present scenes that are integrated into viewers' series of receptions and judgements affecting the relations between the reader and the text that can contribute to the development of the reader's moral responses and development.

Justified and the story it is based on focus on the personal and professional relations of Raylan Givens, a Deputy United States Marshal played by Timothy Olyphant. He is reassigned from Florida to Harlan County, Kentucky, where he was reared but has no desire to return. His relocation is due to his handling of an incident in Miami, and to the Marshals Service's pursuit of Boyd Crowder. Raylan is likened to, and styles himself on, the lawmen of the Old West: cowboy hat and boots, his badge signaling his possession of a gun and his readiness to use it, when justified. His duties bring him face-to-face with his past: where he grew up; where he first worked; his family, friends and associates; what he kept and left behind. Boyd, Raylan's main antagonist, an acquaintance form childhood and later a co-worker in the mines, is involved in robbery and drugs in Harlan County.

The pilot episode initiates many of the plotlines, themes and issues developed throughout the series. It follows Leonard's short story closely, using much of the dialogue with little modification. In this episode, there are three shootings that fit or approximate the pattern of a shootout. Some person has committed some characteristic action that offends a moral code. An ultimatum is issued to that person: either leave the place by a given time or risk being shot. Sometimes there is an option to change behavior, but the relevant behavior is generally such a deep character trait that its loss would signify a death of sorts. The option to flee is a rhetorical device, it is expected that time will elapse or behavior be repeated. This excess results in a standoff, a face-to-face encounter at the appointed place and time, at which someone shoots and somebody is shot. The shootouts are narrated in different ways, presented on screen or conveyed indirectly, with details later elaborated through dialogue.

The series *Justified* opens with the camera following the back of a man wearing a light-colored suit and a cowboy hat in strong sunlight. Those familiar with the filmic conventions of the Western recognize the figure cast before the viewer as a

---

[13] Hans Robert Jauss, *Toward and Aesthetic of Reception*, Minneapolis, MN: University of Minnesota Press, 1982.

[14] Martha Nussbaum, *Love's Knowledge: Essays on Philosophy and Literature*, New York, NY: Oxford University Press, 1992.

representative of what is good, right or just, drawing the viewer towards tentative ethical judgement. The use of light also points to, but does not yet confirm the moral character of this person. Those getting to know the conventions may make and test associations of white and light with what is good. However, some incongruity between the man and the spatial and temporal frames disturbs easy associations that conventions may suggest. He pauses at the foot of a rooftop pool and a contemporary scene is revealed. He then proceeds between the pool, sun loungers and people enjoying the promise of both. But the figure projected has a foot in other times and places, his hat and suit against the swimsuits and cocktails, his stride against the salsa and gangsta fusion, but catching something of its rhythm. What authority might his presence and style have here?

His estrangement from the people and the environment is ambiguous: it might support or undermine him in what he has come for; it might make his motives and actions personal or impersonal; it might mean that he is here to issue a counterclaim in his own name or on behalf of someone or something else—a victim, a code or a feeling. Seated at a sheltered table in a corner of the rooftop there is a dark-suited man framed by a glass balustrade, beyond which a horizon of sea and cloudless sky is visible. The moral structuring of place through play of sun and shadow complements that of character. The men are not yet explicitly identified with the law or crime. The man in the light-colored suit approaches the man at the table and says: "Airport's a good 45 [minutes] from here, but I figure you'll be all right if you leave in the next two minutes" (1:1).[15] Raylan had given Tommy Bucks, a local gun thug, twenty-four hours to get out of Dade County, Florida, or else he would shoot him on sight. By the conventions of the Western this triggers the shootout, a meeting of the threat of violence with violence, a return of the duel and the *noblesse d'épée*. Martin Shuster explains this standoff as a challenge for justice and authority that is tied to the project of America. For him this show represents a working through of the problems of a distinctly American form of life as it relates to persons, norms and moral justification.[16]

The confrontation between Raylan and Bucks represents a collision between two characteristic and antagonistic versions of the American dream: cowboy, gangster and their ethics. In the exchange with Raylan, Bucks seeks to establish his claim to place. At first, he responds to Raylan banning him by appealing to precedence and affection, offering explanatory reasons for not leaving: "I been coming here ever since I was a kid, ever since this was nothing but old Jews and old Cubans"; "to tell you the truth, I love it here. I really do, I loved it then, and I love it now". He offers hospitality: "have a meal with me." Raylan's "45" exerts temporal pressure with the shadow of a gun, intensifying the experience of time and place; they coagulate around the site of standoff and shootout. It is a dramatic device where the impression of commanding time counts more than its actual passage. This scene is a staging of the last two minutes of Bucks' life as reckoned by Raylan without reference to any timepiece.

---

[15] *Justified*. 2010-2015. DVD: Sony Pictures Television Inc. and Bluebush Productions, LCC. Developed for television by Graham Yost. 1.1 means season 1, episode 1, etc.

[16] Shuster, "Boyd and I".

Bucks competes for control of time's passage. Extending his authority through narrative and question, he identifies Raylan as a character, not a person:

> You, you're a character. I was tellin' my friends this morning how yesterday you come to me an' [making a gun with his hand] "If you don't get out of town in the next twenty-four hours I'm gonna shoot you on sight." Come on, what is that? They thought it was a joke and sorta started laughing. (1:1)

As this scene unfolds, the music changes from apparently diegetic salsa to salsa infused with a gangster rap and later to non-diegetic Western strains.[17] These musical shifts disturb the viewer and invite her/him to consider what elements belong to the scene and what has been added, by whom and to what effect. What fusions and confusions are presented here? Cameras alternate between Raylan and Bucks, generally focusing on the face of the one speaking, but sometimes lingering on Bucks' response, thus intensifying the face off. The camera is frequently angled upwards towards Raylan's face, elevating him from the viewer's position; but Bucks is often viewed at eye-level, framed between Raylan's shoulder and the rim of his hat. The tracking, the shots and dialogue contribute to the drama, suggesting different available moral perspectives, but seem to align the viewer with Raylan.

Differences between the gangster and the Westerner often emerge slowly. Using *Scarface* as an example, Robert Warshow describes their attitudes:

> [T]he gangster [...] may at any moment lose control; his strength is not in being able to shoot faster or straighter than others, but in being more willing to shoot. "Do it first," says Scarface expounding his mode of operation, "and keep on doing it." With the Westerner, it is a crucial point of honor not to "do it first"; his gun remains in its holster until the moment of combat.[18]

The Westerner, according to Warshow, does not draw reluctantly, he is partially defined by his readiness and skill to shoot and kill his enemy, and it may be that in such action he manifests destiny, duty and justice, doing "what a man's gotta do."

Bucks attempts to establish a morality, to initiate or appeal to a value system based on a locus of belonging: the personal value of place. He invokes childhood memories, presence since some originary time, love and offers hospitality. For Raylan, these are insufficient grounds on which to found justice, so Bucks fuses memory and reciprocity in a further effort to create a shareable code: "Does nothing count, that I let you live?" He imports events, a common history, and reasoning from another time and place. This is almost worthy of being considered a basis for ethical deliberation and judgement. The principles of reversibility—only act in accordance

---

[17] The title music is by a group called Gangstagrass whose music is a fusion of gangster rap and bluegrass. Such a fusion of musical traditions accentuates the proximity of competing moral conceptions, the struggle of each for sovereignty and the possibility that in one there may be elements of the other.
[18] Robert Warshow, "Movie Chronicle: The Westerner", in Jim Kitses and Gregg Rickman, eds, *The Western Reader*, New York, NY: Limelight Editions, 1998, 35-48 (38), article originally published 1958.

with how you would wish others to treat you—and universalizability—act only in ways that you would want all people to act in such situations—tend to be present in many theories of normative ethics and in minimum conceptions of rationalist ethics.[19] Bucks' request for reciprocal treatment approaches a justificatory reason, one that implies some standard, a moral principle, value or virtue. However, closer examination and recollection of a previous remark invalidate the principle invoked, making it less categorical command than caprice: "maybe I should have killed you, huh? Maybe I made a mistake." This reveals that the decision to spare Raylan's life in some prior encounter was not based on some understanding of the value of human life, some sound ethical grounds or even fate, but on a whim.

This groundwork for a mobster moral does not prohibit the taking of life. It permits Raylan to act in accord with the aleatory nature of such morality, or to import some other moral code. Bucks' appeal that Raylan extend him the same consideration reduces reversibility to an economic transaction, or selects the principle without accepting the ethical reasons for that principle, or to preference or egoism, simply because it is personally beneficial at that point. Raylan responds by saying that he is giving Bucks the same consideration, which can be read as performing within Bucks' code, or on another principle, or with a deeper sense of reciprocity. During the dialogue between them, another man is mentioned whose death reveals the nature and limits of Bucks' supposed generosity. Raylan had tracked Bucks to Managua, Nicaragua. There, Bucks captured Raylan and made him watch as he brutally killed the other man.

Perhaps Bucks senses the flaw, the paradox, in his emergent version of a moral code and changes tack. He asks Raylan to consider the social and professional standards that cover this place and Raylan's actions: "In front of all these people, you're gonna pull out a gun and you're gonna shoot an unarmed man?" Bucks presumes that Raylan is bound by moral, social, legal, personal and professional codes not to shoot him. This is ironic. Bucks seeks protection by the law from the law and his own code. Like many felons in the series, he seems unaware that being a bandit or outlaw puts them beyond the power of sovereign law to protect them.[20] They are unethical characters who appeal to another person's sense of fairness or justice, or to an institution or code of practice, to save them. It is a special case of the myth of American exceptionalism, where Bucks desires exceptional consideration and exemption from the code by which he lives, or to be protected by a code that he does not accept. In the end, Bucks draws a gun from under the table. Raylan draws his in response. He shoots Bucks before Bucks can pull his trigger. Afterwards, Raylan says to his boss: "He pulled first. I shot him", which is offered as the simple, necessary and sufficient official justification as Raylan himself faces the disciplinary power of law enforcement and its internal gatekeepers.

Though at a remove from the world, fiction is, nevertheless, a qualified response to the world:

---

[19] Stewart Rachels, *The Elements of Moral Philosophy*, New York, NY: McGraw-Hill, 2013.

[20] Giorgio Agamben, *Homo Sacer: Sovereign Power and Bare Life*, Stanford, CA: Stanford University Press, 1998

> [I]t presents reactions to and attitudes towards the world we live in, and it is these reactions and attitudes that constitute the reality of a literary text. [The literary text] establishes its reality by the reader's participation and by the reader's response.[21]

Literary texts mediate gaps between the external world and the reader's worlds of experience and anticipation. Through reading and viewing, literary media allow for transactions between those worlds and for ethics to develop. Part of the educational potential of this opening exchange lies in the transactions between Bucks and Raylan, its presentation of dialogue, a socially situated act in which people seek recognition from and relevance to another, which is part of the function of stories.[22] There is a weave of memory, reason, feeling and imagination in the presentation of the self as an author and bearer of a moral code. The code being composed by Bucks approximates a morality: it presents shared standards, a system of values operating as a frame of reference for guiding and evaluating thought, feeling and action. Bucks submits his case for scrutiny by Raylan. Raylan, at times, mirrors it back to Bucks, with the intention of revealing its implications, flaws and alternatives; at other times he rejects it, showing it to be little more than Bucks' expression of preferences for how he be treated.

The viewer, critical of Bucks and what he stands for, may not be convinced of the rightness of Raylan's thinking and acting. The viewer's judgement should make reference to criteria and be tentative. Both criteria and the judgement should be resubmitted for further scrutiny. This can be done by comparison. The exchange with Bucks is referred to several times within the first and subsequent episodes, it also features in each of Leonard's stories with Raylan Givens.[23] Elements of the pattern of the exchange between Raylan and Bucks are repeated: a conflict between those who have committed or are about to commit an offence and those who wish to bring justice or prevent the crime. Often there is some verbal exchange between them where appeals are made with respect to a moral system or code of behavior. This can develop as a moral dialogue between the characters. So long as the dialogue continues there is a possibility that justice may prevail. Failure of dialogue in the Western and in crime drama frequently results in violence. When dialogue is sustained there is a chance that the offender pauses long enough to be apprehended or to apprehend the sources or consequences of his/her action. Each episode of the series presents some variation on the conflict between lawmen and felons and an attempt to resolve it through dialogue. In the seventy-eight episodes, Raylan kills twenty-nine people.[24]

---

[21] Wolfgang Iser, *Prospecting: from Reader Response to Literary Anthropology*, Baltimore, MD: Johns Hopkins Press Ltd, 1993, 7.

[22] Jack Zipes, *The Irresistible Fairy Tale: The Social and Cultural History of a Genr*e, Princeton, NJ: Princeton University Press, 2013.

[23] The character Raylan Givens appears in a number of Elmore Leonard's fictions: *Pronto*, London: Phoenix, 2008, first published 1993; *Riding the Rap*, London: Phoenix, 1995; *Raylan*, London: Weidenfeld & Nicolson, eBook, 2012.

[24] This information is based on the fan site justified.wikia.com, http://justified.wikia.com/wiki/Raylan_Givens

This suggests Raylan has a preference for a peaceful resolution through talk, but that there can be times where killing may be justified. The series insists that the viewer return to questions of justification and issues of judgement.

Ava Crowder's shooting of her husband, Bowman, as he eats his dinner at their table is an incident that presents a different version of a moral conversation and the relations between belonging and morality. Unlike the shooting at the Cardozo Hotel in Miami, this is not portrayed on screen. Tim Gutterson, Raylan's colleague, provides the initial details. It does not appear to map neatly onto the pattern of the shootout, usually scheduled for a public place. It may appear that no option or ultimatum were given. It happened at home, and the home is considered special under the law with respect to what can transpire there and to the defense of self and property.[25] Bowman, like Bucks, was eating, which may signify a claim to certain public and private rights, possession of and authority over place and contents. Yet options were offered and an ultimatum was issued. Ava told Bowman that she wanted a divorce: grant or refuse. Refusal compels the ultimatum towards a shootout, of sorts. Ava is telling Bowman to stop beating her, and this is categorical. She does not state limits of time or behavior, they are implicit: never again. Bowman understands this, and responds by threatening to make her disappear. In her account of events to Raylan, Ava summarizes her relationship with Bowman, his aspirations and disappointments, blaming and beating her. Ava realized that she should not tolerate his behavior towards her and she determined to shoot him. She knows Raylan works with the Marshals Service. Her story offers explanatory reasons, outlining a sequence of events in which the outcome seems inevitable. The justification she offers to Raylan, "I did what I had to do", mirroring Raylan's to his superiors, added to satisfy official scrutiny and to keep things simple.

There have been American Westerns in which women are as or more capable than men in the use of the gun, but generally female characters have to find ways around reaching the limit point of the shootout in which justice depends on speed and accuracy with a gun, or luck. A woman may need to take the initiative, to jump the gun, in order to orient the odds in her favor, and live to tell the tale. In her own way, Ava manipulated the impression of time by not specifying a temporal limit, thus forcing the moment to its crisis. However, on a more personal and post hoc level, Ava speaks to Raylan as a person from her past, a new present and possibly future. In her greeting of Raylan, in the story she tells, Ava appeals to his reason, feeling, memory and imagination and to what was, is and can be shared.

The account of this second shooting plays against the first: the roles of host and guest, the sense of entitlement over property and place, the presumed right to select and arrange the values. Bucks and Bowman choose values on the bases of appetite and preference. They both believe that they have the right to exercise violence to enforce their values. Indeed, to some extent violence is one of their values. If the reader associates Bucks with Bowman in this regard it is likely that they reject their

---

[25] Justin A. Joyce, "The Warp, Woof, and Weave of This Story's Tapestry Would Foster the Illusion of Further Progress: Justified and the Evolution of Western Violence", *Western American Literature*, 47:2, Summer 2012, 174-199.

mutual value systems. This rejection may be prior to meeting them in the text, but the encounter allows the reader to review the rejection and to consider similarities between gangsters and wife-beaters and the emptiness of their ethics on the grounds of reversibility and universalizability. Alternatively, or in addition to this, the viewer might be sympathetic to Ava's experience and suffering. This moral feeling might be enhanced by the account she relates to Raylan of her marriage, it may even be that she has structured her account in order to solicit Raylan's sympathy. This affective moral response may coincide with or be supported by reason. How Bowman has treated her, violated her dignity as a person is unjust, vicious. Ava may be associated with Raylan, in sharing her story with him, or aligning her with a particular conception of justice, or in the justification she gives for shooting her husband. As with Raylan, some viewers might have reservations about the moral code that Ava responds with, or the degree of violence used. However, she/he would be inclined to see Ava as justified, and hence deem killing justified in some contexts on reasonable grounds.

The viewer may continue the quest to discern the relevant features of the contexts and criteria by comparing characters, actions and justifications presented in this with the initial scene and with the short story. In doing so, she/he has an opportunity to reassess aspects of moral codes with variations in character and situation, to query relations between the particular and general. Ava's home is not on the map and can really only be found by some local knowledge. It is, in some regard beyond the frontiers of the law and technology. She does not feel that law can protect her here. Is the justice code of the American frontier, where justice is rough, appropriate here? Does the fact that Bowman threatened to make Ava disappear mean that he is prepared to accept the same moral terms that he has set? What protections are afforded by this moral code to those less quick on the draw, less accurate in aim or less lucky?

The third shootout of this episode involves Boyd Crowder and Raylan. Boyd is Bowman's brother, and through filiation he feels a right to and responsibility for Ava, but his attraction to Ava is more powerful making him feel a moral obligation. Boyd, like Bucks, is a felon. However, Boyd and Raylan's shared past of working the mines together provides a basis for some shared moral feeling. But Raylan is an obstacle for Boyd, romantically and as an outlaw. Boyd heard through the channels of television news and criminal fraternity of the Bucks incident. With the desire to become known as the man who shot Raylan Givens, Boyd sets up a shootout, replicating features of both the earlier ones. Raylan manages to shoot Boyd first, but does not kill him. When asked to explain, he says it is because they dug coal together. The justification for not killing Boyd, in the series, runs deep in veins. The recurrence of familiar elements places this scene in the viewer's chain of receptions and can lead to the viewer refining or modifying her/his criteria for justification and moral reasoning. Questions of family and friendship now trouble action, judgement and justice.

The older Westerner's confidantes were bar women, fallen women, and widows. He was more stoic, protective or misunderstood when it came to women who represent refinement, virtue and civilization in an American mind.[26] To some degree, Raylan's conversations with women follow the conventions of older Westerns, but not simply or absolutely. Towards the end of the first episode, in the dead of night, Raylan breaks into the home of his ex-wife, Winona, and her new husband. The past that led to his return to Harlan County, and the past that his return awakens, trouble him. He submits himself, his motives, feelings and actions for her scrutiny, not for her approval, but to better understand himself. Troubled by the killing of Tommy Bucks, Raylan tells her about meeting him in Nicaragua and how Bucks had filled a man's mouth with dynamite and lit the fuse. He repeats fragments of his official reason, "He pulled first—so I was justified". But this time he is not offering it as an official explanation for administrative purposes, he is trying to understand himself, his moral code and conduct. He continues: "What troubles me, is what if he hadn't? What if he just sat there and let the clock run out? Would I have killed him anyway? I wanted to. Guess I just never thought of myself as an angry man." To which Winona responds "Oh Raylan! Well you do a good job of hiding it, and I… I suppose most folks don't see it, but, honestly, you're the angriest man I have ever known" (1.1).

In this dialogue, Raylan is reviewing his understanding of justice, his judgement and his actions. The series of questions that follow the initial assertion of justification suggests that he is not satisfied with the rationality of frontier justice, though there is a draw to it. While he presents himself, and wants others to think of him as cool, confident and skilled, in talk and with a gun, underneath he is uncertain. The configuration of this dialogue is different to those above. Raylan is not speaking as a representative of legal authority, nor as a man who has it all worked out. He is not trying to save or seduce the person with whom he is talking, nor is someone trying to win him over. In recounting to Winona the encounters with Bucks, Raylan comes to realize that his morality is a practical fusion of memory, reason, feeling and imagination. But he also catches a glimpse that an excess of any of these—too much past, too cold reason, too passionate feeling—may uncouple justice from being and doing good, and imagination may help him make sense of relations between them.

A number of Raylan's conversations with criminals follow the pattern of that with Bucks. Raylan takes the position of an agent of justice. He hopes talk will defuse the conflict, but is ready to use his gun and confident in his skill with it. Sometimes Raylan succeeds in talking down a potential crime. Other conversations, such as those with Ava, whose killing of her husband is not viewed as a crime by the courts or marshals, serve to reinforce reasons given for killing, moving between explanations and justifications. The dialogues he has with Winona, and similar ones with Art Mullen, his boss and previously a colleague, and with Boyd, are more critical attempts to understand himself, his reasoning, his feelings, actions, belongings and what happens when words fail and guns are fired. Justice, in *Justified*, becomes more than just a legal concept, it is a moral relation

[26] Warshow, "Movie Chronicle: The Westerner".

BIBLIOGRAPHY

Agamben, Giorgio, *Homo Sacer: Sovereign Power and Bare Life*, Stanford, CA: Stanford University Press, 1998.

Aristotle, *Nicomachean Ethics*, trans. Irwin, T. Indianapolis: Hackett Publishing Company, 1999.

Buell, Lawrence, "Introduction: In Pursuit of Ethics", *PMLA*, 114:1, Special Topic: Ethics and Literary Study, January 1999, 7-19.

Fieser, James, "Ethics", in James Fieser and Bradley Dowden, eds., *Internet Encyclopedia of Philosophy*. http://www.iep.utm.edu/ethics/#H4 [accessed 01/02/2018].

Frow, John, *Genre*, Abingdon: Routledge, 2006.

Gert, Bernard and Gert, Joshua, "The Definition of Morality" in Edward N. Zalta, ed., *The Stanford Encyclopedia of Philosophy*, 2015. https://plato.stanford.edu/entries/morality-definition/ [accessed 02/02/2018].

Iser, Wolfgang, *Prospecting: From Reader Response to Literary Anthropology*, Baltimore, MD: Johns Hopkins University Press Ltd, 1993.

Jauss, Hans Robert, *Toward an Aesthetic of Reception*, Minneapolis: University of Minnesota Press, 1982.

Joyce, Justin A., "The Warp, Woof, and Weave of This Story's Tapestry Would Foster the Illusion of Further Progress: *Justified* and the Evolution of Western Violence", *Western American Literature*, 47:2, 2012, 174-199.

Le Juez, Brigitte, "Positive Uncertainty and the Ethos of Comparative Literature", *CLCWeb: Comparative Literature and Culture*, 15:7, Article 2, December 2013. http://dx.doi.org/10.7771/1481-4374.2376 [accessed 01/02/2018].

Leonard, Elmore, "Fire in the Hole", *Fire in the Hole*, New York: William Morrow, 2012, 57-112. Originally published 2001.

Nussbaum, Martha, *Love's Knowledge: Essays on Philosophy and Literature*, New York: Oxford University Press, 1992.

Plato, *Republic*, trans Reeve, C. D. C., Indianapolis: Hackett Publishing Company, 2004.

Rachels, Stewart, *The Elements of Moral Philosophy*, New York: McGraw-Hill, 2013. Scaggs, John, *Crime Fiction*. Abingdon: Routledge, 2005.

Shuster, Martin, "'Boyd and I Dug Coal Together': Norms, Persons and Being Justified in *Justified*", *MLN*, 127:5, December 2012, 1040-1058.

Slatta, Richard W., "Making and Unmaking Myths of the American Frontier", *European Journal of American Culture*, 29:2, July 2010, 81-92.

Turner, Frederick Jackson, "The Significance of the Frontier in American History", *American Historical Association*, 1894. https://www.historians.org/about-aha-and-membership/aha-history-and-archives/archives/the-significance-of-the-frontier-in-american-history [accessed 01/02/2018].

Warshow, Robert, "Movie Chronicle: The Westerner", in Jim Kitses, and Gregg Rickman, eds, *The Western Reader*, New York: Limelight Editions, 1998, 35-48. Originally published 1958.

Zipes, Jack, *The Irresistible Fairy Tale: The Social and Cultural History of a Genre*, Princeton: Princeton University Press, 2013.

Television Shows

Justified, Sony Pictures Television Inc. and Bluebush Productions, LCC, developed for television by Graham Yost, 2010-2015.

Websites

http://justified.wikia.com/wiki/Justified_Wiki [accessed 02/02/2018].

Part II. Intermediality and Innovation

CHAPTER 7

Transmedia Adaptation—A Dialogue of Genres and Communication Media

Narvika Bovcon and Aleš Vaupotič

Adaptation studies focus on the transition of past works and genres—i.e. prototype works—into new works. Even openly declared adaptations in fact should still be considered original creations by an individual or group author. An important theoretical reference for this field of study is the Bakhtinian idea of dialogism as a ubiquitous intertextuality, which, at the same time, preserves the author concept in the role of the one responsible for the work as a complex utterance. Such an approach waters down the difference between an adaptation and a predominantly original work (which in its pure form cannot exist), since every utterance appropriates and reuses past discourses.[1] The creative use of the past is therefore construed as a total reconfiguration of the available discourse fragments in a new consummated whole. Walter Benjamin emphasizes the paradox of the regular and the extraordinary in great works of art: "A major work will either establish the genre or abolish it; and the perfect work will do both."[2] Here a perfect work is an ironic paradox[3] in the domain of the generic units of communication.

Thomas Leitch has notably raised a problematic issue of adaptation studies: "that the field is still haunted by the notion that adaptations [mostly films on literary works] ought to be faithful to their ostensible source texts."[4] Instead, he argues for a wide consideration of adaptation focussing on the identity of the new work and the creative relationship—e.g. as receptive process—between the interconnected works. In conclusion, he argues for the idea of intermediality, widely accepted in Europe but less so in English language theory, that opens the scope of adaptation studies to all possible communication media in all combinations. Peter Weibel theorises the era of

---

[1] Bakhtin's later works consider speech genres as generic entities providing recognizable shapes to the flow of dialogue. See Mikhail M. Bakhtin, *Speech Genres and Other Late Essays*, Austin: University of Texas, 1986.

[2] Walter Benjamin, *The Origin of German Tragic Drama*, London, Brooklyn, NY: Verso, 2009, 44.

[3] Stephen Werner, *Socratic Satire: An Essay on Diderot and* Le Neveu de Rameau, Birmingham, Alabama: Summa Publications. Inc., 1987, 73.

[4] Thomas Leitch, "Adaptation Studies at a Crossroads", *Adaptation*, 1:1, 2008, 63-77 (64). See also Deborah Cartmell, ed., *A Companion to Literature, Film, and Adaptation*, Chichester, West Sussex: Wiley-Blackwell, 2012, 3-4.

the post-media condition, which after the first phase of establishing the equivalence of all media continues into the second phase:

> The new second phase, in an artistic and epistemological sense, is about blending the specific intrinsic worlds of the media. […]
>
> Sculpture can be a photo or a videotape.
>
> An event, photographically captured, can be a sculpture, a text or a picture. The behaviour of an object or a person, video graphically or photographically documented, can be a sculpture, language can be sculpture, language on LED-screens can be painting, can be a book and sculpture, video and computer installations can be literature, architecture or sculpture.[5]

Here the dialogue takes place between artistic disciplines that have turned into media, they depend on "the intrinsic worlds of the apparatuses, the intrinsic characteristics of the media world."[6] The concept of *deep remixability* by Lev Manovich in his book *Software Takes Command* (preprint 2008) refers not only to the remix of subject matter of different media when they enter the uniting digital environment "but also [of] their fundamental techniques, working methods, and ways of representation and expression."[7] This pushes media hybridity to the limit. Most prominent cases of deep remixability are, as Manovich observes, motion graphics projects (e.g. those realized using the Adobe After Effects software) that combine all historical techniques of visual representation: maps, pictograms, hieroglyphs, ideographs, scripts, alphabet, graphs, projection systems, information graphics, photography, modernist language of abstract forms, cinematographic techniques, 3-D computer graphics, algorithmically produced visual effects.[8] Peter Weibel's notion on the second phase of the post-media condition foregrounds the ubiquity of the deep remix in contemporary culture.

The adaptation process can develop on multiple levels. It can cross different media and, as the cases presented in this essay will show, can touch their very core. Considering Benjamin's paradoxical "perfect work", and the problem of faithfulness to the (canonical literary) source raised by Leitch, it becomes clear that the comparison of two works that are not of equal quality can be a problem. Of course, a classical novel renders a substantially more complex readerly experience than a Hollywood production. It is extremely difficult to make a film version of Shakespeare's play that could compete with the source text—Peter Greenaway's *Prospero's Books* (1991) could be such an adaptation of *The Tempest* (1610-11)—however the price to pay for a success like this is the circumstance that Greenaway, a trained painter, does not consider himself a film director but somebody working with

---

[5] Peter Weibel, "The Post-Medial Condition", *Arte Contexto*, 6, 2005, 11-15 (14).
[6] *Ibid.*, 13.
[7] Lev Manovich, *Software Takes Command*, (preprint) 2008, 25. http://softwarestudies.com/softbook/manovich_softbook_11_20_2008.pdf [accessed 30/01/2018].
[8] *Ibid.*, 27.

images in general, which confirms the Benjaminian insight.[9] For this reason the essay attempts to show and explore the most extreme cases of adaptation crossing media boundaries. These cases of adaptation—the links between Dickens, Griffith, Eisenstein; or, the second case, Dickens, David Simon, the theory and art practice of the author of this text—link artistic creativity with a scholarly approach. This reduces the alleged objectivity and increases the creative potential, which is achieved in a hybrid approach.

This essay is composed of two parts. The first chapter reflects on (more or less) an anecdote about the genesis of film language, and in this context, considers the reception of Dickens' works. Next the text turns to borderline cases of adaptation: genre/media hybrid, deep remixability, and allusion. The notions of genre and media are considered as only quantitatively different, not qualitatively, both instances of discourses and apparatuses considered by the theory of discourse (Bakhtin, Foucault etc.). The second part of the text presents an artistic inquiry—concepts and ideas used in production of artworks by the authors of this essay—that sheds light on the possible methods of studying adaptations. Two aspects are foregrounded: the ideas of the transformation of the source text into an archive of fragments that are subsequently put in new meaningful constellations, and the use of Shakespeare's works in the role of a mediator in the understanding of the language of new media art.

DICKENS, D.W. GRIFFITH, DAVID SIMON—THE OUTER BORDERS OF THE FIELD AND ITS EXTENSIONS

The relationship between the source work and the work that enters a dialogical exchange with it can be grounded in formal or even media-specific layers of the two works. Such is the case of David Wark Griffith using Dickens's novelistic technique from 1908 into the 1920s, i.e. in the earliest examples of modern film montage. In the famous article from 1944, "Dickens, Griffith, and the Film Today", one of the key authors and theorists in film history Sergei Eisenstein claims that Dickens was the source for Griffith's pioneering understanding of film language and for "film craftsmanship in general":

> From that steely, observing glance, which I remember from my meeting with him, to the capture *en passant* of key details or tokens—indications of character, Griffith has all these in as much a Dickens-esque sharpness and clarity as Dickens, on his part, had cinematic "optical quality," "frame composition," "close-up," and the alteration of emphasis by special lenses.[10]

---

[9] He claims this often, e.g. in the introduction included in the DVD release of *The Draughtsman's Contract* (1982).

[10] Sergei Eisenstein, "Dickens, Griffith, and the Film Today", in *Film Form, Essays in Film Theory*, ed. and trans. Jay Leyda, San Diego, New York, London: Harcourt Brace Jovanovich Publishers, 1949/1977, 195-255 (213).

Eisenstein develops two lines of argument: he points to similarities between Dickens's novels and Griffith's modern film, as in the quote above, and he also lists documents testifying to the conscious and direct reference to Dickens as recorded in Griffith's biography. Namely, in an interview from 1922, Griffith states that he once gave his employers an ultimatum: he insisted that they let him use parallel action, which he found in Dickens, or they should dismiss him altogether.[11] In Eisenstein's article the relationship to a particular literary tradition meets the birth of a new communication medium in the reflection of a third element, a revolutionary film director, who together with other Soviet authors fundamentally transformed film language (e.g. by problematizing the narrative film montage, introduced by Griffith, in the idea of intellectual montage in Eisenstein's own works or in the experimental films of Dziga Vertov).[12] The source—Dickens—and the target—modern film—meet with a specific emphasis, the soviet avant-garde culture. The need for a particular reference-point in such an intermedia collision is even clearer in the twenty-first century, when the film montage is in decline and the languages of new media, such as digital compositing in computer-based visual effects are taking over, and the shots building a diegetic film-space become mere simulations. The mediated interpretation, on the one hand, problematizes the direct link between two artistic practices (i.e. Dickens' works and the modern film montage), but on the other, it gives it sharp contours by theorising them (e.g. in Eisenstein's terms). The film was not a replacement for the realist novels of the nineteenth century. Eisenstein more likely argues for a concrete source, which had enormous influence, but was not acknowledged as such. For Eisenstein, the study of Dickens to correctly evaluate the modern film montage is essential, while for Dickens' scholars, on the other hand, the "Griffith-esque montage" in the novels is an interesting interpretative starting point, too. The article is, above all, a pointer that should guide the reflection, and much less a factual historical narrative. This may sound ambivalent, but it is integral to Eisenstein's methodology. He claims that the successor "played an enormous role in heightening the tradition and cultural heritage of preceding epochs", which refers to two relationships: Griffith—Dickens, and the "Soviet school of film-making"—Griffith.[13] In Eisenstein's case the Marxist idea of historical development provides the framework for the transformation between world-views of different epochs, however in general, from the point of view of the early twenty-first century, the connection between an individual literary author and a medium of communication, such as film, demands a more elaborate explanation.

The famous historical cases of Dickensian adaptation—Griffith's insistence on using Dickensian technique of parallel action for his film editing, which resulted in modern film montage, and Kafka's blunt claim that his novel *Amerika* would be a copy of Dickens: "The 'Stoker' a mere copy of Dickens, the planned novel seems even more so"[14]—have contemporary equivalents. Today, a total reconceptualization

---

[11] *Ibid.*, 203.

[12] See Pascal Bonitzer, *Le Champ aveugle*, Paris: Cahiers du Cinéma/Gallimard, 1982.

[13] Eisenstein, "Dickens, Griffith, and the Film Today", 233.

[14] "Der 'Heizer' glatte Dickens-Nachahmung, noch mehr der geplante Roman." Franz Kafka, *Tagebücher 1910-1923*, 8 October 1917, http://gutenberg.spiegel.de/buch/-162/10 [accessed 30/01/2018].

of Dickens's work as a source is discussed in reference to the TV series by David Simon, *The Wire* (HBO, 2002, 2003, 2004, 2006, 2008). *The Dickensian Aspect* is the title of the 6th episode of the 5th season, and, ironically, in this particular instance, it is used erroneously to refer to a sentimental, self-righteous journalistic style, whereas, in fact, the whole series, with its dialogized polyphony, relates more evidently to Dickens's works. Mikhail Bakhtin himself explains his key notion of heteroglossia using Dickens' novel *Little Dorrit* (1855-57), and a Bakhtinian analysis of the dialogue of voices in Dickens' novels shows the coexistence and isolation of different world-views (either linked to the characters or the narrators).[15] In this sense *The Wire* series could be considered a conglomerate of highly compacted ideologies that coexist but never blend. Of course, sentimentality is part of Dickens' world but is arguably not the world-view linking all the diverse phenomena and issues of the world into one complete whole (e.g. in *Bleak House*, 1852-53, the sentimental narration is strictly limited to one half of the novel: one narrator, Esther Summerson, embodies a first-person sentimental perspective, whereas the third-person narrative, the other half of the novel, is highly ironical). There is another similarity between Dickens' way of addressing his audiences and *The Wire.* Simon finds a particularly appropriate embodiment for a complex description of contemporary reality in the format of the TV series, which solves the problem that a standard film is much too short to reach the level of complexity of a realist novel. This is mirrored in the serialized character of Dickens's works, the novels were written on the fly (with approximately one instalment between the one being written and the published one), the audiences could even react to the novel as it was written, which is today uncommon in the novel-based communication favouring solitary reception of a finished book. As in the case of the Dickens-Griffith-Eisenstein link, the Dickens-Simon-"this argument" link rests on similarity between Dickens and David Simon's project and on explicit references to Dickens in the series itself, and in the critical texts and interviews,[16] an important ingredient being the Bakhtinian idea of dialogism which construes reality as a flux of voices creatively and responsibly transforming one another to make sense of reality.

Borderlines of Adaptation

The relationship between Griffith's pioneering use of film language and Dickens' novels could be construed as an extreme case of adaptation. The genre rules and even medium-specific levels of different works and different artistic media are combined in a new whole, a new cultural medium. More often, however, adaptation is considered from the point of view of subject matter transition from one work to another: e.g. a film follows a story or narrative strategies from a novel. The adaptation as a

---

[15] See Aleš Vaupotič, "Realism revisited—Dickens' *Hard Times* as a narrativized archive", in: *Fortunes et infortunes des genres littéraires*. *Echinox. 16.* Cluj: Phantasma, 2009, 175-185.

[16] Paul Owen, "The Wire re-up: season two, episode two—David Simon hits the Hay", *The Guardian,* 2 June 2009, https://www.theguardian.com/media/organgrinder/2009/jun/ 02/wire-season-two-episode-two-david-simon-hay. David Simon, "Interview by Jesse Pearson", *Vice magazine*, 1 December 2009, http://www.vice.com/read/david-simon-280-v16n12 [both accessed 25/10/2016]. Note the active engagement with the Dickens reference which a serialized format makes possible.

substantial inclusion of a past reference into a new work can spread from a content level to deeper levels. The borderline cases of adaptation, where it begins to be indistinguishable from an original work, are particularly interesting: such as genre hybrids and allusions.

A *genre/media hybrid* is, for example, Gerhard Richter's artist's book *Eis* (Ice, 2011).[17] It combines Richter's photographs—well known from his paintings and his sheets with photographs and other graphic material in his famous project *Atlas*—with the text from the *Allgemeine Encyklopädie der Wissenschaften und Künste* from 1871. The reader is faced with a collection of encyclopedia entries on Greenland, on its geology, animals, inhabitants, history etc. The reader has to decide which cover page is the front one, since text and pictures run in either direction. On a two-page spread there may be pictures turned upside down or not, the texts as well, but in the case of pictures, the viewer records each upside-down picture as somehow different from the same picture as seen "correctly"—this occurs, when the reader-viewer finishes reading the book in one direction and turns the book around, to read the second text in the other direction. The reading experience is highly unusual: the reading of the text makes the reader visualize the concept of Greenland, the Vikings, places etc., but the text does not become a narrative. Instead, it builds a mental visualization, which is fragmentarily and in a cold, objective way juxtaposed to Richter's stunning photographs. The reading experience is not an illustrated narrative, but functions as a media hybrid, where images and fragments of text work together on a conceptual level, as mental visualizations. In comparison to iconotexts, e.g. *Austerlitz* (2001) by Winfried Georg Sebald or *Istanbul* (2003) by Orhan Pamuk, Richter's artist's book *Eis* puts the images first, before the text, which is not surprising, since the author is a painter and a photographer who creates images, while the text is—and is perceived as such—"just" a quote of an encyclopedia entry. A similar approach is used in Richter's artist's book *War Cut* (2004) where close-up photographs of one of his paintings are juxtaposed to texts from the German newspaper *Frankfurter Allgemeine Zeitung* from the beginning of the Iraq war.

Allusion is another interesting aspect of adaptation, where the source work is barely recognizable in a new original work. Allusion to Shakespeare's *A Midsummer Night's Dream* (1595-96) is evoked in the Slovenian film *Varuh meje* (Guardian of the Frontier, 2002) by the director Maja Weiss. The film does not belong to any one of the traditional film genres, but it compiles a number of sharply dissociated genres—such as a *Deliverance*-type thriller, a Disney fairytale, an allegoric satire—and unites them in a new polyphonic whole. In the film the homogeneity of the objective world, and consequently of the subject, is dissolved. The film can be understood as an ordered group of separate utterances (in a Bakhtinian sense) that are not feminist in themselves, but the film as a whole gives them a feminist ideological charge, and they can be understood as manifestations of the threatened positions that women regularly find themselves in, although any picturing of violence in the film is

---

[17] The conception of an artist's book generally refers to the practice of using book-format in the fine arts: the artefact nature is foregrounded and the visual language is typically more important than the text. See Johanna Drucker, *The Century of Artists' Books*, New York: Granary Books, 1995.

avoided (to resist any voyeuristic enjoyment of the film audience). Without such a feminist perspective, the film turns out chaotic, fragmented, not able to represent any real situation or world-view, as opposed to a more common approach in films that are socially critical and create representations of coherent and recognizable situations. In this latter case, there is a caveat though, since the spectacular repetition of problematic social phenomena in artworks may turn out to make such social injustices more acceptable, as argued in general terms by Adorno.[18] In the film by Maja Weiss, to hold the disparate fragments of reality together, the complicated plot of Shakespeare's comedy *A Midsummer Night's Dream* is additionally used, but only as an allusion. For example, the wild night of Titania and Bottom, transformed into a donkey, is alluded to in the *Guardian of the Frontier* with the love affairs of three young protagonists, allowing thus a spectrum of romantic and grotesque interpretations—of course, the viewer is also explicitly reminded of Shakespeare's text with an abrupt digression into poetic monologue, which by the change in language register asks for more significance than explicitly given by the plot. A way of explaining the link between the film and the classic play is that the Shakespearean reference is offered to an attentive viewer, who needs to add a substantial amount of knowledge on Elizabethan theatre. However, it may be argued, that such reception strategy is of key importance for understanding the general theme of the film. In Shakespeare, we have many parallel cases of love, whereas in the film the interpersonal relationships are much more dissonant, but nevertheless resound one against the other.

Artistic Research in Transmedia Adaptation

The following two sections are specific from the methodological point of view: cases of transmedia adaptation will be presented that are a product of artistic research by the authors of this essay, and the outlines of artistic projects argue for possible theoretical frameworks for adaptation studies.[19] The works presented are connected to specific Shakespeare texts. The subchapter *R III* will look at different derivative works gathered in the project *R III* (2002), which relate to Shakespeare's play *King Richard the Third* (1592). The second subchapter will explain, how in the exhibition titled *Jacques* (2009) the individual new media projects were either originally related to Shakespeare's works, or Shakespearean themes were used for the transformation of art projects subsequently, i.e. in the user-viewers' reception in the frameworks of the exhibition as an art installation.

---

[18] Ernst Bloch, Georg Lukács, Bertolt Brecht, Walter Benjamin, Theodor Adorno, *Aesthetics and Politics*, London: NLB/Verso, 1977, 189.

[19] All the artistic projects that are presented were conceptualized and realized by the authors of this essay. Technical aspects of the interactive projects were solved in collaboration with computer engineers and other collaborators.

R III

The project *R III* is a hermeneutical crossing of territories that establish the discursive unit of Richard III—from Shakespeare's history play to his entire works and a plethora of theatrical and cinematic performances, to English Renaissance Studies, contemporary and modern paintings, that along with the versions of the *R III* project are situated between text and interpretations in different media. The project *R III* is based on the concept of integration of media, where specific media function as discursive formations[20] and the content (always already mediated), when transferred from one medium to another, changes fundamentally. The project was realized in three versions. The main version is the videotape that translates the history play into the medium of video with its specificities. Of course, the history play itself as a discursive formation nowadays is not isolated in a transhistorical vacuum, but was influenced throughout history by a plethora of transformations in different media, theatrical performances, films, paintings, narrations, interpretations [...]. The videotape did take into account these several and heterogeneous traditions in order to get to the virtual core of the play and present it in a contemporary form.

As a first step, the text was analyzed and five main themes were selected: (1) the horse, (2) the pledges and the curses, (3) the friendship, (4) the winter, (5) the queen. The themes are not ordered in a temporal succession and may reappear at different points in the text. They are organized in a pentagram of relations to represent the concept of reading and the script for the video. Although a videotape is a temporal, linear medium (duration of *R III* is 10 min. 30 sec.), the fact that the themes in *R III* videotape do not evolve from each other in a cause-effect series or a narrative, gives the viewer the impression that she is watching fragments of a structure that exist simultaneously and are interrelated to produce action on another level, which is not explicitly shown, but merely pointed to, since the viewer may know the story from the original play. The key idea is that the five themes that produce the action in the play are presented as a conceptual diagram in a spatialized two-dimensional form without a temporal vector.

The video is a remontage of authors' recorded footage, of excerpts from different theatrical and film adaptations of the play, and of animated text. The video montage techniques are used to focus the viewer's attention on the spoken text (mostly the original drama text, but taken from different sources) by presenting it separately from the image: animated masks open parts of the screen to show segments of the action, split screen image combines two images simultaneously in order to make them both relative, repetition of tiny bits of action alienates it and makes it mechanical, frozen image stops the illusion of a real recorded action, moving image with cut-out frames creates an arhythmic, paused and broken stroboscopic motion. Both image—and with it the space that it shows—and time—as perceived in the moving image—are manipulated and therefore artificial. The concept of the relational diagram (based on the already mentioned five themes) comes to the fore also by deliberate employment of these video montage techniques.

---

[20] See Michel Foucault, *The Archaeology of Knowledge*, London, Tavistock, 1972.

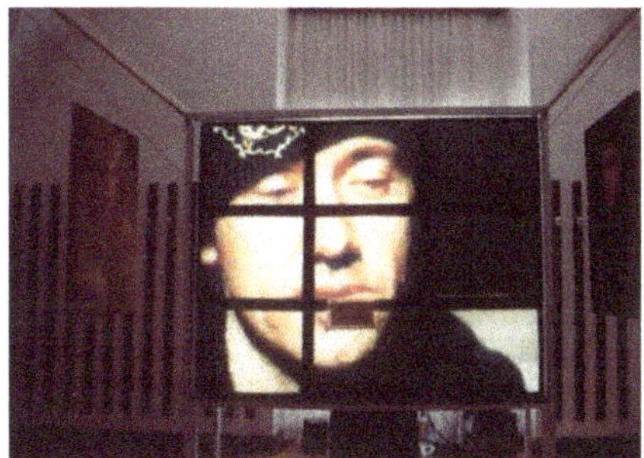

Image 1: Video installation *R III*

The second version of the project is the video installation. Its constitutive parts are the video tape that runs on a 9-screen video-wall, the book with Shakespeare's plays, two portraits (acrylic paint on canvas, 50 × 70 cm) of King Richard the Third and the Duke of Buckingham, and a metal cube that holds the parts in place. The experiences of different media in the installation function in connection to each other. The installation embodies the spatialized media relations.

The third version of the project translates the text into the medium of Internet communication, i.e. of hypertext and hyperimagery (hypermedia).[21] The placement of content on the Internet cannot be "pure" and isolated, but it is always connected to other web pages (at least as soon as we use a browser), therefore the network of Shakespearean studies and research about the King Richard III are thematized.[22] The web site is composed of two pages, the page with textual connections and the page with linked images. The hyperimagery page is organized as a Shakespearean theatre, where on the lower stage there is an interactive image map: the user navigates on the flat surface of the image map and by clicking on visually more interesting parts of the map discovers links that trigger the videos that are shown on the upper stage of the theatre. The short videos correspond to the five themes from the conceptual diagram.

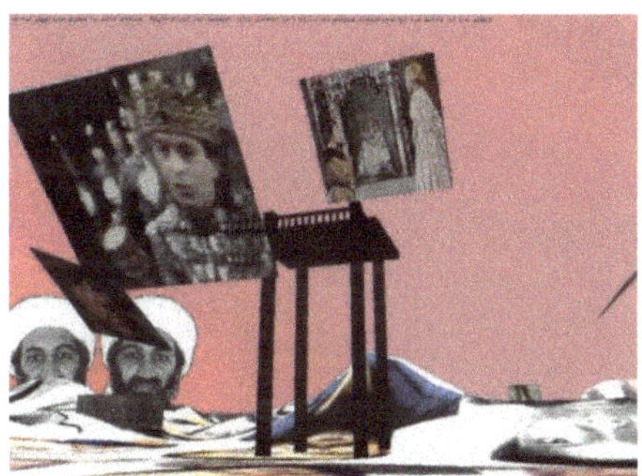

Image 2: *R III* integrated in *VideoSpace*

[21] http://black.fri.uni-lj.si/riii [accessed 30/01/2018].

[22] This project was realized ten years before the increase of pages on Richard the Third theme on the Internet following the discovery of the historical king's remains in 2012.

In *VideoSpace* (2003), a 3-D computer-generated virtual space, the project *R III* is integrated as the element of language, while the other two elements, the human and the matter, are represented by two other art projects: *Javornik* (2001), which thematizes performance and body art, and *VSA* (2002), which shows the measurements of the cosmic background as recorded by the Very Small Array telescope on Tenerife island, and the institutional exchange of the artists with the researchers at the Cambridge University.[23] In *VideoSpace,* as in the *R III* project, the elements are set in spatial relations and fixed in a frozen moment in time, the reading of the content in this virtual space is purely conceptual and spatial. The viewer moves in the space as in a first-person view computer game and watches or listens to media content that is arranged at different meaningful spatial locations: on the interactive multiple-screen video walls inside the house, connected to the marble blocks that spread over the whole territory in the form of a square grid, as video screens that float in the sky and can be watched in another way, by climbing a lift and thus gaining also a different perspective over the whole space. The conceptual diagram for this project is a triangle of the three factors that constitute the interaction in the navigable virtual space: the landscape, the objects in the space, and the first-person camera view. The three factors correspond to a second triangle of territory, nodes, and trajectory.

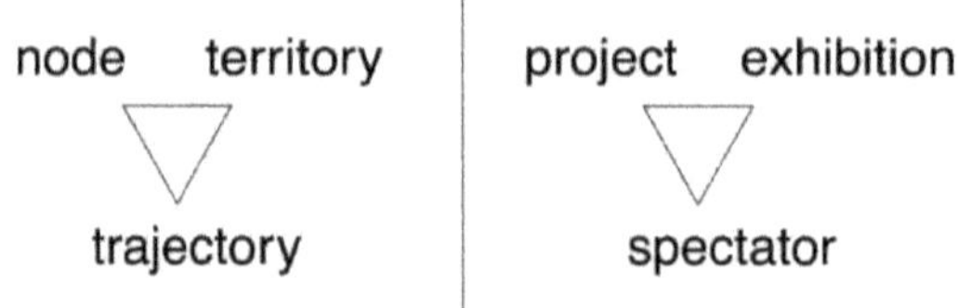

Image 3: Conceptual diagram: territory, node, trajectory

The model of the territory, node, and trajectory as the defining aspects of a navigable virtual space was also tested in a real space installation *Friedhof Laguna* (co-author Gašper Jemec) at the 50th International Art Exhibition Venice Biennial in 2003. The alternative reality of our virtual space of the Deep Sea Water Voyagers was introduced through the spatial vector in real space that traversed the vector of the walking path of Biennale visitors (that typically move from Giardini to Arsenale) and was directed towards the laguna. Two organic hydrodynamic shapes were placed in the exhibition crossing the visitors' trajectory. A version of *VideoSpace* was used as a point of view of the artwork-creature, as an alternative reality. In the *FriedhofLaguna* project the conceptual triangle translates thus: territory into exhibition (the whole Biennale and *VideoSpace*), node was our art project (the interaction with the video-installation), the trajectory of the viewer was proposed as an alternative trajectory that led from the real space of the Biennale exhibition to the virtual reality in our project (represented by a modified version of *VideoSpace*).

---

[23] http://black.fri.uni-lj.si/javornik, http://black.fri.uni-lj.si/videospace/vsa [accessed 30/01/2018].

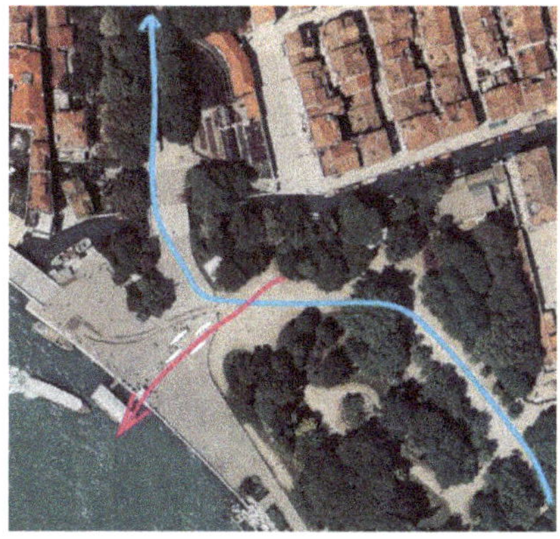

Image 4. Trajectory vector in the exhibition: the usual visitors' trajectory is the blue line, the alternative trajectory introduced by the project is the red line.

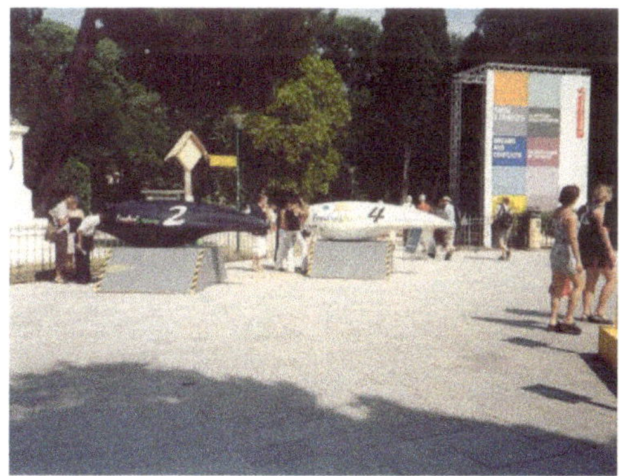

Image 5: *Friedhof Laguna* installation at the 50th Venice Biennale

The project series *R III*, *VideoSpace*, and *Friedhof Laguna* is founded on a decomposition of sources, the Shakespearean texts and other materials. The isolated fragments are then put in different constellations that relationally reconfigure their meanings. The new discursive constellation is static and is opening a space[24] for insight into the remix-like nature of these artworks. The source material fundamentally changes by being included into a new whole, but nevertheless retains its mark of heterogeneity as part of an *ad hoc* archive.

A later derivative of the *R III* project is the digital animation *To Brecknock, while my fearful head is on!* (2006)—it shows a digitally animated photorealistic character of King Richard the Third at the turning point of the drama, when he breaks

[24] "In other words, the archaeological description of discourses is deployed in the dimension of a general history; [...]; what it wishes to uncover is the particular level in which history can *give place* to definite types of discourse, which have their own type of historicity, and which are related to a whole set of various historicities." Foucault, *The Archaeology*, 164-165. Emphasis by the authors.

friendship with his loyal cousin Buckingham, as Buckingham hesitates to kill the young princes (act 4, scene 2). King Richard pretends to listen to the strikes of the clock and not hear the request of Buckingham, which he also subsequently declines. The animation shows a computer-generated king, rendered in a *chiaro-scuro* technique, sitting on the throne in a portrait shot; the facial expression is animated in subtly bored and avoiding grimaces and his fingers are animated as in an impatient motion. Finally, he speaks the sentence: "Well, let that rest."

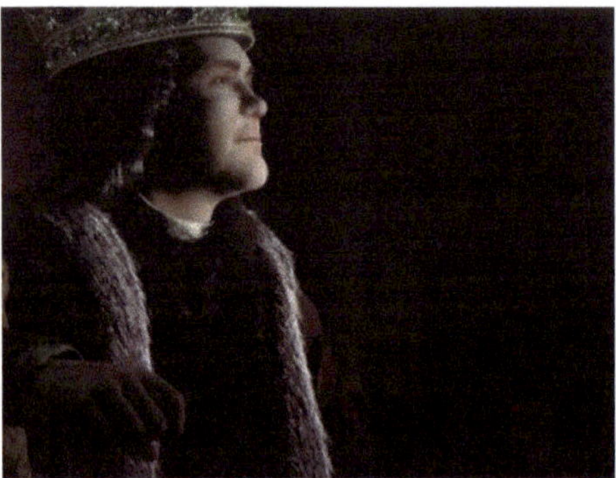

Image 6: A frame from the digital animation *To Brecknock, while my fearful head is on!*

This animation was never shown together with the works based on Shakespeare's *King Richard the Third* presented above. It was integrated in a smart-space installation *Presence* (2008)—a part of the *Jaques* exhibition.

JAQUES [DʒEɪ'KWIZ]

This section emphasizes two themes from Shakespeare's comedy *As You Like It* (1599) in their relationship to new media objects that were part of the *Jaques* exhibition:[25] first, the temporary suspension of violent conflict that happens when the characters flee into the Forest of Arden; and, second, the reading of an environment that "speaks" or is inscribed with texts. Both themes are transposed into concrete manifestations of several aspects of new media reality as they appear in new media art works, such as virtual spaces, interactive installations where the viewer assumes a part in the dialogue, real objects with doubled existence in the Internet of Things, and 3-D printed objects. The individual new media projects by the authors of this essay were either based on Shakespeare's works, or the Shakespearean themes were used as metaphors for gaining insight into contemporary mixed reality. Thus, a literary classic assumes the role of a mediator in the understanding of the language of new media.

Shakespearean studies attempt to explain the Forest of Arden through numerous sources: The Forest of Arden in Warwickshire, central England, where Shakespeare spent his youth. Also, the Ardennes forest in Belgium, in which the play supposedly

[25] Vžiglica Gallery, Ljubljana, 6 February—3 March 2009.

takes place. By mentioning Robin Hood, Shakespeare compares it to the Sherwood forest. Additional meaning can be found in the maiden surname of Shakespeare's mother, which was—Arden. The Forest of Arden could be an example of Arcadia or the Garden of Eden, but as opposed to the forest in *A Midsummer Night's Dream* it is not inhabited by fairies and elves, but by rural people and individuals who escaped the outside world of politics dominated by the fight of all against all. The play does not start in the forest; it begins at the duke's court. The duke has eliminated his older brother so that he would be in possession of all the power and riches. Even more violent is the relation between Oliver and his brother Orlando, for Oliver wants to murder Orlando, who subsequently escapes into the Forest of Arden—which is where everybody who is in disfavour and still manages to survive finds him- or herself sooner or later. The inhabitants of the forest suffer not only exile but also Adam's penalty, i.e. the four seasons in which they are tortured by the freezing winter cold. However, the expelled old duke states that any kind of suffering is a friendly "counsellor" compared to the dangers of the envious court.

The violence taking place at the royal court is portrayed in many of Shakespeare's plays. One of them, *King Richard the Third*, was used as the starting point for an interactive computer installation titled *Presence*,[26] which recreated the turning point of the dramatic action of this history play, i.e. the moment when King Richard rejects his cousin, and partner in crime, the Duke of Buckingham. King Richard is digitally animated and projected in the gallery space—the abovementioned video *To Brecknock, while my fearful head is on!*—while Buckingham's position is taken over by the viewer, who becomes thus a substitute for the character in the play as well as for the body of the actor on the stage. The theatre is used as a mediator while the model of a new-media smart-space is being established. Like in the everyday use of smart devices in mixed reality, in this installation too the visitor finds her- or himself in a gallery space and in a narrative reality at the same time. The king's presence becomes even more immersive, since the computer vision software is capable of recognizing what is going on in front of the projection. On the wall in the gallery there is the inscription from the play (act 2, scene 7): "All the world's a stage," which signals the importance of the visitors' moves in the monitored space. The system adjusts the content of the video to fit the viewer's behaviour: one should not look the king in the eyes and the installation does "not work" if we look at it directly—it does not play the whole animation. Only if the visitor approaches the projected king respectfully, with a lowered gaze and head half turned down and to the side, the animation plays the whole dialogue, which ends with the spoken words of the king. A third type of behaviour is also predicted, an intrusive approach too close to the king, which results in a violent flashing light on the projection that should repel the visitor and make him/her move away.

---

[26] See Narvika Bovcon, Aleš Vaupotič, Borut Batagelj, Damir Deželjin, Franc Solina, "Presence: The Integration of Classical Artistic Media in a Smart Space Prototype", in: *VSMM 2009 - Proceedings 15th International Conference on Virtual Systems and Multimedia*, Los Alamitos, California, Washington, Tokyo, IEEE Computer Society & CPS, 98-103.

The two-stage use of computer vision is important for this installation. The first change occurs when a viewer enters the shot of the surveillance camera in the active field of the installation (a defined zone of the gallery) as a smudge. At this level the system is a simple sensor; however as soon as the computer learns that it is seeing a human being and not a faceless object, its vision becomes (to a certain degree) similar to human gaze and the computer starts to play a role in the ideological field in front of the installation. *Presence* thus addresses the complex issues of artificial intelligence that—with a high level of smart analyzing—surpasses the mere recording of surveillance cameras and consequently poses questions as to the ideological connotation of the supposedly unbiased view of the machine.

Of course, there is a great difference between the apparent rejection of Buckingham's dramatic role and the actual rejection of the viewer in the gallery to whom the installation decides not to show the video, if his behaviour is not correct. Outside of the Forest of Arden—in the bloodthirsty world of the history play *King Richard the Third*—all consequences are final, while in the Forest of Arden, like in an art exhibition, they stop on the level of debate, without losing the complexity of political and ideological dilemmas. This middle ground is represented in *As You Like It* by the former nobleman, the "melancholy Jaques", who exchanged the aristocratic material possessions for the openness of the abstract forest and decided to permanently live in it. Shakespeare emphasizes this particular condition in the theory of seven levels of argument presented by the court jester, Touchstone, in act 5, scene 4. He establishes that the argument can be calmed down up to level six, which is followed on level seven by a duel and serious injuries. However, Jaques replies to the fool that his argument is caught in a contradiction, for he stated that he avoided the duel on the seventh level, even though he previously stated that it can be solved only up to the sixth level. On the seventh level, the fool explains, the argument can be solved on the level of debate, a dialogue, when the argument is understood on the level of a discourse, into which one can add an "if" or two. Of course, this means that the seventh level demands that the entire reality be shifted to the level of discourse, thus momentarily stopping the unstoppable flow of time that performs the consequences of human actions. This can be stopped in such a way only within the Forest of Arden (or in an exhibition space), never outside of it. In the exhibition, a reminder of such suspension of real consequences of actions is also the sculpture *Dragonfly*, a computer generated 3-D object that was printed on a machine for rapid prototyping. It was conceptualized as an innocent materialization of any virtual model or computer information as such, but several years ago, it got a more sinister appeal as the first actual firing guns were 3-D printed and their virtual models with instructions were put on the Internet. The reality has started to re-enter the cyberspace.

The Forest of Arden is a semiotic forest that the melancholic philosopher Jaques does not leave even after the happy outcome of the comedy-plot: he does not mind the fact that he is confronted with an exceptionally complex forest of meanings—for he sees people from all classes and with various problems—in which nothing carries a meaning any more. On the contrary, Jaques boldly faces the given variety of meanings and tries to make new sense out of it, for instance in the form of a critical approach to violence towards animals.

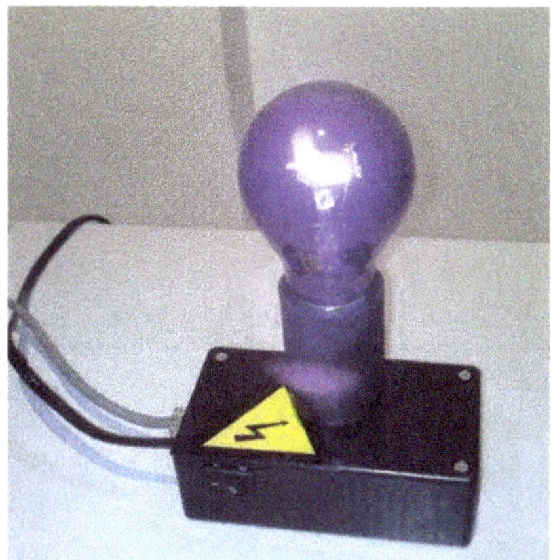

Image 7: *IP Light*

At the exhibition, the fictive Jaques faces a challenge in a new media object, a light that is at the same time in real space as well as a unique entity on the Internet—it has its own IP address in the same way as servers do. The *IP Light* has at least two practical uses: it can be used as a reading light, or it can transfer a message as it is turned on and off on the Internet.[27] In 2009, the project contemplated the future Internet of Things, where each of our possessions will exist in real space and in cyberspace at the same time. This will result in the fact that these objects (and the people who are linked to them) will be easily traceable and their actions documented, as everything will be reflected in the changes of the positions and conditions of objects. Furthermore, the objects in the Internet of Things are accessible through computer manipulation, and this increases human capabilities to magical limits. An important consequence arises: as we will be regularly faced with smart responsive walls, non-living matter will be given life. The feeling for materiality will change, because we will read it as an interface object in our dialogue with the environment—in fact with other people, who contribute to communication on the Internet.

The exhibition *Jaques* reflects the changed world after cultural transcoding has subjected all objects to algorithmic manipulation. This is an idea Lev Manovich presented in *The Language of New Media.* Vast domains of culture are now digitized which allows one to treat culture as a new media: it is governed by five principles—numerical representation, modularity, automation, variability, and transcoding. With regard to the last principle Manovich adds that transcoding is not limited to "computer layer" but also encompasses the "cultural layer", the rules and the intuitive algorithms of culture.[28] A defining aspect of this global change is examined also in the concept of "techno imagination" (a term used by Vilém Flusser in the seventies), which deals with the acceleration of mankind's performance of procedures. For instance, the world appears in different dimensions when viewed through a Google search than

[27] Software and hardware: Matevž Grbec, Marko Ilić, Samo Mahnič.
[28] Lev Manovich, *The Language of New Media*, Cambridge, Mass., MIT Press, 2001, 45-48.

while perceived solely through human senses. The world has disintegrated into a mass of bordering and permeated archives, forming a space that is not homogenous. This space is inhabited by people and objects, both of which exist simultaneously in the real world as well as in cyber reality. The movements around this space require displacements also on the level of meanings, desires and constraints. The metaphor that we (as authors of the projects) have chosen for this experience is Shakespeare's Forest of Arden from the comedy. A person in the Forest of Arden "finds tongues in trees, books in the running brooks", which is not merely a metaphor, but also a hard and solid fact, when the besotted Orlando carves love songs into trees and hangs poems on branches.

The two thematic elements from *As You Like It*: the suspension of violence and the readability of environments define the *tertium comparationis* in the relationship between the Forest of Arden and the characteristic discursive model of a new media object. Manovich's classical definition of a new media object as a series of interfaces to a database[29] foregrounds the access to the elements of an archive—that do not annihilate each other—and to the problem of correctly understanding the "tongues in trees, books in the running brooks,/ Sermons in stones and good in everything./ I would not change it", says Duke Senior in the Forest of Arden (act 2, scene 1).

Shakespearean themes were used as metaphors for gaining insight into contemporary mixed reality. Here Benjamin's insights from *The Origin of the German Tragic Drama* again come to mind, the meaninglessness of the world in German counter-reformation baroque *Trauerspiel*—and in Benjamin's own time—is in Shakespeare's works, and e.g. in Calderon's, compensated with the reflection of the fragmented reality, its artistic elaboration.[30] The art conquers the problematic reality, looming in Benjamin's interwar world. For the reflection to be possible, the reality has to become frozen, given to extra-temporal contemplation, available as an archive, and readable as language. The art projects presented have shown the way source texts are adapted in new works by participating in a new whole, which is at the same time asserted and radically fragile, based on authors answerability.

The adaptation, as a working method for creating new original content or even inventing new artistic mediums (which are increasingly enabled by invention of new information communication technologies), was presented in its most far reaching and extended forms: genre/medium hybrids, concept of deep remixability, allusions, and travelling metaphors. The authors' artistic research shows how artists conceptualize these transitions and how they adopt certain aspects for clearly defined purposes in the construction of new original works. The dialogue between artists from different centuries and places goes on, since every artist finds her or his position in the longing for the creation of something new and original and in the belonging to the traditions that she or he knows, the traditions that shaped her or his vision and thinking. The adaptation practices are thus an engine for creating ever new original works and keeping these works understandable to the viewers as artefacts that belong to a shared culture.

---

[29] *Ibid.*, 227.
[30] Benjamin, 228-229, 235.

BIBLIOGRAPHY

Bakhtin, Mihail, "Discourse in the Novel", in *The Dialogic Imagination*, Austin, London: University of Texas Press, 1981, 269-422.

———, *Speech Genres and Other Late Essays*, Austin: University of Texas, 1986.

Bloch, Ernst, Georg Lukács, Bertolt Brecht, Walter Benjamin, Theodor Adorno, *Aesthetics and Politics*, London: NLB/Verso, 1977.

Bonitzer, Pascal, *Le Champ aveugle*, Paris: Chaiers du Cinema/Gallimard, 1982.

Bovcon, Narvika, Aleš Vaupotič, Borut Batagelj, Damir Deželjin, and Franc Solina, "Presence: The Integration of Classical Artistic Media in a Smart Space Prototype", in: *VSMM 2009 - Proceedings 15th International Conference on Virtual Systems and Multimedia*, Los Alamitos, California, Washington, Tokyo, IEEE Computer Society & CPS, 98-103. http://eprints.fri.uni-lj.si/1391 [accessed 30/01/2018].

Bovcon, Narvika, Gašper Jemec, and Aleš Vaupotič, *Friedhof Laguna (website)*, 2003. http://black.fri.uni-lj.si/recyc/flr [accessed 30/01/2018].

Bovcon, Narvika, and Aleš Vaupotič, *Jaques* (catalogue), 2009. http://encls.net/files/jaques_cat_reduced.pdf [accessed 30/01/2018].

———, *R III (video tape)*, 2002. http://black.fri.uni-lj.si/mouseionserapeion/db/video/d_adsl/61-4_r_iii(bovcon,_vaupotic).avi [accessed 30/01/2018].

———, *R III (website)*, 2002. http://black.fri.uni-lj.si/riii [accessed 30/01/2018].

———, *Umetniški arhiv: Dva primera/Artistic Archive: Two Examples*, Maribor: MKC Maribor, 2004. http://black.fri.uni-lj.si/mouseionserapeion/db/objekti/vspcmousserap.pdf [accessed 30/01/2018].

———, *VideoSpace (website)*, 2002. http://black.fri.uni-lj.si/videospace [accessed 30/01/2018].

Benjamin, Walter, *The Origin of German Tragic Drama*, London, Brooklyn, NY: Verso, 2009.

Cartmell, Deborah, ed., *A Companion to Literature, Film, and Adaptation*, Chichester, West Sussex: Wiley-Blackwell, 2012.

Drucker, Johanna, *The Century of Artists' Books*, New York, Granary Books, 1995.

Eisenstein, Sergei, "Dickens, Griffith, and the Film Today", in *Film Form, Esseys in Film Theory*, ed. and trans. Jay Leyda, San Diego, New York, London: Harcourt Brace Jovanovich Publishers, 1949/1977, 195-255.

Flusser, Vilém, *Kommunikologie*, Frankfurt am Main: Fischer Taschenbuch Verlag, 1998.

———, *Kommunikologie weiter denken*, Frankfurt am Main: Fischer Taschenbuch Verlag, 2009.

Foucault, Michel, *The Archaeology of Knowledge*, London, Tavistock, 1972.

Kafka, Franz, *Tagebücher 1910-1923*, 8 October 1917, http://gutenberg.spiegel.de/buch/-162/10 [accessed 30/01/2018].

Leitch, Thomas, "Adaptation Studies at a Crossroads", *Adaptation*, 1:1, 2008, 63-77.

Manovich, Lev, *Software Takes Command*, preprint 2008. http://softwarestudies.com/softbook/manovich_softbook_11_20_2008.pdf [accessed 30/01/2018].

———, *The Language of New Media*, Cambridge, Mass.: MIT Press, 2001.

Owen, Paul, "The Wire re-up: season two, episode two—David Simon hits the Hay", *The Guardian*, 2 June 2009. https://www.theguardian.com/media/organgrinder/2009/jun/02/wire-season-two-episode-two-david-simon-hay [accessed 30/01/2018].

Richter, Gerhard, *Eis*, Cologne: Verlag der Buchhandlung Walther König, 2011.

———, *War Cut*, Cologne: Verlag der Buchhandlung Walther König, 2004.

Simon, David, "Interiew by Jesse Pearson", *Vice magazine*, 1 December 2009. http://www.vice.com/read/david-simon-280-v16n12 [accessed 30/01/2018].

Vaupotič, Aleš, "Realism revisited—Dickens' *Hard Times* as a narrativized archive", in: *Fortunes et infortunes des genres littéraires, Echinox, 16.* Cluj: Phantasma, 2009, 175-185.

Weibel, Peter, "The Post-Medial Condition", *Arte Contexto*, 6, 2005, 11-15.

Werner, Stephen, *Socratic Satire: An Essay on Diderot and* Le Neveu de Rameau, Birmingham, Alabama: Summa Publications. Inc., 1987.

CHAPTER 8

The Tweetbook as a New Frontier of Literary Retellings

Claudia Cao

Retelling and rewriting have characterized literary production since its origins. They have served to preserve the literary tradition and, at the same time, they have been essential to the evolution and transformation of literary *topoi* and *mythoi*.[1]

Each rewriting implies, as Linda Hutcheon points out in reference to adaptations,[2] a repetition with difference, which involves two main agents: the context of the source and target texts, as well as the time. In order for rewriting to be possible, in fact, the source text undergoes a process of appropriation which may have political implications in relation to the context and the time of reception:[3] gendered or postcolonial reinterpretation or, in general, cross-cultural transpositions of a literary classic which usually call into question power dynamics implied by the canonical works in relation to the target culture. In addition, they implement modernizing processes aimed at demonstrating either the vitality of the value system expressed by the source text or its obsolescence.[4]

It is not the aim of this essay to further investigate the large number of issues that the reflection on intertextual relationships evokes. Instead, this short preamble will only recall a number of key concepts that have marked the debate around intertextuality and rewriting in the second half of the twentieth century.

The oscillation between the terms "retelling" and "rewriting" heretofore maintained is no coincidence. What we have witnessed over the past fifteen years

---

[1] See Walter Benjamin, *Illuminations*, London: Fontana Press Berland, 1992: 91: "storytelling is always the art of repeating stories".

[2] See Linda Hutcheon, *A Theory of Adaptation*, New York and London: Routledge, 2006; Gary R. Bortolotti, Linda Hutcheon, "On the Origins of Adaptations: Rethinking Fidelity Discourse and 'Success'—Biologically", *New Literary History*, 38:3, 2007, 443-458.

[3] Curtius speaks of "possession" of a classic when someone reads it, referring to its timelessness (see Ernst Robert Curtius, *Letteratura europea e medioevo latino*, transl. Anna Luzzatto, Mercurio Candela, Corrado Bologna, Firenze: La Nuova Italia, 1992, 22), and the appropriation, according to Iser, begins with each act of reading as a process of representation of what is not explicit (Wolfgang Iser, "The Reading Process. A Phenomenological Approach", *New Literary History*, 3, 1971-1972, 179-199). For more on the context of reception, see also Lubomír Doležel, *Heterocosmica. Fiction and Possible Worlds*, Baltimore and London: Johns Hopkins University Press, 1998; Liedeke Plate, H. G. Els Rose, "Rewriting, a Literary Concept for the Study of Cultural Memory: Towards a Transhistorical Approach to Cultural Remembrance", *Neophilologus*, 97, 2013, 611-625.

[4] These ideas will remain in the background for the following discussion, but they should be considered in reference to the modernizing processes to which works are continually subjected in rewrites through new media.

with the spread of blogs, social networks, and digital media in general is something that takes the experiences of reinterpretation and manipulation of the collective imagery, begun in the postmodern era, to the extreme. Global culture, thanks to the new media, is becoming increasingly participatory, allowing the transformation of the web user into a "prosumer", producer and consumer at the same time. Processes of convergence between old and new media generated by the Web, well-illustrated by Jenkins (2006), are influencing the relationship of the contemporary reader with the literary tradition and the canonical texts: recent instances of fandom, for example, are expressions of the fusion between "high culture" and "low culture" to which Web users continually give life through a variety of textual forms, such as fanfictions. As highlighted by Bolter and Grusin (2000), these new textual forms are based on processes of "remediation" on both the technological and cultural levels that are forcing us to use new critical perspectives to understand the complex mechanisms of this rich production and to rethink our theoretical paradigms. This is also the reason why I have chosen to use both terms, "retelling" and "rewrite": the textual fluidity[5] to which new media have given rise has dismantled the binary opposition between orality and writing, and it is leading to more complex forms of cultural transmission and exchange.[6] As we will see, besides the rewriting itself (intended as an act of resemanticization of a source text) there are various forms of appropriation of the source texts which also make use of creative repetition, thanks to the combination with other codes or to the allusive character that repetition takes on in a new context.

To limit the field of investigation to a single type of text, this essay deals exclusively with the so-called twitterature to focus on the experience of the Italian social reading "TwLetteratura".[7] Departing from Hutcheon's proposals in her *Theory of Adaptation*, I will begin with some questions that illustrate the role of the main factors at play: the source text (what?), the adapters and the context of reception (who? where? when?), the main forms of rewriting (how?) and the effects that these reuses have on the source text in comparison with the types of intertextual relationship to which we were accustomed before the advent of digital media. Before moving to the experiences of twitterature, I will start with a short introduction to the use of Twitter and to the first literary experiments produced on this social medium.

EXPERIMENTS OF NARRATIVE AND RETELLING ON TWITTER

Twitter, born in 2006, is a micro-blog which limits its texts to 140 characters, intended to spread information in real time. Given the possibility of retweeting and indexing the posts under the same label (using the hashtag #), Twitter has an intrinsic narrative and citational potential which has had full expression in numerous collective

---

[5] See John Bryant, *The Fluid Text. A Theory of Revision and Editing for Book and Screen*, Ann Arbor: University of Michigan Press, 2002.
[6] Walter J. Ong (*Orality and Literacy: The Technologizing the Word*, New York: Methuen, 1982) has introduced the concept of "secondary orality".
[7] The term "twitterature", as shown by Paveau, was coined with the editorial experiment *Twitterature* (2009) by Aciman and Rensin, but now includes various narrative types quite different from the rewritings produced by the two American authors.

and individual experiences.[8] In fact Twitter originated at least three types of narrative texts: the serial form, which is distributed over the time—and which can be both "authorial" and "collective"—and the short form, stories which in 140 characters of a tweet condense the "initial situation", the "breaking of the order", and the "conclusion".[9]

If we focus only on the serial type, it is possible to recognize two main peculiarities of these texts: first of all, the immediacy of the micro-blog – that can continually interact with information and daily news – and second, the interaction with users, that can have a much greater effect on the evolution of the plot than in other narrative forms.

A specific feature of the narrative on Twitter is therefore the "verticality" of the medium: on Twitter, in contrast to the conventional literary work, the novel does not work horizontally, but is made of links, jumps forward and returns backward. It is not structured as are the usual plots of start-development-end that we associate with the narrative.[10] The narrative on Twitter is therefore ontologically dynamic, and the writer can reference events that occur in real time, creating links between the real world and the fictional one. This leads to a much greater involvement of the reader in the narration and making the process of interpretation much more complex than in conventional narrative.

These features of the serial narrative should be taken into consideration when we talk about the large number of rewritings originated on Twitter. As Bronwen Thomas notes, "serial forms are used on Twitter to retell classic tales and epics of various kinds" (Thomas 2014: 100). However, while Thomas ascribes rewritings on Twitter only to the authorial serial type, it should be pointed out how the Italian context, within this category, has given rise to a subcategory of collective serial rewritings which I am going to examine more closely.

As useful evidence regarding the categories of adaptation, consider the example given by Thomas about the retelling of *Mahābhārata* (@Epicretold), one of the most famous Indian epic stories.[11] In the introduction, the author states that he has tried to produce an adaptation of the Indian epic tale, underlining with the term "adaptation"

---

[8] For an overview on the narrative production on Twitter see Claudia Cao, "Dai classici letterari a Twitter: alcuni esempi di riscrittura", *Between*, 4:8, 2014, www.betweenjournal.it [accessed 30/01/2018]; Anna Notaro "How Networked Communication Has Changed the Ways We Tell Stories", *Between*, 4:8, 2014, www.betweenjournal.it [accessed 30/01/2018]; Sonia Lombardo, *Narrativa in 140 caratteri. Genesi della twitteratura*, Storiacontinua.com, 2013; Marie-Anne Paveau, "Genre de discours et technologie discursive. Tweet, twittécriture et twittérature", *HAL. Archives-Ouvertes*, 2012, https://hal.archives-ouvertes.fr/hal-00824817/document [accessed 30/01/2018]; Daniele Giampà, *Oltre i confini del libro. La letteratura italiana nell'era digitale*, http://elmcip.net/node/5698 [accessed 30/01/2018].

[9] An example of particular interest of the last typology are the "twisters" by Arjun Basu (http://arjunbasu.com/twisters).

[10] See Sonia Lombardo, "Come (NON) raccontare una storia su Twitter", http://www.storiacontinua.com/scrittura-creativa/come-non-raccontare-una-storia-su-twitter/. Although hypertexts predate Twitter as non-linear texts, these new rewritings are distinctive because they embrace multiple media platforms.

[11] See Chindu Sreedharan, "A 1,000 tweets. In 1,360 days. Ugh", http://www.chindu.net/musings/mahabharata-on-twitter-crosses-landmark/ [accessed 30/01/2018].

that his *Mahābhārata* on Twitter should not be merely considered a rewriting, but an experiment focused on the medium rather than on the hypotext.[12]

A case of individual rewriting such as @Epicretold is also useful to provide a perfect example of the new relationship that the rewriter can establish with the reader community on Twitter. The author creates a reticular relationship between his work and the reader: through comments, answers, blogs, Facebook, and emails, the author plays with the "inferential paths" of the readers,[13] often to disregard them or sometimes to feed them with strategic pauses and advances. The reader, in this way, becomes a full member of the process of production of the text, helping to give a direction to the rewriting throughout different media platforms, demonstrating the efficacy of "courting" the consumer across multiple media platforms.[14]

THE CASE OF TWLETTERATURA

TwLetteratura.org is an example of social reading. A community created in Italy in 2011 by three experts in literature and communication, it organizes the timing for a group reading of a classic, mainly from the Italian literary tradition. Then, it establishes the hashtag for its retelling on Twitter, distinguishing individual chapters with a slash followed by the chapter number (for example, #TwAusten/01, #TwAusten/02, etc.).

Step by step, the participants follow what other readers and rewriters produce, until the publication of a tweetbook (as in the case of #TwAusten) or many tweetbooks (as in the case of #Invisibili, based on *Invisible Cities* by Calvino)[15]. The editor of the tweetbook can be an author who either collects the best rewrites of all the participants—and in this case the collection is often focused on a specific semantic field, suggested by the subtitle of the tweetbook– or his best tweets on a book (as for example @exlibris2012's *TwAusten and Me*).

The webpage dedicated to the method of TwLetteratura clarifies the different forms of retelling accepted: each rewriting can be a paraphrase, a comment, or a free interpretation. The use of different stylistic registers—as found in Oulipo production—allows users to experience a huge amount of combinations of deconstruction and reconstruction of the original text, a system of micro-texts generated in the community in connection with the original work and with the other

---

[12] See Chindu Sreedharan, "Field notes on epicretold", http://www.chindu.net/reports-on-research/field-notes-on-epicretold/, [accessed 30/01/2018]: "[It] brings me to the caveat. Epicretold needs to be seen as an experiment in social media, not in the Mahabharata". The term hypotext is taken from Gérard Genette's *Palimpsests*, and it indicates the source text. The etymology of the neologism emphasizes his "palimpsestuous" idea of "literature in the second degree".

[13] See Umberto Eco, *Lector in fabula. La cooperazione interpretativa nei testi narrative*, Milano: Bompiani, 1979.

[14] See Henry Jenkins, *Convergence Culture: Where Old and New Media Collide*, New York: New York University Press, 2006, 3.

[15] Trytweetbook.com was the most-used twitterature application until July 2016, but Betwyll has since supplanted it. While the tweetbook is no longer available online, it is still possible to find individual tweets on twitter.com.

rewritings (because every tweet is open to other comments, responses, and additions).[16]

The method has already been experimented on various classics such as those by Cesare Pavese, or Pasolini, Emilio Lussu, and Alessandro Manzoni. The choice of texts belonging to the high Italian cultural tradition, the heterogeneity of the participants (adults and young people with different backgrounds), and the agreement on the timing of collective reading of every chapter which they intend to rewrite to facilitate participation and sharing among users, demonstrate the centrality given now to the source text, to the act of interpretation and, even more, to the educational aims that these rewrites are gradually acquiring.

In order to illustrate the different outcomes to which rewrites give rise, I examine the results of the rewriting of two works by Calvino: #Invisibili (2013), the retelling of *Invisible Cities*, and #NidiDiRagno (2015), dedicated to *The Path to the Spiders' Nests*. The first experiment, due to the great variety of tweetbooks published, provides evidence of a new form of serial and collective rewriting, while *The Path to the Spiders' Nests*, as it is primarily intended for secondary schools and proposed by a teacher of literature, offers an interesting example of the extension to the entire social reading community of the "hermeneutical community" proposed by Romano Luperini (2013) in reference to the role of literature at school.

Luperini refers to the idea of the "interpretive community" developed by Stanley Fish in *Is There a Text in this Class?,* but overturning it. Unlike Fish—who interprets the concept of "interpretive community" nihilistically, starting from the relative and conventional definition of literary text and of its interpretation—Luperini defines it instead as a "community with a shared knowledge and a common horizon of values, which can be divided during the act of interpretation. It foreshadows a wider democratic community, national and supranational, and it trains to democracy through the conflict of interpretations".[17] As Luperini clarifies in his essay, offering the experience of the plurality of meanings, of the relativity and infinity of interpretations, the shared reading of literary works shows that finding the truth is a processual act, a dialogical process which includes the contributions of many. In this way, the individual reader increases their awareness of the limits of their interpretation in comparison with the community of readers, and those limits are fully reflected in the rewriting and reinterpretation that they contribute to the social reading. At school, the sharing of the same cultural horizon is given by the selection of the texts already made by the editors of literary history textbooks or by the teachers. In the case of TwLetteratura it is interesting to see how users begin to identify themselves as members of a virtual community around a shared literary base, even with recurring references to other works previously read together and rewritten through the same social reader. The fact that #NidiDiRagno is a school project does not entail a greater homogeneity of users: the two projects that we are examining are indeed characterized

---

[16] This is my translation of the method explained on the website of TwLetteratura http://www.twletteratura.org/2014/02/il-metodo-tw-letteratura/ [accessed 01/02/2018].

[17] Romano Luperini, *Insegnare la letteratura oggi*, Lecce: Manni, 2013, 93. The translation from Italian is mine.

by the same heterogeneity despite their different origins. Elaborated two years apart, the rewriting of the *Invisible Cities* was founded on the desire to celebrate the ninetieth anniversary of the birth of the author, while #NidiDiRagno, two years later, was intended as a moment of reflection on a crucial part of the Italian history, the Resistance, told from an entirely new and original perspective on Calvino's novel.

THE SOURCE TEXTS

To understand the different results produced by the experiments of retelling mediated by the social reader, I begin by introducing the two source texts. *The Path to the Spiders' Nests* is the first novel written by Italo Calvino, in 1947, two years after the end of the Second World War and the Resistance. It is perhaps the only one of his novels attributable to the Neorealist trend, although, as Cesare Pavese remarks,[18] the fairy-tale aura that distinguishes the rest of his production is still present. The two key ingredients for the creation of this fairy-tale atmosphere, despite the historical context, are the choice of a narration with internal focus, from the perspective of a child, the protagonist Pin, and the decision not to delve too deeply into the violent events that marked the partisan struggle against the German occupation. The experiences lived by Pin are therefore marginal compared to the real historical events, not only because he is not involved in the partisan clashes, but also because when he comes face to face with the bloodiest events, he misrepresents them. He sees everything as a great adventure, as a play for adults, those adults whom he wants to imitate. In contrast, *Invisible Cities* reflects the postmodern experimentalism typical of Calvino's later production. With its multi-faceted narrative structure, it is a good example of a novel that anticipates the reticular structure that fiction has acquired in the digital age and the assemblage of texts around the same semantic field, which we will meet again in the tweetbooks originating from it.[19] As Calvino has commented, he wanted to concentrate all of his thoughts and experiences around the same symbol, the city.[20]

The importance of Calvino as a source of inspiration for fiction on Twitter has already been illustrated by Edoardo Montenegro, who honored the author by highlighting on TwLetteratura's blog how Twitter embodies the key principles set forth in the *Lezioni Americane*.[21] These are lightness, due to the necessity of condensing concepts that are often serious and demanding into a few words, through the use of metaphor and allusion; quickness, due to the possibility of using simultaneous information from different sources; exactitude, obligated by the need to express a thought in a few characters and to be clear; visibility, which also originates from that use of images necessitated by the brevity of the medium; and multiplicity, which combines very distant fields of knowledge and creates previously inaccessible bonds.

---

[18] See http://www.twletteratura.org/2015/10/nididiragno-italo-calvino/ [accessed 01/02/2018].

[19] On Calvino's novels as a precursor to the reticular format of the digital age see Arturo Mazzarella, *La grande rete della scrittura. La letteratura dopo la rivoluzione digitale*, Torino: Boringhieri, 2008.

[20] See http://www.twletteratura.org/2013/10/invisibili-citta-calvino-twitter/ [accessed 01/02/2018].

[21] http://www.twletteratura.org/2012/02/lalgebra-di-twitter-appunti-sulle-lezioni-americane-di-italo-calvino/ [accessed 01/02/2018].

The Retellings

To illustrate the main types of rewriting which take life from the factors highlighted previously—the source text, the context of reception, the rewriters, the virtual community that has sprung up from the sharing of readings in recent years on TwLetteratura—is also to explain the way in which each of these factors influences the final result, innovating or maintaining conventional processes of rewriting.

As we have seen from the references to the two source texts, there is a substantial difference between the structure of *The Path to the Spiders' Nests* and *Invisible Cities* that creates a divide between the various types of rewriting experienced so far on TwLetteratura: rewriting a work with a main character and internal focalization allows an automatic cohesiveness of rewriting, and this cohesion generates certain mechanisms of rewriting influenced primarily by the organic structure of the hypotext. Moreover, the presence of a child as a protagonist, and the narration of the facts from the point of view of this "unreliable narrator" (Booth 1983: 339) often have ironic or allusive consequences, which allow a reading between the lines of what the protagonist is not able to understand. Empathy, irony, and allusions are the recurrent features within the retellings, along with the constant process of modernization with reference to the war context in which the story takes place.

For example, we can take the tweets by @exlibris2012 in reference to the second chapter of the book ("You understand, right, @IoSonoPin? From now on, nothing is going to be as before, there will be secrets and no more time for jokes"; "In the end you just have to get rid of that weapon, give it to those who requested it of him. It will be like forgetting, as if nothing happened"; "But I did it, I took the gun, why don't you ask me anything? I want to go back to before, I did it for you!"[22]). Here, the turning point, the moment of transgression that affects the child's future, the theft of a German's gun, is rewritten in the empathic form, often using the first person, turning the internal focusing in identification with the protagonist, with a transvocalization (the shift from the first to the third person),[23] or in the form of an "admonition" for the irresponsible nature of the child. There are also cases of a modernizing rereading of the same episode, such as the tweet by @erikaluna,[24] who, attaching an image of the P-38 gun stolen by Pin, recalls another of the dark moments of Italian history ("The P-38 has for @IoSonoPin a magical connotation. It will return in our *lead* story. pic.twitter.com/aWy8Z9ZXrM", where the word "lead" creates an immediate allusion to the "Years of Lead").

The latter tweet allows us to introduce another of the elements which distinguishes Twitter as a platform for rewriting that is very different from other virtual communities, such as those of fanfiction: the way in which the medium determines the type of rewriting, presenting questions, admonitions, reflections, addressed to each character in the second person or citing it as the last example (@IoSonoPin is, in fact, the protagonist's account). Twitter is the first digital medium

---

[22] @exlibris2012's quotes (my translation) are taken from the tweetbook she edited http://www.trytweetbook.com/book/105714 [accessed 15/07/2016].

[23] See Genette, *Palimpsests.*

[24] Blutrasparente, *I miei #NidiDiRagno*, http://www.trytweetbook.com/book/105707 [accessed 15/07/2017].

to allow ordinary citizens to feel in touch with hitherto unreachable personalities. Now they can receive daily updates by ministers, governors, novelists, journalists, and the most famous people from around the world. Similarly, the rewriting, as a reflection of the reading path of each user, reflects this expectation or tries to realize this possibility of creation and access into a new world where characters of the fictional world and persons from the real world may meet, expressing the questions, doubts, and curiosities which are often at the origin of rewriting itself.[25] We have only to read the posts in the "protagonist's" account to find dialogues which actualize those encounters in virtual form. After the sentence addressed to Pin by Montenegro ("Under the belt that whips you, you desire to receive caresses, @IoSonoPin. And History doesn't give them to you. #NidiDiRagno/03 […]"), Pin answers by involving the students in the discourse. Those students may be little older than he is and might satisfy his desperate search for a trusted friend to lead to the spiders' nests, a search which spans the entire work ("if the caress is given by you, then I trust in it #NidiDiRagno/03 @1aclassicojesi […]"). This actualization of impossible dialogue goes even further, with the interpellation by the character of the author who created it: "Men who eat *abbovati* [like oxen], @Calvino_Italo? You speak too hard"[26] or "It's not the jacket that is too big, @Calvino_Italo, it's you who made me too little to know what I know. #NidiDiRagno/01".

Both in the tweet by Pin and in those addressed to him, we can also find examples of intertextual references to works rewritten during the previous experiments on TwLetteratura such as *Pinocchio* and *Invisible Cities*: the meeting with his employer in prison is compared by Pin to the encounter between Pinocchio and Geppetto inside the belly of the whale ("Now I will say that my meeting with Pietromagro in prison is like that of Pinocchio and Geppetto in the belly of the whale. #NidiDiRagno/04"), or the recall to the closing words of *Invisible Cities*, such as the tweet by @lalagedulce: "Today only this: 'seek and learn to recognize who and what, in the midst of inferno, are not inferno, then make them endure, give them space'".

Moving on to the second of the works in question, we can observe how the fragmentation of *Invisible Cities*, the structuring of the individual imaginary cities like tiles in a mosaic united by the reference to a symbol—the city—led to a myriad of tweetbooks, whose variety of semantic fields reflects their fragmentary nature and the shades of meaning of each city.

To show an example of such a tweetbook, we can consider the case of *Eutropia*, the city described by Calvino in Chapter IV entitled "Trading Cities":

> When he enters in the territory of which Eutropia is the capital, the traveler sees not one city but many, of equal size and not unlike one another, scattered over a vast, rolling plateau. Eutropia is not one, but all these cities together; only one is inhabited at a time, the others are empty; and this

[25] See Jan Connelly, Liping Deng, "Reading in a Participatory Culture: Remixing Moby-Dick in the English Classroom", *Pedagogies: An International Journal*, 9:2, 2014, 173: "Jenkins identifies five basic elements—kernels, holes, contradictions, silences and potentials—that inspire fan interventions. Here, he is offering core components of a participatory model of reading".

[26] This tweet refers to the difficulty to find the term *abbovati* in other Italian texts.

> process is carried out in rotation. Now I shall tell you how. On the day when Eutropia's inhabitants feel the grip of weariness and no one can bear any longer his job, his relatives, his house and his life, debts, the people he must greet or who greet with him, then the whole citizenry decides to move to the next city, which is there waiting for them, empty and good as new; [...] So their life is renewed from move to move... (64)

The subtitle chosen for the tweetbook considered here offers the first interpretative key to these rewritings of the city. *Eutropia. L'eterno intorno dell'uguale* (which means *The eternal (going) around the same*), where "around" in Italian sounds like *ritorno*, "return",[27] a clear allusion to the famous Nietzschean expression "The eternal return of the same". It reveals in advance the meaning given to this city: the impossibility of a real change or the possibility of an only partial change. At the same time, it emphasizes the importance assumed by the allusive and ironic pun of these rewrites.

To understand how this interpretative key finds expression throughout the various contributions, since these are collective works, it is interesting to look through the different forms of rewriting and identify the semantic fields created by the processes of exchange and sharing among the members of the community.

Among the forms of rewriting we can find the simplest case of the quote ("the inhabitants repeat the same scenes with the actors changed") reused in an allusive and satirical key, as the caption of a picture of a war museum, a reminder of the eternal return, in this case, of the tragedies of history.

In other cases the use of the quote becomes more complex and turns to the creation of intertextual relations with other authors: some people choose to quote another writer to offer their own interpretation of the city—as in the case of Seneca's quote "'*Animum debes mutare, non coelum*'", which means "you have to change your mind, not the sky [not the reality around you]"—and those that with their pastiches create echoes and parallels with other authors (as in the Pirandellian reference, "Eutropia, 'on your way, you'll encounter every day millions of masks and very few faces'"). The same happens in the case of *The Path to the Spiders' Nests*, where the physical description and the social status of Pin recall other famous children from the literary tradition, such as Rosso Malpelo by Verga[28] or Ciaula by Pirandello.[29]

Among the most common forms of rewriting in TwLetteratura there are also two other typologies: the satirical retelling—which rewrites the city of Eutropia or the experiences of Pin in the light of the most urgent issues of contemporary Italian

---

[27] See DuFer, *Eutropia—Invisibili/23—l'eterno intorno dell'uguale*, http://beta.trytweetbook.com/book/100796 [accessed 15/07/2016]. All the quotations referring to *Invisible Cities* are taken from this tweetbook.
[28] See ExLibris2012: "It also makes me think about Rosso Malpelo of @verga1840: kids who are not kids, inevitably adults" or another Tweet by a third-year student rodo_3A: "Pin as Malpelo: getting from adults only labor and punches. #NidiDiRagno/01".
[29] See ExLibris2012: "Pin as Ciaula and RossoMalpelo: true! But the magnitude of @verga1840 for me is incomparable #NidiDiRagno/01".

society—and the modernizing one, in which the reinterpretation of the works by Calvino aims to merge with the "here and now" of the real-world community.

Among the satirical retellings, think, for example, of the tweet, "In Eutropia the Nazi criminal was buried here, then there, there, over, and again here. So nobody complained", alluding to the controversy which arose in 2013 around the discovery of Priebke's burial; or "In Eutropia *leghisti* [the Italian political party against immigration] don't exist. Every place is home, every trip is migration, every face is the same", a tweet where the subjects of exchange and equality of the hypotext are mixed with the recent debate on migration and racism.

We notice the same phenomena of satirical allusiveness and modernization in the case of #NidiDiRagno, with the tweets' focus on the themes of war and childhood denied: "It's hard to stay children in war. Forgive us #Pin # NidiDiRagno/01" (by @LepriRoby); "'It must be terrible to be a little beast'. Sometimes it is worst being a child. The world is full of stories of childhood denied #NidiDiragno/02"; "A child forced to grow a bit too fast: don't you think that they also exist today? #NidiDiRagno/04 [...]"; "In #NidiDiRagno/04 you talk about real jail. For prisons of gold we would have to wait until 1988" followed by a link to the archive of *Corriere della Sera*, one of the major Italian newspapers, dedicated to the scandal on the bribes received by politicians to build prisons.

In the case of *Invisible Cities,* the simultaneously visual and metaphorical character of the symbol of the city, the common thread throughout the narrative, finds its full reflection in the constant transcoding that takes place in the process of rewriting. In the case of *Eutropia*, to render the labyrinthine nature of this ideal city, there are many references to the chessboard and the labyrinth, in the texts and also through images and photographs, such as the famous illustrations by Escher and the visual transpositions that three artists performed in collaboration with the rewriting of the Calvinian city on TwLetteratura.[30]

A final project to highlight is #Invisibili/me, born after the rewriting of *Invisible Cities*, which shows how the users have internalized Calvino's intention of transposing their own experiences in symbolic form, choosing to explain their vision of reality by creating additional invisible cities, as a testament to the creative power of rewriting, that "mimetic practice"[31] that comes from reading. These new tweetbooks have mainly preserved the style of Calvino's work, sometimes suggestive, sometimes ironic, sometimes fabulous and evocative, with synesthesia, metaphors, and personifications. This is the project that leads to the full synthesis of *Invisible Cities* and popular culture through allusions and combinations of images spread by the various social media which continuously feed the collective imagery.

To draw together the threads of the discourse, I return to the two key concepts with which I first introduced the processes of rewriting in the social reader TwLetteratura, to illustrate how the two ideas interpenetrate in our examples the redefinition of the concept of rewriting, and the concept of the hermeneutical

---

[30] The works of three artists Alessandro Armando, Elena Nuozzi and Francesca Ballarini were exhibited in various cities in Italy at the end of the project.

[31] Genette, *Palimpsests*, 119.

community. The numerous cases of interpenetration between the real and fictional worlds offer some of the many examples of the dismantling of boundaries made possible by this social reader. First of all, we see the crossing of borders between literature and real life (or the virtual life of social media), as well as the increasingly clear dismantling of all barriers between author and reader, since now it is the readers who write what they would like to read.[32] If this shrinking of distances is the key ingredient for the creation of a hermeneutical community, no less important is the reticular feature that the communication has acquired through the contributions of the many digital media that render the source text, collectively read, shared, and rewritten, a "constellation of texts, an intertextual platform",[33] characterized by the blending of genres, registers, and codes which creates a common knowledge base and a shared value system. I am referring here especially to the second creative phase originated with #Invisibili/me, where many contributions coming from popular culture and many different codes—from street art, photography and other visual arts—helped to create, in the wake of Calvino, new "invisible cities", amplifying the reticular character already acquired by the work in the previous process of rewriting. These new stories created by the hermeneutical community which had just shared the reading of the *Invisible Cities*, still allude to the hypotext through the choice of the style and metaphors.

Collective rewritings, unlike authorial retellings, therefore, do not only testify to the new relationship between source text, rewriter and readers. Even more important, the immediacy of Twitter also allows the chain of literary communication of which every literary work is part to show its full potential and to be taken to the extreme. The reader, first receiver of the original text, becomes the creator of a new text that will be sent to a new receiver, giving rise to the chain of unlimited transmission coined by Doležel. However, compared to the linearity that seemingly characterizes the chain of literary communication, collective Twitter retellings generate new processes of interaction. The object of the rewritings is not only the hypotext, but also the rewritings by other members: imitations, parodies, metatexts, pastiches with other classics or with daily news. In this way, these new hermeneutical communities create an ideal interpretative spiral that replaces the linearity of the conventional process of literary transmission: each receiver, after his reading of the source text, can compare his personal reading of the original work with new reading perspectives by examining others' rewritings, and he can realize his personal rewritings of the hypotext mediated by the filter of other readers' interpretations.

BIBLIOGRAPHY

Aciman, Alexander, Rensin, Emmett, *Twitterature. The World's Greatest Books Retold Through Twitter*, London: Penguin, 2009.

Barthes, Roland, *S/Z*, Paris: Seuil, 1970.

---

[32] See Roland Barthes, *S/Z*, Paris: Seuil, 1970; Donata Meneghelli, "Jane Austen: tra brand e desiderio", *Between*, 4:8, 2014. http://ojs.unica.it/index.php/between/article/view/ 1358/1315 [accessed 01/02/2018].

[33] Meneghelli, "Jane Austen", 11. Translation is mine.

Basu, Arjun, *Twisters*. http://arjunbasu.com/twisters [accessed 29/01/2017].

Benjamin, Walter, *Illuminations*, London: Fontana Press Berland, 1992.

Blutrasparente, *#Invisibili/me 09 – L'altlante delle città*. beta.trytweetbook.com/ book/101267/pdf [accessed 15/07/2016].

———, *I miei #NidiDiRagno*. http://www.trytweetbook.com/book/ 105707 [accessed 15/07/2016].

Bolter, Jay David, Grusin, Richard, *Remediation: Understanding New Media*, Boston: The MIT Press, 2000.

Booth, Wayne C., *The Rhetoric of Fiction*, Chicago: The University of Chicago Press, 1961.

Bortolotti, Gary R., Hutcheon, Linda, "On the Origins of Adaptations: Rethinking Fidelity Discourse and 'Success'—Biologically", *New Literary History*, 38:3, 2007, 443-458.

Bryant, John, *The Fluid Text. A Theory of Revision and Editing for Book and Screen*, Ann Arbor: University of Michigan Press, 2002.

Calvino, Italo, *Invisible Cities*, Transl. William Weaver, New York: Harvest, 1974.

———, *Romanzi e Racconti*, Milano: Mondadori, 2004.

———, *Lezioni americane. Sei proposte per il prossimo millennio*, Milano: Mondadori, 2010.

Cao, Claudia, "Dai classici letterari a Twitter: alcuni esempi di riscrittura", *Between*, 4:8, 2014. http://ojs.unica.it/index. php/between/article/view/1330 [accessed 01/02/2018].

Connelly, Jan, Deng, Liping, "Reading in a Participatory Culture: Remixing Moby-Dick in the English Classroom", *Pedagogies: An International Journal*, 9:2, 2014, 172-178.

Curtius, Ernst Robert, *Letteratura europea e medioevo latino*, Transl. Anna Luzzatto, Mercurio Candela, Corrado Bologna, Firenze: La Nuova Italia, 1992.

Doležel, Lubomír, *Heterocosmica. Fiction and Possible Worlds*, Baltimore and London: Johns Hopkins University Press, 1998.

DuFer, Rick, *Eutropia—Invisibili/23—l'eterno intorno dell'uguale*. http://beta.trytweetbook.com/book/ 100796 [accessed 15/07/2016].

Eco, Umberto, *Lector in fabula. La cooperazione interpretativa nei testi narrativi*, Milano: Bompiani, 1979.

Exlibris2012, *#NidiDiRagno*. http://www.trytweetbook.com/book/105714 [accessed 29/01/2017].

Fish, Stanley, *Is There a Text in This Class? The Authority of Interpretive Communities*, Cambridge: Harvard University Press, 1980.

Genette, Gérard, *Palimpsests. Literature in the Second Degree*, transl. C. Newman, and C. Doubinsky, Lincoln and London: University of Nebraska Press, 1997.

Giampà, Daniele, *Oltre i confini del libro. La letteratura italiana nell'era digitale*. http://elmcip.net/node/5698 [accessed 15/12/2017].

Hutcheon, Linda, *A Theory of Adaptation*, New York and London: Routledge, 2006.

Iser, Wolfgang, "The Reading Process. A Phenomenological Approach", *New Literary History*, 3, 1971-72, 279-99.

Jenkins, Henry, *Convergence Culture: Where Old and New Media Collide*, New York: New York University Press, 2006.

Lombardo, Sonia, *Narrativa in 140 caratteri. Genesi della twitteratura*, Storiacontinua, 2013 (ebook).

———, *Come (NON) raccontare una storia su Twitter*. http://www.storiacontinua.com/scrittura-creativa/come-non-raccontare -una-storia-su-twitter/ [accessed 15/12/2017].

Luperini, Romano, *Insegnare la letteratura oggi*, Lecce: Manni, 2013.

Mazzarella, Arturo, *La grande rete della scrittura. La letteratura dopo la rivoluzione digitale*, Torino: Boringhieri, 2008.

Meneghelli, Donata, "Jane Austen: tra brand e desiderio", *Between*, 4:8, 2014. http://ojs.unica.it/index.php/ between/article/view/1358/1315 [accessed 01/02/2018].

Notaro, Anna, "How Networked Communication Has Changed the Ways We Tell Stories", *Between*, 4:8, 2014. http://ojs.unica.it/index.php/between/article/view/1341 [accessed 01/02/2018].

Ong, Walter J., *Orality and Literacy: The Technologizing the Word*, New York: Methuen, 1982.

Paveau, Marie-Anne, "Genre de discours et technologie discursive. Tweet, twittécriture et twittérature", *HAL. Archives-Ouvertes*, 2012. https://hal.archives-ouvertes.fr/hal-00824817/document [accessed 15/12/2017].

Plate, Liedeke, Rose, H. G. Els, "Rewriting, a Literary Concept for the Study of Cultural Memory: Towards a Transhistorical Approach to Cultural Remembrance", *Neophilologus*, 97, 2013, 611-625.

Sreedharan, Chindu, *A 1,000 Tweets. In 1,360 Days. Ugh.* http://www.chindu.net/musings/mahabharata-on-twitter-crosses-landmark/ [accessed 15/07/2016].

———, *Field Notes on Epicretold.* http://www.chindu.net/ reports-on-research/field-notes-on-epicretold/ [accessed 15/07/2016].

Thomas, Bronwen, "140 Characters in Search of a Story Twitterfiction as an Emerging Narrative Form", in *Analyzing Digital Fiction*, eds. Alice Bell, Astrid Ensslin, Hans Kristian Rustad, New York: Routledge, 2014, 94-108.

CHAPTER 9

Poetry and Code as "Sister Arts" in Eavan Boland's "Code" (2001)

Nina Shiel

In 1975, Frederick Brooks, in his collection of essays on software development, drew a distinct parallel between the work of the computer programmer and the poet. "The programmer, like the poet, works only slightly removed from pure thought-stuff. He builds his castles in the air, from air, creating by exertion of the imagination."[1] Although, these days, we tend of think of programming as an activity that firmly belongs in the area of science, the comparison between programming and poetry is more apt than might initially be expected. At the heart of any kind of computer-generated material lies programming code, these days usually only called "code", which consists of several different forms known as "languages" and the production of which is called "writing". Through such terminology and the process of creation through text, we can immediately see a conceptual connection with production of literary text. Further, the highly-structured rules of code can be compared with poetic metres: a defined set of parametres govern the production of the writing in order to achieve the desired effect. However, contrary to poetic metre, which can be broken for an even greater effect, broken code simply will not work.

This resemblance between poetry and programming has not gone unnoticed among practitioners. Stanford University has hosted code poetry slams, inviting and presenting submissions "ranging from human language poems incorporating concepts and gestures from programming, to poems written entirely in compilable code".[2] Other recent projects dedicated to code poems and available online include code{poems} (http://code-poems.com/index.html), a collection intended by its editor, Ishac Bertran, to explore the potential of code to communicate at the level of poetry, and a code poetry competition on sourcecodepoetry.com, which requires entries, in some manner relatable to Shakespeare, to be compilable code in any programming

---

[1] Frederick P. Brooks Jr., *The Mythical Man-Month: Essays on Software Engineering*, anniversary ed. Boston: Addison Wesley Longman, 1995, 7.

[2] "Code Poetry Slam: programmers and poets: create! compose! compile! (+ pizza)", Stanford University Division of Literatures, Cultures, and Languages. https://stanford.edu/~mkagen/codepoetryslam/ [accessed 25/01/2017].

language.[3] These examples demonstrate the readiness of poets and programmers to treat coding as a creative artform that strives towards expression and representation. As such, coding closely operates with literary writing, even as it, at the same time, maintains a distinct border with its adopted relation.

The concept of sibling-like correspondences between the arts, first brought to prominence in the aesthetic theories of the eighteenth century, and persisted in various ways until the present day, is explored in this essay in the context of the 2001 poem "Code" by the Irish poet Eavan Boland.[4] While the original concept of the Sister Arts focused on poetry and painting, the parallels between poetry and coding, drawn in the poem and established by the other examples mentioned above, allow us to treat the two latter ones in an equivalent manner. We are offered a comparative methodology by H.J. Jensen, who suggests three ways of comparing the arts: (1) historical exploration, which considers the historical context of the arts; (2) similarities of effects in the different arts; and (3) how each art uses imagery from the others and how one relies on the other arts.[5] In order to fully contextualize the relationship between poetry and coding in Boland's poem, it is necessary to briefly discuss the parallel relationship between poetry and painting: the text and the visual. The close reading of the poem is supplemented by material drawn from interviews with the poet, as well as from her 2003 essay titled "Virtual Syntax, Actual Dreams", in which she describes her discovery and love of computers in the 1990s.[6]

Comparing Poetry and Its Siblings—From Painting to Coding

The early modern aesthetic concept of the Sister Arts assumed direct parallels between the composition and purpose of distinct artforms. Most typically, such correspondences were drawn between painting and poetry, although parallels with the above were also created with music.[7] The roots of the concept were seen as lying in antiquity. In the late sixth century BCE, Simonides described poetry as speaking painting, or painting with a voice, and painting as silent poetry. The first century poet Horace, in particular, seemingly provided support to the notion of parallels between

---

[3] Bertran's statement of intention is available on his website, http://www.ishback.com/codepoems/index.html [accessed 25/01/2018]. For a profile of Bertran, see Jonathan Keats, "Code isn't just functional, it's poetic", *Wired*, 16 April 2013, https://www.wired.com/2013/04/code/ [accessed 25/01/2018].

[4] Eavan Boland, *Code*, Manchester: Carcanet Press, 2001.

[5] H.J. Jensen, *The Muses' Concord: Literature, Music, and the Visual Arts in the Baroque Age*, Cloomington: Indiana U.P., 1976, 166.

[6] Eavan Boland, "Virtual Syntax, Actual Dreams", *PN Review* Vol 29 issue 4, 2003, http://www.pnreview.co.uk/cgi-bin/scribe?item_id=1440 [accessed 04/02/2018].

[7] Peter Jan de Voogd, in *Henry Fielding and William Hogarth: The Correspondences of the Arts* (Volume 30, Amsterdam: Rodopi, 1981, p.52) provides a useful summary of the history of the concept of the "sister arts." The concept was introduced in England by John Dryden in 1695, when he included "An Original Preface Containing a Parallel betwixt Painting and Poetry" to his translation of Charles Alphonse Du Fresnoy's treatise *De Arte graphica*. The concept is further extensively discussed in the seminal work of Jean Hagstrum, *The Sister Arts: The Tradition of Literary Pictorialism and English Poetry from Dryden to Gray* (Chicago: University of Chicago Press, 1958). See also Jensen 1976, and Richard Wendorf (ed), *Articulate Images: The Sister Arts from Hogarth to Tennyson*. Minneapolis, University of Minnesota Press, 1983.

artforms with his line, "*ut picture poesi*", "as painting, so is poetry". Interestingly, the full context of the quote by Horace reveals that he is talking about the response of the reader or the viewer. He is not interested in the content, but points out that regardless of the medium, the response to a work of art depends on a number of factors. In effect, he advises the artist to present the work in the appropriate circumstances to show it at its best.

According to the notion of the Sister Arts, the creative processes behind painting and poetry were fully comparable. Peter Jan de Voogd describes the correspondences between the two according to the eighteenth-century writings as follows.[8] The materials required for each were different, which led to the difference in the methods of creation, but the end result of each was the culmination of the same parallel process. The "plot" of the poem—its design—matched the composition of the painting and the verbal expression in the poem was akin to the use of colours in the painting: the poet, in effect, was painting with words, while the painter did so with the brush. Both artforms had the same purpose: to move and to instruct their readers and viewers. At the same time, because the representative mechanisms of the two were not one and the same, there were clear differences: the painter was limited to showing a static image, a slice in time, whereas the poet was able to construct a series of scenes from one place or situation to another. The static nature of painting versus the dynamic nature of poetry were at the core of the challenge to the Sister Arts theory in 1836 by the English translation of G.E. Lessing's highly influential work *Laocoon, An Essay Upon the Limits of Painting and Poetry.*[9] Lessing did not outright deny the comparableness between the two, but argued that writing was fundamentally superior to visual representation and hence the two should not be assessed at an equal level.

The "painting" power of poetry (as with any creative literature) lies in the process of poetic techniques drawing out a visual image in the mind's eye. We can compare a person imagining a vivid mental image to a person viewing a work of visual art. Each experience has the power to arouse emotion through affective mental association. Since the Classical times up to the present day, this evocative power of words has been the subject of scholarship on the concept of ekphrasis, the idea that a vivid visual image or situation can be represented by means of words. As such, ekphrasis sits at the heart of the notion of the Sister Arts and illustrates the correspondences and differences between the two artforms.[10] By doing so, ekphrasis also brings into discussion the conceptual tension between the Sister Arts, based on their discrete means of representation, and rooted in the valorized dualistic division established by Lessing. His thinking separates the Arts into two mutually opposing streams: one contains poetry, eloquence, the mind, expression, and the masculine, while the other contains painting, silence, the body, imitation, and the feminine.[11] This gendered division entered and persisted in the Western scholarship, so that as recently as in his

---

[8] de Voogd, 52-58.

[9] G.E. Lessing, *Laocoon: An Essay Upon the Limits of Painting and Poetry,* trans. E. Frothingham, Mineola: Dover Publications Inc, 2009 (1836).

[10] See Hagstrum 1958 for a discussion of ekphrasis and its history in the context of the Sister Arts.

[11] Lessing, *Laocoon*. For a concise deconstruction of Lessing's thinking, see W.J.T. Mitchell "The Politics of Genre: Space and Time in Lessing's Laocoon", *Representations*, No. 6 (Spring), 1984, 98-115.

1993 monograph on ekphrasis, James Heffernan presented ekphrasis as having a strongly gendered-power dynamic, which occurs between the active "masculine" viewer and the passive feminized object.[12]

This wholly artificially gendered division views poetry, or the written word, as an active, positive force, while it attributes a negative, passive aspect to painting, i.e. the visual image. The active/passive division is drawn from the idea that text can move the reader along several consecutive scenes, while an image depicts one single moment and place. Additionally, an image is present in the immediate and requires no special effort, whereas words, in evoking a mental image, introduce additional cognitive step to reach the desired end result. Murray Krieger sees this desire for the preference of the immediacy of the visual over the mediation of the text as a result of a semiotic desire for the "natural sign", a written sign that would have "the world captured in a word": a sign that would, at the same time, be the signified itself.[13] Such unreachable maximum simplicity would reduce writing and visual depiction obsolete, as any communication or creation of art would be conducted using concrete objects—but abstract concepts would present a difficulty.

Yet, computer code contains within itself that which it represents. As a set of instructions to the computer, it is "written" as a series of letters, numbers and other symbols understandable to humans. It uses specific rules in terms of syntax and grammar in order to function properly. Once run through a compiler, transforming into machine-readable form, that same code is perceived in other formats: it becomes graphics, or music, or anything else displayable by a computer. A piece of code can, therefore, be seen at once as a representation as well as that which it represents. This is a major difference between coding, writing and other artforms. No other artform can similarly extend its representative power over others. Evocative text can cause mental images in the reader, but the text itself cannot become images and images cannot generally become text.[14] Yet, code, depending on its intended function, creates other forms of art from itself, although, in its raw form, it is best compared with writing.

Like traditional writing, coding can be understood as an active form of creating meaning, as its creation and execution generates texts, images and even spaces available to us through the various instances of digital media. Branding coding as a purely scientific/mathematical subject does it a disservice. The field of programming consists of several different programming languages, which operate through predetermined syntax and grammar. Daniel Punday extensively discusses the parallels and differences between coding and writing, as traditionally understood, in his recent work *Computing as Writing*.[15] On the one hand, he criticizes the view of Steve McConnell, who has voiced his discomfort concerning the parallel between writing and coding. McConnell suggests that comparing coding to writing makes the former

---

[12] James Heffernan, *Museum of Words: The Poetics of Ekphrasis from Homer to Ashbery*, Chicago: University of Chicago Press, 1993.

[13] Murray Krieger, *Ekphrasis: The Illusion of the Natural Sign*. Baltimore, Maryland: The Johns Hopkins University Press 1992, 11.

[14] Consideration of non-Western and non-alphabetic scripts is beyond the scope of this essay.

[15] Daniel Punday, *Computing as Writing*, Minneapolis: University of Minneapolis Press, 2015.

sound like writing a casual letter, which is written without much thought from start to finish.[16] Instead, McConnell feels that coding requires planning and management. Punday puts forward that comparing coding to the writing of a novel would more accurate, as both activities involve dealing with complex details with a lot of planning. On the other hand, Punday cites Donald Knuth, who argues for programming as a literary activity, a form of communication between people rather than simply between a human being and a machine.[17]

Punday concludes that, while writing is an important model for thinking about computing, particularly in terms of creative activities, we still ought to remember that even traditional forms of writing consist of a number of purposes and methods: creative writing significantly differs from what he calls professional or corporate writing. Therefore, any tensions that can seem to arise between traditional writing and coding can also be explained by examining the purposes of the writing in question, with creative work and non-creative work requiring different approaches, levels of planning and methods of execution, regardless of whether the work involves digital or non-digital production. Such tensions are familiar to us from the concept of the Sister Arts, which use different methods and approaches to reach a related goal of transferring information in one form or another, as discussed above. Paradoxically, while code remains a form of writing, due to its qualities brought about by its essential relationship with the computer, it is sufficiently different from traditional writing to merit an exploration in this essay as a Sister Art to poetry: strongly related, but one that uses different methods in order to deliver an equivalent purpose.

It is also worth briefly considering the gendered aspect of the Sister Arts. As we saw, the traditional division between poetry and painting links the former with the masculine, and the latter with the feminine, with the former considered in favour of the latter. In the past thirty years, coding has transformed from a highly specialized professional skill to a fashionable pastime promoted to school children through workshops known as coder dojos. As part of this push, girls in particular have been encouraged to pick up coding, as a result of the activity having gained strong masculine associations, as is the case with STEM subjects across the board. Alongside this effort, it has been pointed out that originally coding was seen as more suited for females, comparable to secretarial work at typewriters, before its prestige grew and it was appropriated by male programmers, who developed into an elite class in the information society. As an integral part of its discussion of poetry and coding, Boland's poem presents one of the coding pioneers, Grace Hopper. As discussed below, Boland draws a strong parallel between the female programmer and herself, a female poet, thus moving away from constricted gender roles of the artforms.

---

[16] *Ibid.*, 57.
[17] *Ibid.*, 61

THE POET AND THE COMPUTER PROGRAMMER: EAVAN BOLAND AND "CODE"

In "Code", Eavan Boland compares and contrasts poetry and computer programming as creative arts, suggesting that both manifest the power of language in different but related ways. Beginning with the poem's title, Boland alludes to the many meanings of the word "code" – a system of rules that govern information for communication or storage, in cryptography, cognition, semantics, or in the process of computer programming, which has become synonymous with "coding". Poetry, similarly, is a code of sorts, which uses specific conventions as poetic operations to convey meaning through a set of symbols. The poem is dedicated to the American mathematician Grace Hopper, who is identified in the dedication as the "maker of a computer compiler and verifier of COBOL". The dedication puts forward the poem as an ode, but the overall sense of the text is that of a highly personal letter, as the first-person voice of the poem directly addresses Hopper throughout, in intimate, almost plaintive, evocative tones, as discussed below.

Rear Admiral Grace Murray Hopper (1906-88) was a computer scientist, who worked on early programming languages. In the 1950s, she developed the first computer compiler, which became a turning point in the history of programming. A compiler "translates" between the computer and the human, so that commands entered using a "high-level language", one that employs natural human language elements, are converted into a "low-level", or machine language, which is then read and "understood" by the computer. Machine languages consist of binary code, in which all data is represented as a series of ones and zeroes. The conversion process enables the execution of a computer program.

In conjunction with the concept of the compiler, Hopper developed the first programming language that syntactically used statements derived from natural English, as opposed to commands solely designed for computer use. This language, called FLOW-MATIC, later evolved into the better-known programming language of COBOL (acronym for common business-oriented language). A hierarchy of sections, paragraphs and sentences gives COBOL a syntax that resembles that of English. Its commands tend to use recognisable English words, such as "ACCEPT", "DISPLAY" and "MOVE", rather than mathematical symbols, such as x and y. COBOL also has an unusually high number of "reserved words", terms that have specific purposes in the language and cannot be used for any other purpose. Hence, they create a complex "grammar" for the language. Thus, Hopper's evolved creation brings together elements from hard coding and from natural language.

In an interview published on the website of the poetry publisher Carcanet Press in 2007, Boland briefly talks about the poem as an expression of the connection she feels with Hopper, in terms of using language and symbols at public and private levels.[18] She finds a poignancy in Hopper's lonely work to enable a new kind of language, but she also expresses envy at the computer scientist's freedom from the struggle of

[18] "Interview with Eavan Boland", 20 July 2007, Carcanet Press. http://www.carcanet.co.uk/cgi-bin/scribe?showdoc=28;doctype=interview [accessed 04/02/2018].

poetic ideas and reflections of power in language. Boland's feeling of connection with Hopper lends a strong personal layer to the poem, expressed in its language and themes, as discussed in the rest of the essay.

This personal aspect is emphasised further by Boland's subsequent essay of 2003, titled "Virtual Syntax, Actual Dreams", on her own discovery of computers in the early 1990s. Although the essay does not mention Hopper, it discusses the parallels between the syntax of programming and the syntax of poetry, as well as poetry and coding as two different cultures of language. Effectively, the essay functions as a companion piece to the poem, providing supplementary background information by means of prose. Importantly, by returning to the themes of "Code", it confirms that the poetic voice in the poem is Boland's own. It is interesting that Boland noted in the 2007 interview that she herself does not know how to program; yet, her treatment of the code and the coder in the poem implies at least a certain level of familiarity with the topic.

In the essay, Boland suggests that a poet is particularly well prepared to comment on new technology, because that technology shares the themes of time, power and language with poetry. She evokes the image of a poet engaged in a struggle with language in order to make things happen – to shape the world. She speaks of longing for the way poetry "re-orders a moment" through a feeling of order and force. A computer, she maintains, is primed with power and language: "When I sat down at the computer, turned it on, issued the dark and plain commands of its operating system, I began to feel that I was not simply instructing a machine but constructing a reality."[19]

So, as a writer, as a creator of literary realities, Boland begins the poem as one colleague to another, "Poet to poet" (l.1), although it is immediately made clear that the relationship is one-sided and illusionary, as the writer Boland imagines the "writer" Hopper: "I imagine you/at the edge of language" (l.2). The structure and form of the poem occupies that very same edge of language, as we see at first glance: every second stanza is written with stacked indentations, as code often would be, and the remaining stanzas, placed in dialogue with the others, retain the unindented line structure more typical of traditional writing. The structure reflects the content of the poem, in which Boland speaks of herself writing poetry, while envisioning Hopper "writing code". Another structural aspect dialogically addresses the chronology of the two writers: in the first half of the poem Boland evokes the vision of Hopper, comparing and contrasting the American computer scientist with herself, before moving on, in the second half, to discuss the shared creative nature of their respective occupations.

In the first part, the parallel images of the two writers are carefully situated in specific times and places. Hopper is "at the start of summer/in Wolfeboro New Hampshire" (l.2), later emphasised as "west of me and in the past" (l.25), while Boland is decades in the future: "The line of my horizon [...] appears at last fifty years away" (l.16-17). She names her own place of residence, as she often does in her poetry: "this Dublin suburb" (l.20). The image of Hopper is evoked as still, through the negated sentences of time and through a series of repeated perfect tenses that

[19] Boland, "Virtual Syntax, Actual Dreams", no page number available.

imply completion, even as the poem states with finality that "Atoms, energies have done their work/have made the world, have finished it, have rested" (l.13-14). In contrast, Boland's Dublin has a sense of subtle movement: leaves stir, there is "air and invertebrates and birds" (l.21). Boland, in her own time, is alive, while her summoned image of Hopper is still, a brief vision of imagination.

At the same time, the exact geographical and chronological contexts, expressed by the poetry, are contrasted with the timelessness of the code that the Hopper of the vision is writing, "compiling binaries and zeroes" (l.28), the binary code of ones and zeroes at the heart of every computer. In her essay, Boland describes her first computer as "this seasonless machine", which contains and surpasses the limits of history.[20] The computer is a machine of memory: "Each pattern [of bytes] was instructing the computer to do something. To read. To compare. To remember."[21] In the poem, the negations of time also express the existence of code outside the reference frame of the human world: "You have no sense of time. No sense of minutes even./They cannot reach inside your world/your grey workstation/with *when yet now never* and *once*" (l.4-7).

At first, the italicized words look like code statements, or words of a programming language that cause specific operations to take place. On more careful inspection, these words, all of which pertain to time, are, in fact, not typically found in code at all. Even as code looks like it is connected to what, in the words of the poem, "we call this Creation" (l.15), it exists on a slightly different conceptual plane. The italicized words are not useful as code operators, because the functioning of code is not dependent on the human perception of time. Instead, they are time operators applicable to the human world, the world of poetic language. At the end of the first part of the poem, Boland explains what Hopper is doing with her work. "The given world is what you can translate." (l.29) The significance of the compiler is that, in a manner of speaking, it translates between human and machine languages, between the human world and the world of code, between the languages of poetry and code – it is the very "edge of language" at which the poem sees Hopper work, as noted above.

In the second part, the poem moves away from the perspective that is directly focused on Hopper and her work. Here, the poet-voice comes into her own, realising her own power of language, after a period of admiration for Hopper's creation of a new language. "Let there be language –" (l.31) exclaims the poet, mimicking the biblical words of creation, which harkens back to the world as Creation, as discussed in the first part of the poem. A moment of brief hesitation follows from the poet's part, as the text reflects on Hopper's achievements laid out in the first part: "even if we use it differently" (l.32). The poet-voice acknowledges that the coder and the poet both use language, but in different ways, and for this brief moment of insecurity, the poet is not sure that her own use of language rates as high as Hopper's: "I never made it timeless as you have./I never made it numerate as you did" (l.33-34). We can extend the poet's momentary anxiety to be reflective of today's public climate, which values the language of coding above the language of poetry. Effectively, the poet seems to

---

[20] *Ibid.*
[21] *Ibid.*

find herself asking: In the face of such achievements, what good am I? What good is my work?

"And yet", comes the answer straight away (l. 35). The power of the poetic language is to also create things anew. The poet imagines a situation in the past, which provides her with inspiration in the present, and, using her own language, as a result she preserves the real memory of Hopper, and her own imaginary memory of Hopper at her desk:

> And yet I use it here to imagine
> how at your desk in the twilight
> legend, history, and myth of course
> are gathering in Wolfeboro New Hampshire
> as if to a memory. As if to a source. (l.35-39)

In her essay, Boland describes the impression that her first computer made: "even then I could see that somehow there had crept into this casing every dream of language, of power, of magic that human beings had ever had."[22] To her, a computer enables the process of creation and manipulation through the syntax of code, which she compares to the feeling of control she felt when she worked on the syntax of her Latin exercises as a teenager: "that old magic of language I had first found in my Latin grammar".[23] When the commands she issued to her computer were executed into events, she felt that that magic created a bridge of sorts between her human self and the machinery in front of her. She describes the process as "nearer to myth than technology [...] in my imagination at least". Specifically, this "myth of meaning", as she puts it: "was the exchange of language between one who understood it and one who could enact it", an Orphic effect on nature achieved by means of artistic language.[24] In the poem, the poet's magic of language conveys an image of Hopper at her workstation, in her hometown, gathering the initial seeds for her own language, the syntax of which will later elicit the response of legend and myth in Boland. Hopper becomes the source of the magic, the "maker of the future", as she is addressed in the second last stanza (l.40).

The aspect of memory in the poem is underlined in the last two stanzas, as the poem discusses the fading of the past and its voice longs for Hopper as a mother figure. Before a fuller analysis of these stanzas, it is useful to consider Hopper's position in the history of computing. In the Carcanet interview, the interviewer calls Hopper "the forgotten inventor of COBOL". [25] Such a designation is perhaps somewhat unfair, and certainly exaggerated for effect. Although less known that many male figures in computing history, Hopper is remembered, to a degree. For instance, the website of the Computer History Museum in Mountain View, California, includes Grace Hopper and her work on the compiler in its timeline of computing

---

[22] *Ibid.*
[23] *Ibid.*
[24] *Ibid.*
[25] "Interview with Eavan Boland".

milestone.[26] Nonetheless, it is worth noting that despite its significance in the history of computing, COBOL has never been a popular programming language, due to its perceived inflexibility and verbosity. Hopper is hardly a household name, but then again, few figures in the history of computing are, with the possible exception of Alan Turing and the recent CEOs of global multinationals.

Although Boland does not mention the issue of Hopper being "forgotten" directly, the fleetingness of the past is a palpable force throughout the poem. On the one hand, this is in contrast to the timelessness of code, but on the other hand, it serves as a reminder of the separation between the framework of code and the framework of the poetic language. The chronological gap between Hopper and the poet-voice is emphasized through imagery of shadows and darkness. When the poet notes that Hopper is geographically and chronologically removed, at the same time "Dark falls. Light is somewhere else" (l.26). In the poet's imagination, Hopper sits at her desk in the twilight. In the second last stanza, the motif of the fading light comes to be directly associated with fading memory: "if the past/is fading from view with the light/outside your window" (l.40-42).

As a response, another instance of the poet-voice's newfound confidence provides reassurance: "There is still light/in my suburb and you are in my mind" (47-48). The memory of Hopper persists in the poet's mind and expression through poetic language, symbolized by the absence and presence of light, as well as the promise of light earlier on in the poem. The line of the poet's horizon, fifty years removed from Hopper, is "the first sign that night will be day [...] in this Dublin suburb" (l.19-20). The final stanza brings the two characters juxtaposed together in the play of light and its absence. The image of Hopper in the poet's mind, surrounded by the light in the suburb, is "head bowed, old enough to be my mother –/writing code before the daylight goes." The separation in time is doubly stressed through the difference in age and through the imagery of the rapidly fading light.

The expression "writing code" line five of the final stanza, is immediately paralleled by the poet's statement: "I am writing" in the next line, with the implication that she is writing poetry. The placement of the two present participles at the centre of the stanza that represents the two writers in the poem next to each other also situates the two crafts of language in an equal position. The positioning affirms the beginning of the final stanza, which carries over from the previous one as the only example of enjambment between stanzas in the poem: "let it make no difference". The syntax of the poem, which here verbally expresses the syntax of the code, breaks in order to draw attention to the poem's conclusion. It does not matter if memory fades, it does not matter if the syntax of code (or poetry!) is not perfect, it need not make a difference. The poet preserves the memory of Hopper through her own writing, in her own light of a memory brought about by a new time. "I am writing at a screen as blue/as any hill, as any lake" (l.51-52), here picking up again the earlier reference to a future horizon of blue: the bluish light of a modern computer screen – a machine of language, and a machine of memory.

[26] "Timeline of Computer History", Computer History Museum, Mountain View, http://www.computerhistory.org/timeline/?year=1952 [accessed 04/02/2018].

At the end of the poem, time blurs one more time. The poet states her internal purpose here, in contrast to the external purpose expressed in the dedication of the poem, "to show you how the world begins again" (l.53). Up until now, time has been linear: on the one hand, the poet and the computer scientist have occupied clearly defined points of time, well removed from each other. On the other hand, it has been meaningless, to an extent, in the framework of code itself. Suddenly, "the world begins again" (l.53), time twists into itself and becomes cyclical, even as the sense of continuity from one cycle to another persists. This continuity is stressed through the repeated word "still": "We are still human. There is still light." (l.46) The separate pronouns of the addressive "you" and the first person "I" have joined together into a "we", for a brief singular instance in the imaginary connection between the two writers, before being separated again. A world begins through an act of creation, an act of writing, whether poetry or code: "One word at a time" (l.54). As the final expression of the cycle of history and language, the poem closes in the same way as it started, but by now a new intimacy has been found. The collegial "poet to poet" (l.1) becomes "One woman to another" (l.55), perhaps, in part, to acknowledge that women writers of any kind have historically been more subject to general forgetfulness than their male counterparts.

What arises from the poem is a strong connection, even a kinship of sorts, between the creative processes that inhabit the writing of poetry and the writing of code. Computer programming in today's society is seen as a strongly mathematical pursuit, typically perceived as a "masculine" activity. In its emphasis on the womanhood of the two writers present in the text, Boland's poem recalls a time in which computer programmers were often women, even as it highlights the creativity behind the "numerate" language of coding and the purely verbal language of poetry alike. The poem clearly distinguishes the two modes of language as having different functions and different expressions, but, at the same time, it sees both modes as being of equal value as powerful methods of creating anew, in ways that can felt by new generations in the future, or, as the poem wistfully hopes, to even be felt in the past through the longing of the future writers.

BIBLIOGRAPHY

Bertran, Ishac, *code{poems}* http://www.ishback.com/codepoems/ index.html [accessed 04/02/2018].

Boland, Eavan, *Code*, Manchester: Carcanet Press, 2001

———,"Virtual Syntax, Actual Dreams", *PN Review* Vol 29 issue 4, 2003, http://www.pnreview.co.uk/cgi-bin/scribe?item_id=1440 [accessed 04/02/2018].

Interview with Eavan Boland, 20 July 2007, Carcanet Press. http://www.carcanet.co.uk/cgibin/ scribe?showdoc=28;doctype=interview [accessed 04/02/2018].

Brooks Jr., Frederick P., *The Mythical Man-Month: Essays on Software Engineering*, anniversary ed. Boston: Addison Wesley Longman, 1995.

Code Poetry Slam: programmers and poets: create! compose! compile! (+ pizza), Stanford University Division of Literatures, Cultures, and Languages, https://stanford.edu/~mkagen/codepoetryslam/ [accessed 25/01/2017].

de Voogd, Peter Jan, *Henry Fielding and William Hogarth: The Correspondences of the Arts*, Amsterdam: Rodopi, 1981.

Hagstrum, Jean, *The Sister Arts: The Tradition of Literary Pictorialism and English Poetry from Dryden to Gray,* Chicago: University of Chicago Press, 1958.

Heffernan, James, *Museum of Words: The Poetics of Ekphrasis from Homer to Ashbery*, Chicago: University of Chicago Press, 1993.

Jensen, H.J., *The Muses' Concord: Literature, Music, and the Visual Arts in the Baroque Age*, Cloomington: Indiana U.P., 1976, 166.

Keats, Jonathan, "Code isn't just functional, it's poetic", *Wired*, 16 April 2013, https://www.wired.com/2013/04/code/ [accessed 25/01/2018].

Krieger, Murray, *Ekphrasis: The Illusion of the Natural Sign*. Baltimore, Maryland: The Johns Hopkins University Press, 1992.

Lessing, G. E., *Laocoon: An Essay Upon the Limits of Painting and Poetry,* trans. E. Frothingham, Mineola: Dover Publications Inc, 2009 (1836).

Mitchell, W.J.T., "The Politics of Genre: Space and Time in Lessing's Laocoon", *Representations*, No. 6 (Spring), 1984, 98-115.

Punday, Daniel, *Computing as Writing*, Minneapolis: University of Minneapolis Press, 2015.

Timeline of Computer History, Computer History Museum, Mountain View, http://www.computerhistory.org/timeline/?year=1952 [accessed 04/02/2018].

Wendorf, Richard (ed), *Articulate Images: The Sister Arts from Hogarth to Tennyson*, Minneapolis: University of Minnesota Press, 1983.

CHAPTER 10

The House as Work of Art: Edmond de Goncourt between Catalogue, Historiography and Autobiography

Massimo Fusillo

In the late nineteenth century, the dominant pattern of the Realist novel is gradually deconstructed and transformed. Proliferating details, anecdotes, documents and descriptions undermine the central role of narration, and prepare the way for modernist experimentation. In his last novel, the most significant figure of this phase and ideal model of Naturalism, Gustave Flaubert, drastically reduces the presence of a well-structured narrative plot, giving space instead to an infinite catalogue, a provocative and sceptical encyclopedia. The text we will deal with, similarly "impossible", was written by one of the two Goncourt brothers, Edmond.[1] *La Maison d'un artiste* is a text not conceived as a novel, in which the catalogue and the description (two different techniques, both non-narrative) are intermingled with autobiographical evocations, historiographical digressions, and essayistic elements. In order to focus better on this unclassifiable text, we will deal first with the long-lasting tension between narration and description in the history and theory of literature, and then with a literary genre, ekphrasis, and a cultural phenomenon, fetishism, quite different of course, but in a way interrelated. To describe a work of art is an extremely ancient literary praxis which basically derives from an attraction for the inanimate and the inorganic which is also at the core of fetishism, apart from its myriad historical and cultural declinations. In late modernity, when commodification, urbanization, and fashion radically changed the relationship with the realm of objects, fetishism becomes more and more a pervasive cultural phenomenon, going beyond its religious, anthropological origin, Marxian classification, and Freudian sexual interpretation. We will conclude with some glimpses into our own age, in which the fluidity between different genres (art criticism, ekphrasis, autobiography, narration, historiography) has reached its extreme results.

In every classicist aesthetic, description has always been considered a subordinate element functional to the main narrative logic and the structure of the plot. This rigid hierarchy is imbued with a productive and economical vision: every useless detail must be avoided, every element must serve the development of narration,

---

[1] Edmond and Jules de Goncourt are the authors of a still canonical naturalist novel, *Germinie Lacerteux* (1865).

representation, and characterization. Being nonlinear and non-sequential, description is perceived as a dangerous and disturbing factor that introduces infinity and openness into an otherwise closed and coherent system.

Largely neglected by ancient rhetoric, which considered it an ornament finalized to a vivid effect (*enargheia*), description is considered the "servant of narration" (*ancilla narrationis*) by Matthew of Vendome (twelfth century) in his *Ars versificatoria*, and is usually classified by Medieval rhetoricians as a procedure of amplification (*amplificatio*). The most radical and canonical expression of the hierarchy of narration over description comes after a period of flourishing detail and long descriptive digressions, that is, during mannerism and the baroque age, which were characterized by a distinctly experimental attitude, the subversion of classical harmony, and a strong visual nature. Nicolas Boileau's *Art poétique* is certainly the most rigorous expression of European classicism and, at the same time, the strictest criticism of baroque descriptive compulsion, including the widespread topos asserting the reader's right to skip descriptions.[2] We find here a principle which will play an important role in Lukács's aesthetic of realism: selection.[3] The author must choose only the important and essential details, which must clarify settings, characters and actions. Description can only be a good background, never an autonomous element or an independent creative strategy.

A century later, the article entitled *Description* in Diderot's *Encyclopédie* still stresses the accidental and chaotic nature of description, strongly opposed to the more logical nature of definition; the supplement published in 1776, written by a belletrist and theorist, Jean-François Marmontel, however, highlights the emotional and pictorial qualities of this rhetorical figure, presenting a more dynamic vision, based on the different points of view, but still confined to a subordinate and ornamental role.[4]

The same features return in other rationalist moments in literary theory: for example in Lessing's *Laocoön*[5] with its sharp distinction between the spatial character of painting and the temporal character of literature (a distinction totally refuted today by visual studies); or in Paul Valéry's aesthetics of coherence, which rejects the random and arbitrary nature of description, whose order can always be reversed; or even in functionalist narratology, in which description is merely a catalyst, an inessential element which fills voids in the central narrative logic;[6] and finally especially in the abovementioned *Narrate or Describe?* by Lukács.[7]

---

[2] Nicolas Boileau, *Satires, épîtres, art poétique*, Paris: Gallimard, 1985.

[3] Georg Lukács, *Erzählen oder beschreiben?* (1936), in *Werke* 4, *Probleme des Realismus* 1, Neuwied-Berlin: Luchterhand, 1971, 197-243; *Narrate or Describe?* in Georg Lukács, *Writer and Critic and Other Essays*, trans. Arthur Kahn, London: Merlin, 1970, 110-148.

[4] The supplement to the *Encyclopédie ou Dictionnaire raisonné des sciences, des arts et des métiers* was reprinted in the section « Grammaire et littérature » of the *Encyclopédie méthodique*, Paris: Pamcoucke, 1782, vol. 1. See also Johanna Stalnaker, *The Unfinished Enlightment. Description in the Age of the Encyclopedia*, Ithaca: Cornell University Press, 2010.

[5] Gotthold Ephraim Lessing, *Laocoön: An Essay on the Limits of Painting and Poetry,* trans. Edward Allen McCormick, Baltimore: Johns Hopkins University Press, 1984.

[6] Paul Valéry, *Autour de Corot* (1932), in *Œuvres,* Paris: Gallimard, 1960, t. 2, pp. 1323-1324. I am following the rich theoretical and historical analysis by Philippe Hamon, *Du Descriptif,* Paris: Hachette,

This essay thus belongs to a long-lasting theoretical tradition, rationalist and classicist, characterized by the vision of a literary text as a closed and harmonic system that refuses the excesses of ornamental detail and celebrates the dynamism of narration. Lukács interprets this vision in his own ideological and poetical terms, particularly in his nostalgia for the epic and for ancient Greece, which is found at the core of his *Theory of the Novel.* This influential work develops Hegel's critical myth of the epic as the primeval form par excellence, the genre that inaugurated and established national identity through its choral, impersonal and totalizing poetry; and of the novel, instead, as the preeminent secondary form, a fragment longing for a lost totality. The opposition between narration and description recalls, in a way, the one between epic and novel.

Narrate or describe? expresses a clearly outdated vision of literature and an interpretation of the recent history of the novel. In choosing Flaubert as the initiator of a negative trend too focused on description and details, Lukács paradoxically anticipates a now widespread critical view, which sees in *Madame Bovary* the sharpest turning point in modern Western narrative, even sharper than the modernist experimentation at the beginning of the twentieth century. In his *Politics of Literature*, Jacques Rancière brilliantly defines Flaubert's style as "democratic", since it abolishes the hierarchy between noble and humble, narration and description, persons and things.[8] His writing is deeply characterized by a pervasive presence of details, objects, fetishes, and by a complex mixture of subjective and objective: anti-hierarchy does not imply, as a matter of fact, anarchy, and contains various gradations.

The concept of turning point implies that several significant trends depart from Flaubert's multifarious production. *Madame Bovary*'s proliferations of details prepares naturalistic descriptions; *Salammbô* and *La Tentation de saint Antoine* anticipate aestheticism and exoticism; the deconstruction of the *Bildungsroman* made in *L'Éducation sentimentale* preludes to the inept anti-heroes of the twentieth-century novel, and its fragmentation of identity. But it is especially his last and unfinished work, *Bouvard et Pécuchet,* which is also, as often happens, his most radical, that has found the greatest refraction in posterity. This nihilistic encyclopaedia reduces writing and narrating to an infinite catalogue, and is difficult to classify from the point of view of forms and genres. If Flaubert's novels, focussed on the search for a perfect idiosyncratic, individual style, never belong to a specific trend or literary movement, his last work challenges the very concept of literary genre, and of the novel itself.

We will deal now with another "impossible" text, basically based on the principle of the catalogue. Published in 1880 by Edmond de Goncourt, *La Maison d'un artiste* defies any clear genre classification. It is a room-by-room guided tour of a house which was conceived as a work of art. In one of the autobiographical passages, Goncourt declares that his ideal job would be as interior designer for a wealthy person, a job which, interestingly, did not exist at that time. From this point of view

---

1993 (revised version of *Introduction à l'analyse du descriptif,* 1981); and his anthology *La Description littéraire,* Paris: Macula, 1991; see also Pierluigi Pellini, *La descrizione,* Roma-Bari: Laterza, 1998.

[7] Lukács, *Narrate or Describe?*

[8] Jacques Rancière, *Politique de la littérature,* Paris: Galilée, 2006; *Politics of Literature,* trans. Julie Rose, Cambridge-Malden: Polity, 2011.

this text anticipates the British aesthetic movement and art nouveau, although the Goncourt brothers did not show a true consonance with contemporary art. Since the house was specially bought by the brothers to find an adequate place for their enormous collections of eighteenth-century prints and Japanese art, the text is chiefly a catalogue of individual works of arts, made of technical descriptions and stylistic introductions to the various personalities of the artists.

Together with the catalogue, which also has a practical function (after Goncourt's death it will serve for the auction that will finance the Academy and the famous prize), we find a first genre which is part of the hybridization at the core of this text, full of fictional, subjective, and critical material: art criticism.[9] *La Maison d'un artiste* is certainly a book on eighteenth-century engravings, on Oriental and Japanese art, on bookbindery, and on other similar issues. And at the same time, it is also a book of literary criticism, since the brother's huge collection of books is also catalogued, and produces several digressions. We can give two noteworthy examples: the passage in which Goncourt declares his passion for writers with an unregulated imagination and extravagant concepts, and quotes the preface of one of those "crazy" books, which has a very strange title, *Cataractes de l'Imagination, Déluge de la Scribomanie, Vomissement littéraire, Hémorragie encyclopédique, Monstre des Monstres* (1779); and the long passage devoted to Balzac and his poetics of money as an axis for the architecture of realism.

Finally, *La Maison d'un artiste* belongs to another prose genre, historiography, and to a particular methodological approach which was to become a significant trend in twentieth century, the so called micro-history, which works on traces, indexes, details. The Goncourt brothers, Edmond and Jules, published several works on eighteenth century based on this method; in our text Edmond catalogues and quotes many and various kinds of minor and short texts: proceedings of the Academy of Painting, playbills, illustrated pages and papers and especially short letters, "billets", which advertise musical shops or other activities, or announce a social event. Especially this last neglected genre, usually richly decorated with imagery, vividly evokes eighteenth-century everyday life, social relationships and artistic milieus.

If catalogue and criticism stay on the side of description, autobiography plays the (marginal) part of narration: it produces some fascinating and lyrical breaks in a prolix and sometimes almost unreadable book (like all catalogues, it is better to browse it). They are impressive moments, which come quite unexpectedly and unpredictably: the evocation of war and hunger, the remembrance of the intense and ferocious struggle with language and style together with his brother at the writing desk, a confession about his compulsive collecting and the narration of the origin of

---

[9] On the hybrid nature of *La Maison*, see Geneviève Sicotte, "La maison-texte de Goncourt", in *House / Text / Museum, Image & Narrative* 16, 2006; Juliet Simpson, "Edmond de Goncourt's décors—Towards the Symbolist maison d'art", *Romance Studies*, 29:1, January 2011, 1-18; Ead, "From Exquisite to Transgressive Moderns? The Goncourt's "Decadent" Eighteenth-Century Art Revival", *Nordlit* 28, 2011: 159-172, who describes a paradigm of "decadence" in a series of Goncourt's texts: "They become hybrid material and "fictional" elements in the creation of interior and internalizing aesthetic "décors" that code new subjective worlds and expanding fictions of them" (167).

this passion in his childhood, and finally the moving description of his brother's disease.

The autobiographical matrix of this work is clearly stated in the Preface, in which Goncourt expresses his strong preference for the "lovable" century, the eighteenth, and theorizes collecting as a substitution for the declining role of women in male thinking, and as consolation for the desolate and hard times. The first motivation about gender sounds quite strange, and certainly universalizes a personal feeling into a historical change: Edmond's scarce involvement in love relationships is well known, in opposition to Jules' remarkable erotic success and can have much to do with the homoerotic substrata of their relationship, which comes out from their letters and other evidence. Apart from the stereotype about the decline of the present age, the second motivation of collecting immediately evokes a crucial category: fetishism, especially in its Freudian version, focussed on symbolic substitution.[10] The Preface ends by highlighting the "almost human tenderness towards things" ("*la tendresse presque humaine pour les choses*"),[11] as an extremely new sentiment, produced by the visual education typical of the nineteenth century, which created a new phenomenon of mass collecting. In this single positive admission towards his own age, we feel the new dimension described by Marx as the fetishism of commodities, later developed by Benjamin through another crucial category, the sex appeal of the inorganic[12], and nowadays transformed into a massive cultural phenomenon, beyond the classical substitutive function of a lost object, "spectralized", as Slavoj Žižek has described it.[13] This new dimension, which culminates in the Universal Expositions, gave an extraordinary impulse to literary and artistic fetishism: to visual descriptions, details, representations of collecting, poetics of the object and so on; a trend that has Goethe, Flaubert, Huysmanns, Woolf, DeLillo and many other writers as most important figures, and uses manifold expressive strategies, such as synaesthesia, theatralization and animation of the inanimate.[14]

From this point of view, *La Maison d'un artiste* presents some interesting features and must be compared with another literary genre which is part of its

---

[10] Sigmund Freud, *Fetichismus* (1927), in *Gesammelte Werke,* 26, Frankfurt: Fischer, 1948; *Fetishism,* trans. James Strachey, in *The Complete Psychological Works of Sigmund Freud,* 21: 147-157, London: Hogarth, 1961. Freud argues that a fetish is a special form of phallus substitute, which arouses when the boy apprehends his mother's (and other women's) "lack" of a penis as the representation of his own possible castration. From this too limited and deterministic vision we can deduce, however, a more general pattern of interpretation, valuable for female fetishism as well.

[11] Edmond de Goncourt, *La Maison d'un artiste,* 2 vols., Paris: Charpentier, 1881; eds. Christine Galantaris and Dominique Pety, Dijon: Echelle de Jacob, 2003, 3.

[12] Walter Benjamin, *Das Passagen Werk,* edited by Rolf Tiedemann, Frankfurt am Main: Suhrkamp, 1982; trans. Howard Eiland, *The Arcades Project*, Cambridge (MA): Harvard University Press, 2002.

[13] Slavoj Žižek, *The Plague of Fantasies,* London: Verso 1997. On the "spectral turn" see Esther Peeren and María del Pilar Blanco (eds), *The Spectralities Reader: Ghosts and Haunting in Contemporary Cultural Theory*, New York: Bloomsbury, 2013. See also Emilie Apter and William Pietz, eds, *Fetishism and Cultural Discourse*, Ithaca and London: Cornell University Press, 1993.

[14] I analyze more broadly this trend in Massimo Fusillo, *Feticci. Letteratura, cinema, arti visive,* Bologna: Il Mulino, 2012; trans. Veronic Algeri and Angelo Pavia, *L'objet-fétiche. Littérature, cinéma, visualité*, Paris: Champion, 2014; trans. Thomas Simpson, *The Fetish: Literature, Cinema, Visual Art*, London: Bloomsbury, 2017.

hybridization: ekphrasis, the description of a work of art, or, more precisely, the "verbal representation of a visual representation".[15] This practice, which goes back to the *Iliad* and therefore is a characterizing topos of epic (from Virgil to Ariosto, from Tasso to Milton, in every poem of this genre) becomes then an autonomous minor genre in the Second Sophistic of the Imperial age: a rhetorical exercise which would develop into a success in later literatures, not only in the baroque period, fascinated by illusionism, but also in Romantic and fantastic literature, in modernist experimentation and finally in the postmodern era. The writers who described works of art often focussed on the archaic and magical power of image, as well as on the limits of representation, while in our age, too easily labelled as a civilization of the image, ekphrasis deals with multifarious new media, and with the moving images of performance and cinema (after all, since the Homerian ekphrasis has always sought dynamized description).

From a stylistic point of view, this corpus can be easily divided into two basic trends: on one hand a precise, detailed and analytic approach, which stays close to the verbal reproduction of the visual data; on the other hand, a free rewriting of the visual work, which is interwoven with narrative expansions, autobiographic insertions, essayistic reflections, and other hybrid forms. In *La Maison d'un artiste,* the first trend is certainly dominant, because it is basically a catalogue that aims at illustrating an impressive collection, conceived as a work of art produced by balanced editing. But we also find parts clearly belonging to the second, freer trend, which is the most literary and the most fetishistic one: lyrical evocation of Japanese landscapes, melancholic remembrances of the times and situations in which a piece was acquired, empathic portraits of historical figures. Generally speaking, Goncourt's style, sometimes purely objective and detached, is more frequently based on a complex synesthetic interaction between verbal music (several alliterations, for example), chromatic description (an impressive number of nuances), a theatrical dimension and emotional responses. The hybrid nature of this ekphrastic style was summarized by Paul Verlaine as a prose poem written by a painter, a definition which re-echoes Horace's motto *ut pictura poësis* ("as is painting, so is poetry").

La Maison d'un artiste does not thus belong to a single genre and cannot be classified in a univocal way, since it mixes art catalogue, criticism, historiography, autobiography, and ekphrasis. This sense of formal non-belonging is profoundly related to a thematic and biographical issue, which can be labelled with an etymologically and symbolically related term: longing. The house in Rue Montmercy, recently renovated and transformed into the *Maison des Artistes et de la Littérature* after a period of decay, was chosen in 1868 by the two brothers after a long search, in order to find the best location for their collections. Immediately after they moved in, when the furnishing was still unfinished, in 1869 Jules' nervous disease had its beginning, and after a terrible period of suffering (he could no longer speak nor recognize his brother), he died in 1870, at the age of 39. Their relationship was extremely close, not only because of their practice of writing in tandem. Even in

[15] James W.A. Heffernan, *Museum of Words: the Poetics of Ekphrasis from Homer to Ashbery*, Chicago: University of Chicago Press, 2004, 3.

social life they used to call themselves with a single common mixed name, "Julesmond", and to mutually finish their sentences in conversation. Therefore, *La Maison d'un artiste* is an act of longing: a working out of trauma through a huge collection of memorial objects, which is the most typical fetish, at the core of many modern novels, from Goethe's *The Elective Affinities* to Orhan Pamuk's *The Museum of Innocence.*

At the end of the long tour of the house, before the epilogue on the garden, Edmond de Goncourt evokes his brother's death in two intense and moving pages. Starting from his room as student, where Jules decided to die and where the surviving brother exercises "the painful pleasure of remembering" ("*la douloureuse jouissance de me ressouvenir*"),[16] the moving description of his brother's delirium culminates in a chromatic and vivid description of his facial expression which he compares to a work of art, to a mysterious inhuman figure in an obscure angle of a non-specified painting by Leonardo. The expression fades away in the final moment, substituted by "the desolate regret of the interrupted Work" ("*le désolé regret de l'Œuvre interrompu*"):[17] a sentence which condenses the longing for an intense and unique common creativity. The epilogue about the garden, a liminal space between interior and exterior, is a brilliant description of the different appearances of the different seasons, full of emotional undertones: the closure of the paragraph and the entire book introduces another kind of belonging and not-belonging: from the garden Edmond feels "a kind of pleasure in feeling myself so close and at the same time so distant from Paris" ("*j'éprouve comme une jouissance de me sentir, à la fois, si près et si loin de Paris*").[18] An ambivalent relationship with the centre of cultural life by the divided self of a lonely writer, saved by the house, as Emile Zola once declared.

Even in its very idiosyncratic nature, *La Maison d'un artiste* shows an interesting dissemination in the history of hybrid forms. Four years after its publication, in 1884 Joris-Karl Huysmans, who had appreciated Goncourt's style in describing Goldensmith's Oriental pieces, published the most canonical work of aestheticism: *À rebours* (*Against Nature*), also based on claustrophilia, collecting, fetishism, and ekphrasis, in a continuous hybridization with criticism which can be read, as Stefano Ercolino recently did, as the beginning of the novel-essay.[19] A quite close parallelism can be made with a book by an Italian scholar and critic, specialist of late Romanticism and aestheticism, Mario Praz. His *La casa della vita* (1979) shares with Goncourt the structure of a guided room-by-room tour, a similar mixture of descriptions, memories, and criticism, and finally a strong focus on collecting (in this case especially conversation pieces).[20] But *La Maison d'un artiste* evokes more generally experimental works at the border between narration and visuality: for example Perec's *La Vie: mode d'emploi,* equally focussed on the spatial structure of a

---

[16] Goncourt, *La Maison d'un artiste, 2.370.*

[17] *Ibid.,* 2.371.

[18] *Ibid.,* 2.382.

[19] Stefano Ercolino, *The Novel-Essay, 1884-1947,* New York: Palgrave Macmillan, 2014.

[20] Mario Praz, *La casa della vita* (1958), Milano: Adelphi, 1995; trans. Angus Davidson, *The House of Life,* Boston: David. R. Godine, 2010.

building, and on collecting as totalizing passion.[21] We can conclude with a last example coming from a contemporary novel, published in 2014, which belongs to a rich trend of contaminations between novel and art criticism, Enrique Vila-Matas' *Kassel no invita a la lógica.*[22] Invited by the famous and prominent exposition of contemporary art, *Documenta,* which takes place every five years in Kassel, to be a living work of art and to write every day in a Chinese restaurant, the author exploited the opportunity to create a unique mixture of travel diary, autobiography, and art description, which is in this case of course totally different from Goncourt's and extremely challenging from many points of view. Extremely difficult to classify from the point of view of genre, Vila-Matas' book confirms how description, catalogue and art criticism can subvert the classical form of narration, and can give expression to an unstable sense of form and genre: to a mix of belonging and not belonging.

BIBLIOGRAPHY

Apter, Emilie and Pietz, William, eds, *Fetishism and Cultural Discourse*, Ithaca and London: Cornell University Press, 1993.

Benjamin, Walter, *Das Passagen Werk,* ed. Rolf Tiedemann, Frankfurt a.M.: Suhrkamp, 1982; *The Arcades Project,* trans. Howard Eiland, Cambridge (MA): Harvard University Press, 2002.

Boileau, Nicolas, *Satires, épîtres, art poétique*, Paris: Gallimard, 1985

Ercolino, Stefano, *The Novel-Essay, 1884-1947,* New York: Palgrave Macmillan, 2014.

Freud, Sigmund, *Fetichismus* (1927), in *Gesammelte Werke,* 26, Frankfurt: Fischer, 1948; *Fetishism,* trans. James Strachey, in *The Complete Psychological Works of Sigmund Freud,* 21: 147-157, London: Hogarth, 1961

Fusillo, Massimo, *Feticci. Letteratura, cinema, arti visive,* Bologna, Il Mulino, 2012; trans. Veronic Algeri and Angelo Pavia, *L'objet-fétiche. Littérature, cinéma, visualité,* Paris: Champion, 2014; trans. Thomas Simpson, *The Fetish: Literature, Cinema, Visual Art*, London: Bloomsbury, 2017.

Goncourt, Edmond de, *La Maison d'un artiste,* 2 vol., Paris: Charpentier, 1881.

Hamon, Philippe, *Du descriptif,* Paris: Hachette, 1993 (revised version of *Introduction à l'analyse du descriptif,* 1981).

———, ed., *La Description littéraire,* Paris: Macula, 1991.

Heffernan, James W.A., *Museum of Words: the Poetics of Ekphrasis from Homer to Ashbery*, Chicago: University of Chicago Press, 2004.

Lessing, Gotthold Ephraim, *Laocoön: An Essay on the Limits of Painting and Poetry*, trans. Edward Allen McCormick, Baltimore: Johns Hopkins University Press, 1984.

Lukács, Georg, *The Theory of the Novel. A Historico-Philosophical Essay on the Form of Great Epic Literature,* trans. Anna Bostock, MIT Press: Cambridge (MA) 1971.

———, *Erzählen oder beschreiben?* (1936), in *Werke* 4, *Probleme des Realismus* 1, Neuwied-Berlin: Luchterhand,1971, 197-243; trans. Arthur Kahn, in G.L., *Writer and Critic and Other Essays,* London: Merlin, 1970, 110-148.

Marmontel, Jean-François, *Description*", in *Encyclopedie méthodique*, Paris: Pamcoucke, 1782, vol. 1.

Pellini, Pierluigi, *La descrizione,* Roma-Bari: Laterza, 1998.

---

[21] Georges Perec, *La Vie, mode d'emploi,* Paris: Hachette, 1978; trans. David Bellos, *Life: A User's Manual,* Boston: David. R. Godine, 1988.

[22] Enrique Vila-Matas, *Kassel no invita a la lógica,* Barcelona: Seix Barral, 2014; trans. Anne MacLean and Anne Malsom, *The Illogic of Kassel,* New York: New Directions, 2015.

Perec, George, *La Vie, mode d'emploi,* Paris: Hachette, 1978; trans. David Bellos, *Life: A User's Manual,* Boston: David. R. Godine, 1988.

Praz, Mario, *La casa della vita* (1958), Milano: Adelphi, 1995; trans. Angus Davidson, *The House of Life,* Boston: David. R. Godine, 2010.

Rancière, Jacques, *Politique de la littérature,* Paris: Galilée, 2007; trans. Julie Rose, *The Politics of Literature,* Cambridge: Polity, 2011.

Sicotte, Geneviève, "La maison-texte de Goncourt", in *House / Text / Museum, Image & Narrative* 16, 2006.

Simpson, Juliet, "Edmond de Goncourt's décors—Towards the Symbolist maison d'art", *Romance Studies*, 29:1, January 2011, 1-18.

———, "From Exquisite to Transgressive Moderns? The Goncourt's "Decadent" Eighteenth-Century Art Revival", *Nordlit* 28, 2011: 159-172.

Stalnaker, Johanna, *The Unfinished Enlightment. Description in the Age of the Encyclopedia*, Ithaca: Cornell University Press, 2010.

Valery, Paul, *Autour de Corot* (1932), in *Œuvres,* Paris: Gallimard, 1960, t. 2, 1323-1324.

Vila-Matas, Enrique, *Kassel no invita a la lógica,* Barcelona: Seix Barral, 2014; trans. Anne MacLean and Anne Malsom, *The Illogic of Kassel,* New York: New Directions, 2015.

Žižek, Slavoj, *The Plague of Fantasies,* Verso: London, 1997.

CHAPTER 11

Voilà mon cœur: It's Been To Hell and Back! José Leonilson's and Louise Bourgeois's Poetic Images on Longing and Belonging

Ana Lúcia Beck

> In the resonance we hear the poem, in the reverberations we speak it, it is our own.[1]

> People ask me—what do
> you mean—and I answer
> what do you think of when
> you see the image.[2]

POETIC IMAGES

This essay investigates José Leonilson Bezerra Dias' (Brazil, 1957–1993)[3] and Louise Bourgeois' (France/USA, 1911–2010) creative processes regarding the poetic images used in the expression of longing and belonging in their œuvres. This discussion presupposes that both poems and visual pieces elaborate poetic images, following Paul Valéry's style: on the one hand, deliberate and intent on the production of one's work; on the other, merging personal, obscure reminiscences and all human faculties.[4] Furthermore, in poetry as in visual arts, the meaning is strongly related to what Bachelard would call the value of poetic images—which will be investigated later. Furthermore, in Bachelard's thought, as reflected in the opening quote, the elaboration of meaning operates through resonance, which can be understood as an approximation between the poem's images and those of the reader. It is in this sense that the creative processes of poetry and visual arts may be considered similar, notably in relation to the elaboration of poetic images and their meanings as originating from interpretative efforts on verbal and visual languages. If such an assumption is correct, it would be possible, as proposed through this essay's methodology, to investigate poetic images of longing and belonging by working on a correlation between visual and poetic pieces. Thus, the discussion on Leonilson's and Bourgeois's poetic images on longing and belonging will be developed in comparison with those elaborated in the poem

---

[1] Gaston Bachelard, *Poetics of Space*, Boston: Beacon Press, 1994.
[2] Louise Bourgeois, *Louise Bourgeois Archive*, New York, LB-0021, undated loose sheet, circa 1989, apud Kulf Ulster, *Louise Bourgeois*, Ostfildern: Hatje Kantz Verlag, Kindle Edition, 138.
[3] a.k.a. Leonilson.
[4] See Ion Gheorghe, *Les Images du poète et de la poésie dans l'œuvre de Valéry*, Paris: Minard, 1977, 105.

"Towards the break of day" by W.B. Yeats (Ireland/France 1865–1939). If poetry and the visual arts are similar human efforts on language and subjectivity as a means to elaborate on our being in the world, a comparison between poetic and visual pieces may illuminate our understanding of similarities between creations expressing longing and belonging.

Given the subjective dimension present in many poetic and art productions, as is the case with Leonilson and Bourgeois, the necessity identified by Bachelard that the viewer/reader witness the developing realization of poetic images and be aware of their singularities seems justified, as it underlines the role of subjectivity in the constitution of poetic images. As Bachelard states:

> In order to clarify the problem of the poetic image philosophically, we shall have to have recourse to a phenomenology of the imagination. By this should be understood a study of the phenomenon of the poetic image when it emerges into the consciousness as a direct product of the heart, soul and being of man, apprehended in his actuality.[5]

Bachelard's account on poetic images accurately reflects the elements of longing and belonging in both Leonilson's and Bourgeois's œuvres. Their poetic images share some characteristics, but these do not pertain solely to visual art and can also be observed in poetry, as in Yeats' "Towards the break of day". This poem in fact seems to echo Leonilson's and Bourgeois's productions so much so that it enables us to envision their significances:

> Was it the double of my dream
> The woman that by me lay
> dreamed, or did we halve a dream
> Under the first cold gleam of day?
>
> I thought: 'There is a waterfall
> Upon Ben Bulben side
> That all my childhood counted dear;
> Where I do travel far and wide
> I could not find a thing so dear.'
> My memories had magnified
> So many times childish delight.
>
> I would have touched it like a child
> But knew my finger could but have touched
> Cold stone and water. I grew wild,
> Even accusing heaven because
> It had set down among its laws:
> Nothing that we love over-much

---

[5] Bachelard, *Poetics of Space*, xviii.

Is ponderable to our touch.

I dreamed towards break of day,
The cold blown spray in my nostril.
But she that beside me lay
Had watched in bitterer sleep
The marvellous stag of Arthur,
That lofty white stag, leap
from mountain steep to steep.[6]

On the verging line separating night from day, a man whose desire is not named as such expresses longing through multiple contrasting images. Tensioning childhood and manhood, past and present, dream and reality, Yeats' subject wonders about the desire to retain things precious to him. In the poem, the emotional dimension is marked by memories whose value is revealed by a child's perception, thus reinforcing the bond between recollections of events and the significant places where these occurred. "Towards the break of day" expands the sense of both longing and belonging on two fundamental grounds: the poetic space as derived from primordial perceptions of certain places, and the closely overlapping correlation between the perception of a place and the perception of another body.

A fond image of the mountain unfolds in the third stanza where it is suggested that the perception, the reality even of such a place in its materiality, cannot be retained. Hence, something apart from its substantiality is responsible for the greatness of the place. However, the relation addressed in the first stanza between the self and the other is also suggested as fundamental for such emotional grounding. Accordingly, the child's memories and the experience of the grown lover intertwine in the perception of the relation between humans and their natural environment: body and stone, flesh and waterfall, longing and belonging, all correlate in their significance.[7]

When analyzing Yeats' poetry, Webb considers the poet established a poetic gesture enabling him to deal with certain aspects of his own feelings and personality through the characterization of specific voices and characters within the poems.[8] Thus, the poet's subjectivity left traces in the poetic production. Webb's analysis opens a perspective on Yeats' poetry which, taking into account "Towards the break of day", is significant in terms of resonance with Leonilson's and Bourgeois images of longing and belonging due to the fact that those artists' productions also strongly incorporate a subjective dimension. Sharing some further aspects, like the use of

---

[6] W.B. Yeats, "Towards the break of day", *Collected Poems*, London: Macmillan London Limited, 1984, 208.

[7] When analyzing Yeats' last poems, Aleksandra Jasínska identifies, metaphors about poetry itself which are also elaborated on the connection between a "place" and emotions. As she states: "They [Yeats' metaphors on his notion of poetry] tell us that it is contact with the soil, lust fear, and rage that become the source of poetry." Jasínska, Aleksandra. The Metaphors of poetry in Yeats last Poems. *Studia Anglica Posnaniensia*, v 25-27, Poznan: Adam Mickiewicz University, 1991-1993, 282.

[8] Timothy Webb, "Introduction", Timothy Webb (ed), *W.B. Yeats Selected Poems,* London: Penguin Books, 2000, 10-30.

verbal information within the visual, or the elaboration of textile pieces, Bourgeois and Leonilson claimed that their relationships were especially relevant regarding their subjectivities' presence within works, which is why a comparative approach of their œuvre is pertinent to the understanding of their creative process, as well as to any debate around longing and belonging in their fundamental human dimension.[9]

JOSÉ LEONILSON AND LOUISE BOURGEOIS

Born in France in a family dedicated to tapestries production and repair, Louise Bourgeois became an important reference for any discussion regarding the relation between art and the self, despite having been recognized quite late in life.[10] Nowadays, the significance of Bourgeois's work is fully acknowledged and much attention is paid to the strong psychological dimension attached to her emotional life, her childhood especially.[11] In her words: "My childhood has never lost its magic, it has never lost its mystery, and it has never lost its drama."[12]

Bourgeois claimed that much of her creative process was driven by a wish to recreate strong and deep emotional states salvaged from her original family circle. She underwent psychoanalysis therapy in a process she saw as a journey to hell,[13] which may partly explain the emotive crudity of some of her works: "My subject is the rawness of the emotions, the devastating effect of the emotions you go through."[14] In such regard, "With analysis, the suppressed feelings experienced in her childhood emerged. Bourgeois regarded these feelings as driving forces behind her art and her need to express herself."[15]

José Leonilson was one of the most important names of *Geração 80* (*80s Generation*), a significant moment in the Brazilian visual arts scene history. The name given to this generation, derived from the exhibition *Como vai você, Geração 80*? (*How are you doing, 80s Generation?*), was significant for marking new perspectives in Brazilian art inspired by a return to an earlier tradition of painting, and contrasting with preceding decades of strong conceptual productions. Within that generation, Leonilson's work in fact became a solitary endeavour for he was the first artist to overtly incorporate personal intimacy and emotional history in his creative output, developing a body of work which soon gained public and commercial recognition.[16]

---

9 See Ana Lúcia Beck; Maria Luiza B. da Silva, "Bleeding words", *Primerjalna književnost* (Comparative Literature), 39.1, Ljubljana: June 2016, 145.

10 Her first major retrospective happened at MoMA in 1982.

11 Such perspective is pivotal in Larratt-Smith's curatorial project *Louise Bourgeois: The Return of the Repressed*, and it is acknowledged in Mignon Nixon's and Juliet Mitchell's essays. See Philip Larratt-Smith, *Louise Bourgeois: o retorno do desejo proibido*, São Paulo: Instituto Tomie Ohtake, 2011.

12 Louise Bourgeois; Marie-Laure Bernadac; Hans Ulrich Obrist, *Louise Bourgeois, destruction of the father, reconstruction of the father*, Cambridge: MIT Press, 1998, 277.

13 Iris Müller-Westermann (ed), *Louise Bourgeois: I have been to Hell and back*, Ostfildern: Hatje Cantz, 2014, 57.

14 "Louise Bourgeois in conversation with Christiane Meyer-Thoss", Müller-Westermann (ed) *Louise Bourgeois*, 242.

15 *Ibid.*, 57.

16 See Adriano Pedrosa, *Leonilson Truth-Fiction*, São Paulo: Pinacoteca do Estado/Cobogo Editora, 2014.

Leonilson considered that his pieces, despite being very personal and speaking about his emotions, would be significant for many people who would establish a relation between their own issues and feelings and his,[17] an idea that can be related to Bachelard's notion of poetic resonance.

Leonilson and Bourgeois œuvres are rich in media and themes which defy categorization. Amongst these, one finds a significant number of textile pieces, elaborated especially from the 1990s on which are especially relevant in terms of the relation with their familial history. These artists' textile productions mark more clearly the relation between the works and childhood as implicated in the development of poetic images, one of Bachelard's most significant considerations regarding their constitution.

Leonilson, despite referring at times to his interest in fashion and his friendship with Marie Rucki,[18] indicated his family as fundamental for the choice of working with fabrics, sewing and embroidery. Son of a textile shop owner, Leonilson grew up in a house where a sewing room was constantly being used and the Northeast Brazilian tradition of embroidery was kept.[19] He was educated in a school run by nuns where he also practiced embroidery.[20] Bourgeois, on the other hand, was very close to the family business which revolved around preparing wool and mending tapestries, activities run by her mother whom she observed closely. She participated actively in the family business from the age of twelve years by executing drawings for the foot of the tapestries.[21]

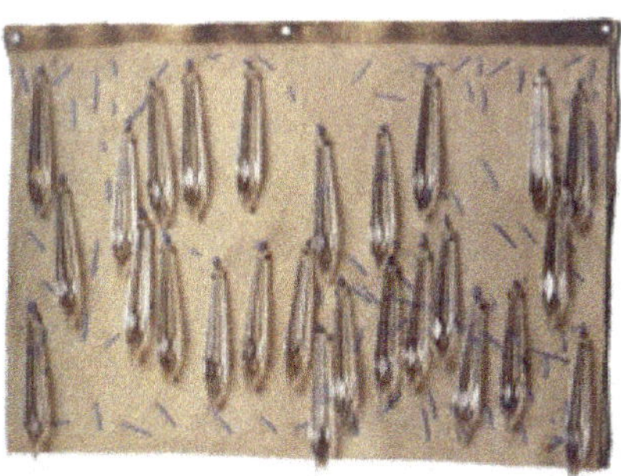

Leonilson, *Voilà mon cœur* (Here is my heart), 1990[22]

---

[17] *Ibid.*, 235.

[18] See Lisette Lagnado, *Leonilson: São Tantas as Verdades/So Many are the Truths*, São Paulo: DBA Melhoramentos/Fiesp, 1998, 132. Marie Rucki was, for many years, the director of Studio Berçot in Paris, a fundamental reference in fashion apprenticeship during the 80s.

[19] The Bezerra Dias family moved from Fortaleza in Ceará state, where Leonilson was Born in 1957, to São Paulo in southern Brazil in 1961.

[20] Lagnado, *Leonilson: São Tantas as Verdades*, 32-90.

[21] Kulf Ulster, *Louise Bourgeois*, Ostfildern: Hatje Kantz Verlag, Kindle Edition, 450.

[22] All reproductions of Leonilson's work are presented courtesy of the Projeto Leonilson foundation. For Louise Bourgeois, © The Easton Foundation/Licensed by VAGA, New York, NY.

CRITICAL SUBJECTIVITY

Whereas Bourgeois's work was recognized during her lifetime and generated a significant critique, a critique of Leonilson's œuvre is still developing. In recent years, two major retrospectives[24] were dedicated to his production bringing to light the necessity to revise fundamental aspects regarding the bond between life and work. Since the first publishing projects dedicated to his production,[25] the idea of it being an emotional diary has been pivotal.[26]

As much as Bourgeois, in interviews and writings, reinforced her art as an act of salvaging the past, Leonilson's public image as a creator was based on the idea of someone who gave his heart out to public view. One of the most emblematic works taken quite literally in such an account is *Voilà mon cœur* (see illustration above), a small felt and canvas piece embroidered with crystal pendants on the reverse of which the statement "Voilà mon coeur, il vous apartien [sic]" ("Here is my heart; it belongs to you") is handwritten, followed by "ouro de artista é amar bastante" ("the artist's gold is to love a lot"),[27] which suggests Leonilson's work is an amorous gift.

Verbal texts, sentences and words are present as both verbal and visual elements in many of Leonilson's pieces. The artist made use of expressions in a number of languages, although generally in Portuguese and English. Verbal elements, like loose words and short expressions, are presented in his pieces usually in readable form, their presence being stressed often enough by the materiality of the embroidered words, or even by their nearly solitary presence within the compositions. However, longer sentences, short poetic expressions and very short poems may also appear, usually in readable form too. In other pieces, resembling palimpsests at times, traces of words and sentences are left behind on the paint or entangled with the drawings' lines, impeding the viewers' ability to read them. *Voilà mon cœur* is especially intriguing as the verbal expressions are not immediately visible, being placed on the back of the canvas, as if the artist felt that his intimate view about creative production ought not to be too plain to see. For contemporary viewers, this information is not accessible, for its current framing does not allow the words to be read. Furthermore, one may suspect that the making of *Voilà mon cœur* is strongly connected with a piece he saw at the Saatchi Gallery in 1990, a piece Leonilson mentions as *The Right Place for the Heart*, possibly by Richard Deacon, in a documentary film by Karen Harley.[28] This is significant as Leonilson wonders how an artist can display his heart for public viewing. However, the same remark, disconnected from the observation about the piece seen at Saatchi, is presented in the first minutes of José Nader's

---

[24] *Sob o peso dos meus amores* (*Under my Love's Weight*) curated by Bitu Cassunde and Ricardo Resende, was presented at *Itaú Cultural* (São Paulo) in 2011 and at *Museu Iberê Camargo* (Porto Alegre) in 2012. *Truth-Fiction*, curated by Adriano Pedrosa, was exhibited at *Pinacoteca do Estado de São Paulo* in 2014 and at *Centro Cultural Banco do Brasil* (Belo Horizonte) in 2015.

[25] Lagnado, *Leonilson: São Tantas as Verdades/So Many are the Truths*.

[26] Years after the release of *Leonilson: São Tantas as Verdades/So Many are the Truths*, Lagnado herself criticized such "docile and tender" or "romantic" perspective stressing that such views on the artist depoliticized the work executed by someone who, in his life, was corrosive and caustic. I refer specifically to the debate *Arquivo e Memória o Legado do Artista* (*Archives and Memories the Artist's Legacy*).

[27] Lagnado, São Tantas as Verdades/So Many are the Truths, 18.

[28] Karen Harley (screenplay, direction and cut), *Leonilson—Com o Oceano inteiro para nadar* (*With the entire Ocean to Swim*), documentary film, 19 min, colored, Brazil: MPC & Associados, 1997: 07.

documentary film, [29] suggesting that this comment was about Leonilson's own production considered in relation to the Brazilian political scene of the time.

Such disconnection did not acknowledge the fact that displaying works related to his own emotional life for public viewing demanded a lot of courage, the courage to face one's sorrows as much as the artistic courage to work these into poetic images. A courage rather similar to that of Bourgeois going to hell and back, or "the courage with which she could open up herself. And the frankness and precision with which she bares her psychological abysses". [30] In Leonilson's case, an affectionate perspective stressed on the dedication of the pieces to loved ones must be taken into account as not necessarily self-evident, but rather as a poetic endeavour taken as a means to accentuate the subjective nature of art as he understood it. At the same time, it represents a meaningful personal experience, an approach similar to Bourgeois's, who went through psychoanalysis before she could become an important artist.[31]

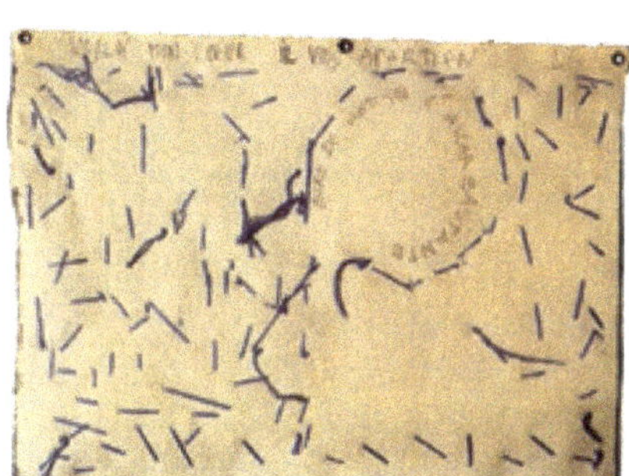
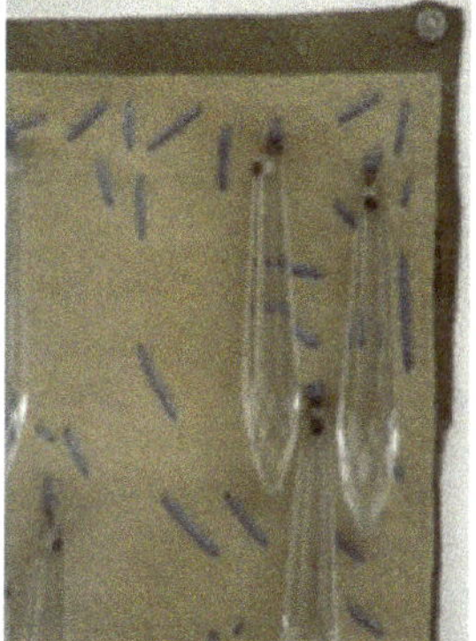

Leonilson, *Voilà mon cœur*, reverse and detail photographed by the author

Yet, neither Leonilson's nor Bourgeois's productions can be reduced to self-centered testimonies.[32] When examining a poet's life and work, Bachelard considers that even though an author like Edgar Allan Poe might have suffered from auditory hallucinations, which might have been the reason for him to write *The Fall of the House of Usher*, his suffering ran against his creative process. In other words, in regard to the relation between a psychological explanation and the poetic images elaborated by the poet "facts do not explain values" for "in works of the poetic imagination, values bear the mark of such novelty that everything related to the past, is lifeless beside them. All memory has to be reimagined."[33]

In Leonilson and Bourgeois, such values demonstrate how the artists had to necessarily surpass their feelings to produce objects that do not simply depict their emotions but are creatively responsive to them. Bourgeois's pieces do not merely

---

[29] José Nader (screenplay and direction), *A paixão de J.L.*, documentary film, 82 min, colored, Brazil: Estudio Já Filmes, 2014.

[30] Ulster, *Louise Bourgeois*, 80.

[31] Juliet Mitchell, "O ciúme sublime de Louise Bourgeois", in Larratt-Smith, *Louise Bourgeois*, 49.

[32] Louise Bourgeois considers that her memories, the ones that "came to her" and were the "seeds" of her creative process (what Ulster calls "the nucleus of something that becomes a work of art"), were "documents". See Ulster, *Louise Bourgeois*, 365-375.

[33] Bachelard, *The Poetics of Space*, 175.

represent past traumatic emotions; they also imaginatively elaborate on their significance, so as not to dwell on them. Bourgeois highlights such active positioning when considering that "Many works begin with a passive role. To be in a passive role is to inhabit chaos. The chaos has to be dealt with and put into order."[34]

Both Leonilson and Bourgeois, therefore, overcame their own sorrows by making fundamental and resolute poetic choices which define their particular styles. In that regard, the notions of longing and belonging help us underline the detachment that was part of their approach, enabling them, while they drew on their personal experiences, to remain sufficiently aloof from their selves in order to perform their creative ideals.

In this sense, if Bourgeois reclaimed past emotions through psychoanalysis to create from them, she also distanced herself from the childhood circumstances that elucidate her perception of the past, confirming what Yeats' poem presented as a non-retainable experience. If an artist addresses emotional experiences, such as those associated with love or pain, the result must be understood as a poetic response expressing a delayed articulation of feelings. It also outlines the gap, one the one hand, between the moment the experience took place and the time one figures it out, and on the other, between the moment the experience took place and the time one responds to it, a distinction astutely highlighted by Bernhard Waldenfels.[35]

Leonilson believed that his work was ignored by Brazilian art critics, which deepened his sense of uneasiness and solitude. During interviews he gave in 1991, he expresses resentment at this lack of recognition and interest[36]—which is revealing concerning his eagerness to grasp his own creation from a less personal perspective, and discussing it from a more theoretical point of view. Viewing his own work as something distinct from previous Brazilian conceptual productions, Leonilson considers that his generation had to "kill the father of conceptual art,"[37] and indicates Bourgeois,[38] amongst others, as a reference in his formulation of his production's specificity.

The fact that Leonilson designates Bourgeois stresses that he recognizes in her work a similar emphasis on the subject's presence within art. In his case, it is a presence claimed through the loose, non-technical stitching in *Voilà mon cœur*, bringing canvas and felt together whilst spreading small blue marks on its reverse, marks as beautiful as the hanging crystal pendants and as indistinct as them in reference to the hand whose gestures created the piece.

Bourgeois also acknowledges such a presence by underlying emotional contents, reinforcing them by incorporating psychoanalytic terminology in her writings,

---

[34] "Louise Bourgeois in conversation with Christiane Meyer-Thoss", Müller-Westermann (ed) *Louise Bourgeois*, 248. For a more extensive approach on the relation between emotional chaos and Bourgeois's creative process as bringing chaos back to order, see Beck and Berwanger, "Bleeding words", *Primerjalna književnost* (Comparative Literature), 39.1, Ljubljana: June 2016, 141-162.

[35] Bernhard Waldenfels, "Responsive Love", *Primerjalna književnost* (Comparative Literature), 39.1, Ljubljana: June 2016, 15-29.

[36] Pedrosa, *Leonilson Truth-Fiction*, 231-234.

[37] Ana Maria Magalhães; Charles Peixoto (screenplay/direction), *Sprayjet*, short movie, 14 min, colored, Brazil: Embrafilme, 1985, 7.

[38] Lagnado, *Leonilson: são tantas as Verdades*, 110-112.

although questioning and subverting them by confronting her own emotional history, sustaining therefore a critical engagement towards subjectivity.[39]

In this sense, it could prove more adequate to consider the relation between the verbal commentaries in Leonilson's and Bourgeois' pieces as resonating with, rather than explain, the visual elements or even the art piece in its entirety.

NOBODY AND *FEMME MAISON*

More recent critical approaches to Leonilson's production (such as Nader's and Pedrosa's) stress distinct perspectives on his production. Whereas Nader emphasizes Leonilson's search for someone to have a relationship with and the dilemmas he faced once he was diagnosed with AIDS, Pedrosa indicates Leonilson's production as tensioned between life and work, or between "truth" and "fiction".[40] Such a critical take is nowhere more evident than in the close proximity between *Ninguém* (*Nobody*) and *Para meu Vizinho de Sonhos* (*To my Dream Neighbour*), works which emphasize the tension between verbal expressions and the visuality of the pieces:

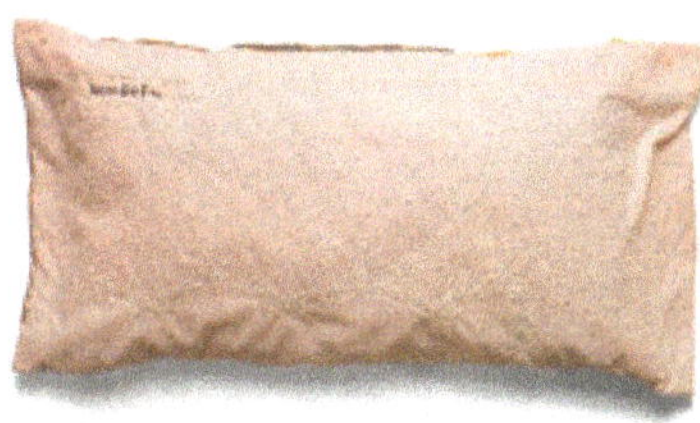

Leonilson, *Niguém*, 1992

Para Meu Vizinho de Sonhos, 1991

[39] Tania Rivera, *O Avesso do* Imaginário, São Paulo: Cosac & Naify, 2013, 276.

[40] After a drawing on paper executed by Leonilson in Amsterdam in 1990 where a sole, small human figure stands amidst the whiteness of the paper accompanied by the words "truth" and "fiction" on either side.

These pieces elaborate the concept of longing by evoking both the desire to "have someone" and the desire to retain sweet memories of love encounters. Longing is conceived as a taut poetic image, which recalls the spectrum considered by Yeats, ranging from images related to the past to those associated with the present. Furthermore, the relation between images and words in these pieces insists on the feeling of longing for something already gone, and also for the non-achieved, contrasting these with the perception of the other in the present, a contrast that somehow suggests an overlay of past and present in the elaboration of poetic images.

Ninguém and *Para meu Vizinho de Sonhos* are made on textile being considered as a live, changeable, malleable element elaborated through actions traditionally acknowledged as feminine like sewing, although presented as an actual object more than a support, like in traditional framed canvases. This poetic choice brings these pieces close to sculpture. In dealing with fabrics and garments, Leonilson presents stitching and embroidery as closely related to ideas of loving and caring. However, in Leonilson's poetics, such procedures are not executed having excellence as a goal. On the contrary, the loose and very apparent stitching and the tortuous embroideries, the very simple gathering of distinct cuts of fabric, not only evoke Bourgeois's textile pieces, but in general the hand behind them and the time implicit in them, thus reinforcing our sense of the artist's devotion.

Leonilson's needle work was done mostly by hand, whereas many of Bourgeois's pieces were executed using a sewing machine, increasingly not even by herself in her advancing years. Nevertheless, especially in pieces depicting human figures and heads, the sewing and patchwork compositions reveal the hand-made parts. These creative choices in Bourgeois' and Leonilson's productions, although implicitly retrieving an emotional dimension marked by the association with childhood, constitute a poetic gesture which reveals itself in the materiality of their presence, never concealed within the fabrics. The creative process must be therefore understood as this ability to work on the verging line which separates longing as desire towards what is not there and the materiality of what is real, that is, the material and the time implicated in the realization of the task, what belongs to the final piece of art. As we will see later, these imbrications can be linked to the significant theme of textiles in mythology and in particular to the figure of Penelope.

Loving, caring, and sewing, generally perceived as feminine attributes, represent the basis for a fundamental development in Bourgeois's poetics. The artist indeed acknowledges sewing's emotional dimension as defying a "mother principle",[41] and uses her own mother as a model.[42] Many of her sculptures and drawings are titled either *Maman* (Mother) or "spider", their association reinforcing their complementary qualities in terms of dedication, caring, and persistence, as related to thread and needle work, and to the mother-daughter relationship—and therefore forming an irreversible symbol of womanhood. In many of Bourgeois's works, the representation of spiders accentuates the relation between their perpetual net-weaving task with Bourgeois's own mother's emotional mending support for the family. The spider, as

---

[41] Ulster, *Louise Bourgeois*, 246.
[42] Müller-Westermann, *Louise Bourgeois,* 240.

related to notions of repair and renewal[43] in Bourgeois's production, is thus associated to feminine tasks and obligations:

> Having to regularly patch holes, in a figurative sense as well, is a woman's fate, according to Louise Bourgeois. The textiles that must be repaired again and again symbolize the burdens which women in particular have to bear and counterbalance.[44]

If Bourgeois's compositions sometimes involve scissors, suggesting a desire to cut off emotional dependency, her work mostly involves coalescing gestures like sewing, mending and weaving, gestures central to her creative process which she acknowledges is a means of resolving personal suffering, transmitting and expelling emotions into her artistic materials. Pieces like *Conscious, Unconscious* (2008),[45] for example, associate needle work and woven objects to the effort of bringing to consciousness heretofore unconscious emotional dilemmas.

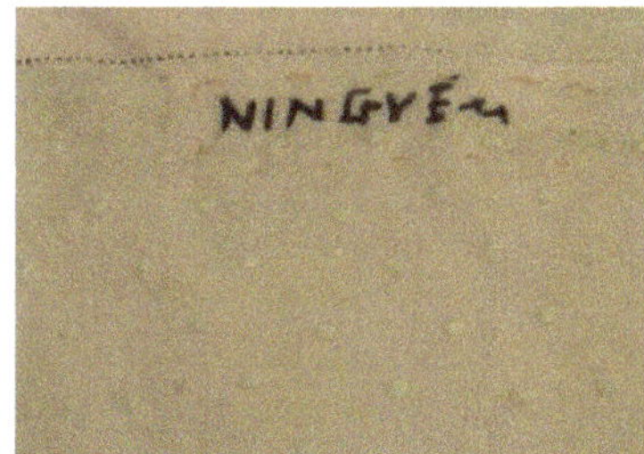
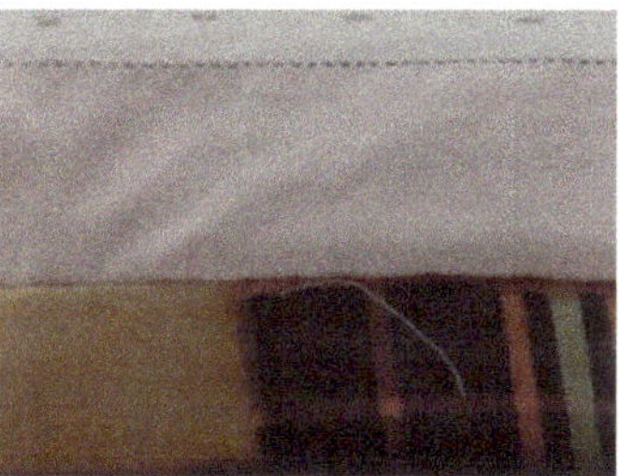

Leonilson, *Niguém*. Detail showing the embroidered word and the sewing between front and back in the pillow photographed by the author.

At a glance, *Ninguém* (*Nobody*) could be viewed as quite literally speaking of loneliness and longing, a sense reinforced by the presence of a solitary word embroidered with a dark thread, which contrasts with the light pink soft fabric. The black letters seem to mark the absence of another being, a sign of the persistence of desire. However, as a visual mark on the fabric, the black lettering seems to discreetly merge into its small embroidered pattern, as if suggesting another poetic value for loneliness. The elaboration of the entire piece, with no matching fabrics in the front and back, seems to respond to a primary sense of solitude, while also acknowledging the realization of the absence of embodied desire. Leonilson subverts this void by giving shape to two distinct absences, the absence of a loved one and the absence of his embodied desire.

---

[43] *Ibid.*

[44] Ulster, *Louise Bourgeois*, 254.

[45] Larratt-Smith, *Louise Bourgeois: o retorno do desejo proibido*, 271. See http://www.hauserwirth.com/exhibitions/743/louise-bourgeois-the-fabric-works/list-of-works/1/ [accessed 19/01/2018].

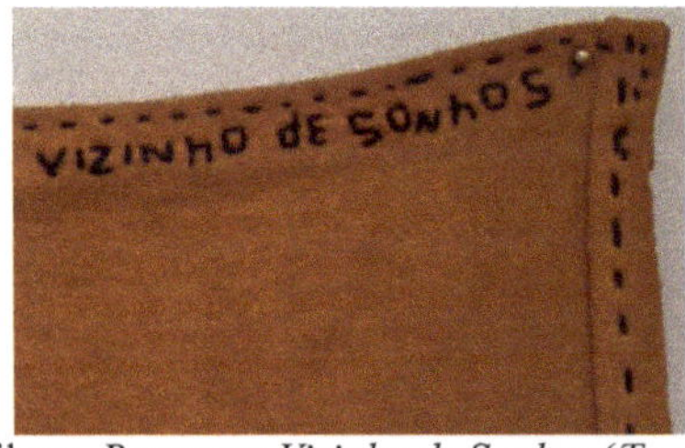

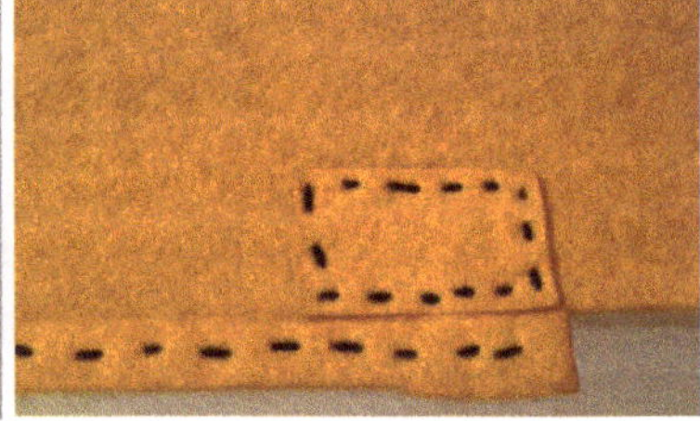

Leonilson, *Para meu Vizinho de Sonhos* (*To my Dream Neighbour*), detail showing the right upper corner and a side stitched square at the left margin, photographed by the author.

Leonilson's elaboration of this small textile is an effective, and affective, act towards the reality of the outer world creating softness and care for someone who is not there. Undoubtedly, loneliness is being addressed in this piece not only by the literal use of the word "nobody", but suggestively too, as a cherished feeling toward a bedfellow, a partner, now only present in one's dreams.

Ninguém faces the viewer with opposing feelings related to desire and sorrow, but also with apparently conflicting ideas of frustration and realization. The sweet longing for companionship and the bitter-sweet taste of solitude are handed to the viewer's gaze and touch at the same time. It seems that Leonilson creates some kind of emotional space, a space enhanced by the proximity of the embroidered words "for my dream neighbor" that may be dedicated to somebody who might have once occupied that space, and whose presence felt like home. This possibility is evoked in the simple creation of an embroidered frame in contrasting black thread, with small dislocated stitched cut offs accentuating the sense of a missing body. The disparate feelings and emotions in the parts composing Leonilson's piece are expressively joined together via cutting and sewing. By doing so, the artist transgresses the absence he feels as a marked longing, to find its exact opposite: the artistic realization that brings him a sense of belonging. In other words, the artist incorporates absence and loneliness in poetic images that produce an embodied presence.

Thus, if solitude may be considered a theme in Leonilson's aesthetics, his poetic images subvert its initial negative, emotional connotation. Regarding the creation of poetic images, Bachelard considers that aloneness experienced in relation to significant places establishes a "centre of solitude", enhancing future lingering "memories" associated to such places. This means that from their very germination, poetic images derive from an associative reflex that brings together feelings and places. In Leonilson's work, significant places are precisely attached to emotional states the artist dives into, in a poetic effort that enables him to subvert such feelings by exploring their less obvious connotations. For loneliness is a rather secluded space much like a forgotten corner in a house or yard, as Bachelard remarks:

> [E]very corner in a house, every angle in a room, every inch of secluded space in which we like to hide, or withdraw into ourselves, is a symbol of

> solitude for the imagination; that is to say, it is the germ of a room, or of a house.[46]

As one would a secluded space, Leonilson's loneliness fences a subjective territory. Many of Bourgeois's pieces carry the mark of similar experiences of isolated spaces as fundamental to the elaboration of poetic images. Thus, the house the artist lived in as a child and its location are visually present in her production, although sometimes figuratively. Bourgeois has created a very large number of drawings and sculptures where two- or three-story buildings, full of windows, with a front door, are represented. Even the choice to work on textile figures from the 80s on was, according to the artist herself, a way to salvage her parents' home whose indoor space was covered in tapestries, hanging on walls, placed on tables or on the floor.[47]

Choisy,[48] the neighborhood where her parents' house was situated, is also evoked in many pieces' titles, and in words and sentences found in pieces like *Ode à la Bièvre* (2002),[49] a 24-page fabric book with different abstract compositions in a variety of forms and colors, organizing time and space through different arrangements, sewn in such a way as to link longing for one's lost childhood to the very process of sewing. Similarly, one notes that the first page of *Ode à la Bièvre* details the presence of the Bièvre river near Bourgeois's family house and describes the variety of plants in its garden. The river is also acknowledged in interviews for its importance regarding the treatment of tapestries fibers.[50]

As a significant place related to the constitution of poetic images of longing and belonging, Bourgeois' childhood home brings us back to the themes of mother and spider: for instance, a giant spider stretching her legs from wall to wall,[51] contrasting with a textile house-woman figure.[52] Bourgeois' images connect here again different and positive poetic images of the weaver, and also nostalgic memories of home, as the bored child chose spider-inhabited corners to cope with her lonesomeness. As Bachelard reminds us, a house becomes memorable by being both a place of living and a place for dreaming:

> The house we were born in is more than an embodiment of home, it is also an embodiment of dreams. Each one of its nooks and corners was a resting-place for daydreaming. And often the resting-place particularized the daydream. Our habits of particular daydream were acquired there. The house, the bedroom, the garret in which we were alone, furnished the framework for

---

[46] Bachelard, *The Poetics of Space*, 136.
[47] Frances Morris, *Louise Bourgeois: teciendo el tempo*, Málaga: Centro de Arte Contemporaneo de Malaga, 2004, 25.
[48] Bourgeois et al, *Destruction of the Father*, 278.
[49] Germano Celant, *Louise Bourgeois—The Fabric Works*, Milan: Skira, 2010, 126-127. http://www.factum-arte.com/pag/135/Louise-Bourgeois 1 [accessed 19/01/2018].
[50] Bourgeois, *Louise Bourgeois*, 280.
[51] http://www.tate.org.uk/art/artworks/bourgeois-spider-al00354 [accessed 19/01/2018].
[52] https://artblart.files.wordpress.com/2013/02/femme-maison-4747-cb-3_lg.jpg [accessed 19/01/2018].

> an interminable dream, one that poetry alone, through the creation of a poetic work, could succeed in achieving completely.[53]

Bachelard considers that poetic images reveal the potency of the imagination. Nevertheless, his approach to the study of such images resides on significant places and our primordial relation to them as constitutive of a poetic imagination of space. Therefore, the house with its corners, attic and basement, drawers, shells and nests, is relevant to the strong relation between place and subjectivity. Bachelard adds that there is a definite connection between our bodily perceptions and our elaboration of poetic images of space.

The endurance of perception of significant places clearly relates to the development of a subjective dimension associated to them. According to Bachelard again, "To inhabit oneirically the house we were born in means more than to inhabit it in memory; it means living in this house that is gone, the way we used to dream in it",[54] which clearly reinforces the connection between experiencing certain emotions in certain places and salvaging the connectivity between those, no matter how diverse or contradictory they may be. This, then, feeds the elaboration of poetic images, of space especially.

The embodied aspect of space perception is also acknowledged in regard to the visual perception of space. When reflecting on the perception of space in daily life, film theorist Jacques Aumont[55], for example, insists that space is not perceived exclusively visually, in particular because distances cannot be measured visually—hence any formulation and understanding of space must be based as much on the perception of one's body in space as on one's sense of dislocation from it.[56] Michel Foucault speaks in similar terms when analyzing Edouard Manet's paintings, stating that "Distance cannot be given to perception; one does not see distance." [57] Any notion of space has therefore tactile and kinetic as much as visual grounding. This means that elaborations on space depend on perceptions of inhabited spaces since, as we saw earlier with Bachelard, places where personal, sensory experience has occurred trigger a subjective imprint.

Loneliness, for example, could be described as being alone in space. But when this space is perceived as so vast as to become unbearable, can it still be addressed as a location, or rather as this limitless vacuum where one finds oneself? Such questions lead us to the poetic significance of Leonilson's *Ninguém*, a piece which incites discussions on the formulation of the embroidered word at its corner.

As we saw earlier, the feelings Bourgeois and Leonilson deal with during their respective creative processes result from a retrieving endeavour to respond to past bodily experiences, defining an inner imprint of different layers of sensations, emotions and concrete equivalents. In this regard, their productions not only illustrate

---

[53] Bachelard, *The Poetics of Space,* 15.
[54] *Ibid.*, 16.
[55] Jacques Aumont, *A Imagem*, Campinas: Papyrus, 1993.
[56] A notion that Zigmut Baumann (*Liquid Modernity*, Cambridge: Polity, 2000) extensively worked on when eliciting the relation between the perception of space and time.
[57] Michel Foucault, *Manet and the Object of Painting*, London: Tate Publishing, 2011, 41.

Bachelard's definition of poetic images of space, but also confirm Johnson and Lakoff's claim about the pivotal role of the body in the creation of categories subsidiary to language development. [58] However, Leonilson's and Bourgeois's operations are not imbedded in rational argument but in emotional diversity. It is for this reason that Morris claims that Bourgeois's œuvre searches for an architectural vocabulary commensurable to "emotions and consciousness states."[59] For Bourgeois's poetic images do implicate a further aspect of the embodied perception of space: one does not perceive one's own body purely in terms of muscles and bones, but also via the emotional flow that goes through it—that subtle, yet forceful, thing we keep struggling to name.

Such conjunction between embodiment and emotion is exactly the kind of relation marked in Yeats', Bourgeois's and Leonilson's images of longing, elaborated on significant places by associating objective and non-objective information, as if marking a blurred line separating body and emotions, reality and affections. Trying to elaborate on longing in relation to places, poetic images propose an approximation between emotional and objective data, both perceived through embodied experiences. Thus, it can be surmised that these creative processes develop the exploration of the relation between embodied language and existential meaning.

This conclusion allows us to examine the concepts of longing and belonging further. Many of Bourgeois' creations evoke the image of a woman longing, closely related to the image of a house in which waiting takes place. Indeed, in a number of drawings, sculptures, engravings and textile pieces, female bodies and houses are brought together, with the house placed on the woman's body or head, thus creating what Bourgeois called *Femme Maison* (*House Woman*). The very wording stresses Bourgeois' questioning of a woman's role, "with her having to be a giver perceivable as being as welcoming and as containing of the other as a home. A responsibility Bourgeois considers not only a burden, but as producing in her feelings of helplessness and hopelessness"[60]—a sense of impotence attached to loneliness, and belonging to a typical, emotional, feminine space.

Penelope

In many respects, the mythical figure of Penelope comes to mind when exploring such a space, and in particular, themes found in Leonilson and Bourgeois, such as the absence of the other and the persistence of desire expressed through weaving. Ulysses' wife is indeed characteristic of feminine, house-wife roles, dutifully weaving while waiting for her husband to return, despite the years passing by. Penelope's

---

[58] George Lakoff; Mark Johnson, *Metaphors we live by,* Chicago: University of Chicago Press, 1980. Lakoff and Johnson's claim may be quite shocking for philosophy-oriented thought, but it is rather fundamental for the arts. Fayga Ostrower acknowledged the perception and verbalization of space as grounded on our embodied being in the world. The best example is the way our standing posture relates to a variety of words signifying mobility and positivity, whereas immobility and negativity are commonly associated to lying. See Fayga Ostrower, *Universos da Arte*, Rio de Janeiro: Editora Campus, 1983.

[59] Morris, *Louise Bourgeois*, 10.

[60] Ulster, *Louise Bourgeois*, 956.

emblematic figure is recaptured by Bourgeois and Leonilson in a way that reinforces the myth while developing new meanings by taking advantage of its potential in regard to longing and belonging. A potential implicitly elaborated on the correlation between the emotional and embodied dimensions of longing and belonging as experienced in waiting.

Bourgeois' elaboration on Penelope is acknowledged by both Müller-Westermann[61] and Ulster who indicates that the artist was very aware of the potency of such imagery, having evoked Penelope in many textile pieces and composed about her as follows:

> Poor sisters how do you put up with the absence of...
> Absence of the other, absence of means, absence of ideal
> absence of interest; an absence is a well that must be filled
> a hole without water – a river dried out.
> There must be ways to fill... that sac
> belly – that lack –
> The lack is much more important than the filled
> One can even take care of it and play to fill it then
> empty it. Children digging a hole in the sand, at
> the beach – The tide fills the hole with water then
> goes out then comes in eternally – Penelope weaves it and
> unweaves it.[62]

On the one hand, Bourgeois here marks the idea of absence of emotional retribution or even emotional reciprocity as perceived in the non-presence of the other's body – an image that resonates with Leonilson's *Ninguém* and *Para meu Vizinho de Sonhos.* On the other hand, this poem suggests the idea of waiting in relation to a desire to "go back" or to "have back" the other in the entirety of the body, so to speak, which would be the fundamental reason for Bourgeois, as much as Yeats and Leonilson, to poetically reclaim the place that is gone forever, the childhood home as much as the mountain and its waterfall or the presence marked in one's bedding. A contrasting yet complementary connection between body and absence whose importance is reintroduced with the images of the hole and river empty of water, for such elaboration implies the idea that the missing body is what defines what the river and the hole are, as much as the missing other, the missing place defines one's own meaning. For the lack here empowers – a key aspect of Bourgeois's and Leonilson's creative practices – and it enables Bourgeois to then further relate Penelope's weaving to an endless effort twined with her life in time. Subverting longing into belonging is a fundamental poetic constituent in Bourgeois's and Leonilson's œuvres, elicited in many textile pieces, some of which recall Penelope by name and enhance the critical engagement of their productions toward subjectivity.

---

[61] See Müller-Westermann, *Louise Bourgeois*, 181.
[62] The Louise Bourgeois Archive, New York, LB-0827, October 29, 1995, in Ulster, *Louise Bourgeois*, 249.

One very evident example in Bourgeois's production is *Hours of the Day* (2006).[63] A 24-page booklet in loose musical score sheets presents, side by side, the image of a 24-hour clock on the right, and short poems in both English and French on the left. These articulate contrasting feelings of anguish and delight towards waiting hours, suggestively named as the waiting for "The Hero" in an allusion to Penelope's waiting for Ulysses. The composition evolves on an extended number of poems which suggest different aspects in someone's relation to the passing of the hours of the day, expressing at times despair in lines like "I am waiting for you; I will not abandon you; I can wait for you; I will wait for you; Do not abandon me", placing these aside the image of a clock whose arrows seem immovable.

However, contrastingly other poems express joy and enchantment with such waiting as in "*J'aimais le jour de Penelope; Oublie-la*" (I loved Penelope's day; Forget her). The immense clock with immovable arrows could suggest anguish in relation to the reality of waiting. However, the sentence praising Penelope's day denies such a perspective, as it meaningfully involves Bourgeois's French childhood to offer a positive outlook on Penelope's wait, distinctively contrasting drawings and poems, to better harmonize anguish and pleasure, as expressed by the complementary media used here.

This combination, explicit in the poems in *Hours of the Day*, is presented more subtly in *The Waiting Hours*.[64] In this textile book, Penelope is not named. However, this revealing composition recalls her endless needle work on thread and time through the variation in sizes, patterns and design in a bluish patchwork sewing. *The Waiting Hours* is a complicated and ingenious needle work whose materiality deeply enhances the sense of beauty found in the passage of time, from dawn to dusk, in a piece that literally embodies evolving moments of the day, and expresses timeless endurance through the intricacy of the compositions. The pieces of fabric sewn together develop time itself to create a poetic image which subverts, like Penelope's weaving, the embodied perception of time in absence into a belonging: the sewn piece itself.

Leonilson's images of Penelope and her longing are elaborated as poetic images closely related to the perception of being in an emotional space. As in Bourgeois, waiting is symbolized by the time dedicated to the needle work. *O Zig-zag* (*The Zig-Zag*) perfectly illustrates this type of representation. It is a textile work adorned with a piece of fabric sewn on a canvas overlaid by hand-embroidered drawings, and small verbal expressions which emphasize the sense of longing for a passionate encounter: "the passionate one", "five minutes, the door", "pearls, hugs without kisses".

---

[63] Müller-Westermann, *Louise Bourgeois*, 175-188. Another version of this work was also produced as an illustrated book: https://www.moma.org/collection/works/illustratedbooks/ 128387? locale=pt [accessed 19/01/2018].

[64] See Celant, *Louise Bourgeois*, 266-267, Ulster, *Louise Bourgeois*, 1075-1084, and http://www.cheimread.com/exhibitions/2011-05-12_louise-bourgeois-the-fabric-works/gallery/checklist [accessed 21/03/2017].

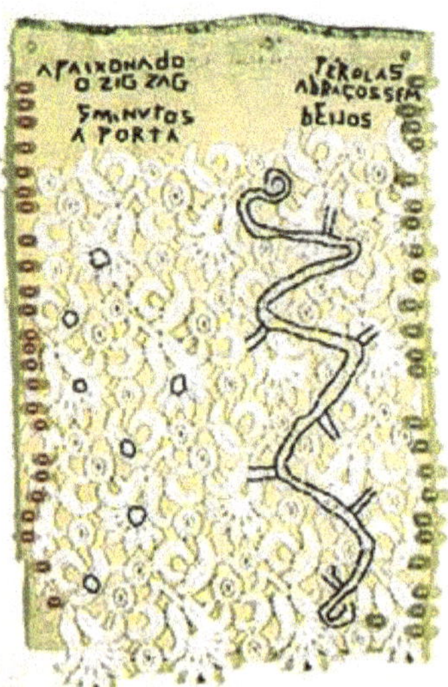

Leonilson, *O Zig-zag*, 1991

Moreover, the relation between Penelope and the translation of waiting into an embodied presence, which is implicit in *O Zig-zag*, is explicitly indicated in other pieces where, as seen in Bourgeois, Penelope is named and the needle work as both a creative action and an emotional maneuver is addressed.

This can be seen in *O Penélope* (*The Penelope*),[65] a patchwork-like textile composition sewn by hand, 220 per 83 centimeters long. The fabric piece was executed in very modest voile patchwork in different white hues where two discreet elements draw attention: a small pleated detail on the right bottom corner and three Portuguese words embroidered with black thread on the left margin. The sheer piece hangs drawing lines on itself due to its own weight. A diaphanous object, it has no other cut of fabric protecting it or enabling more elaborate finishing, as if this could reveal the fragility of the naming interpreted as Leonilson stitching his own longing, identifying with "Penelope". This creation underlines the artist's dual effort, similar to Penelope's, to deal with matter and desire, absence and presence.

Of the four words embroidered, Penelope is the most significant. At the top are the words *segredo* (secret) and *silêncio* (silence) side by side, and in the middle, one reads *sentinela* (sentinel). Altogether, they elaborate a sense of emotional place contrasting with the definite article in front of the fourth word at the bottom, *O Penélope*. However, in Portuguese "o" is a masculine article, which would not be properly placed in relation to a feminine subject like Penelope. Leonilson's poetic use of language plays with basic rules, strengthening his longing for the other as a fundamental aspect of his work, thus showing that his subject matter is inseparable

---

[65] Piece to be found at the Tate Modern: http://www.tate.org.uk/art/artworks/leonilson-jose-leonilson-bezerra-dias-the-penelope-t07768 [accessed 19/01/2018].

from his creative technique.[66] The artist can then introduce a male Penelope who is characterized by his creator's choices and by his gender. This also allows Leonilson to question gender categorizations and expectations, a subject Bourgeois also delves into through her production, as we saw earlier.

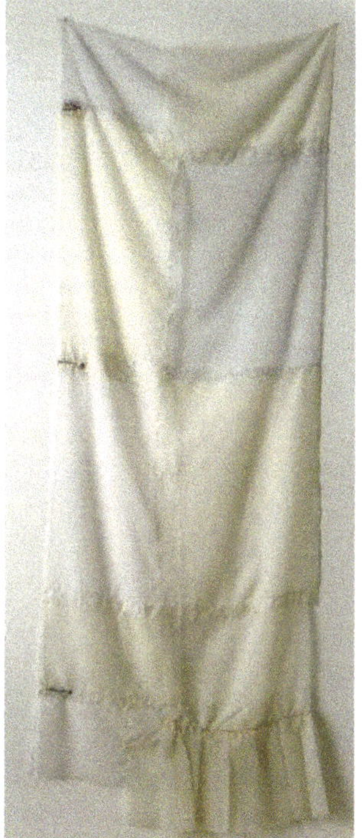

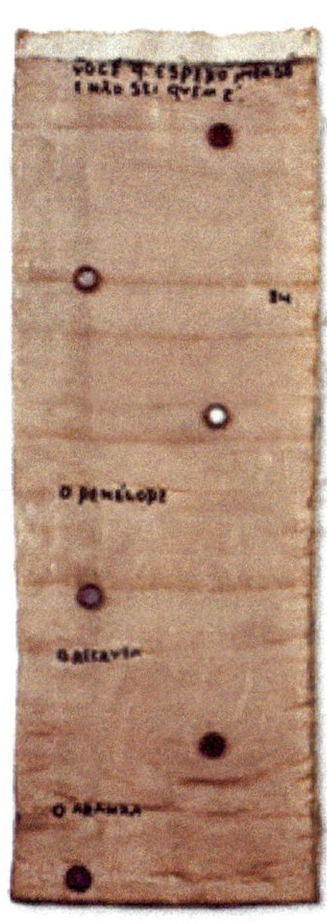

(Left) Leonilson, *O Penélope*, 1993
(Right) *O Penélope, o recruta, o aranha*, 1992

Compared to *O Penélope,* another piece *O Penélope, o recruta, o aranha* (*The Penelope, the Recruit, the Spider*) composed in 1991, also refers to Penelope, although not as sole subject. It stresses Leonilson's longing more literally in the sentence embroidered at the top: *você que espero imenso/ e não sei quem é* (you whom I await immensely/ whom I do not know). However, here, the reinforced back of the canvas and the more finished sewing do not resound as much as the former Penelope with emotional challenge. Another piece, *O recruta, o aranha, o Penélope* (*The Recruit, the Spider, the Penelope*), an embroidery on felt, composed in 1992, addresses the figure of Penelope, but here the character is not considered necessarily as an isolated subject, being contrasted with other characters. Leonilson was fond of giving secret names to people he had relationships with, or people he fell in love with.

---

[66] See Ana Lúcia Beck, Palavras Fora de Lugar – Leonilson e a inserção de Palavras nas Artes Visuais. Dissertation. Porto Alegre: PPGAV/UFGRS, 2004.

This would be the reason for him to refer to subjects recognized by their characteristics through the use of generic names, which would also be accountable for the misuse of articles in regard to gender and grammatical rules, as was done in relation to "the (male) Penelope".

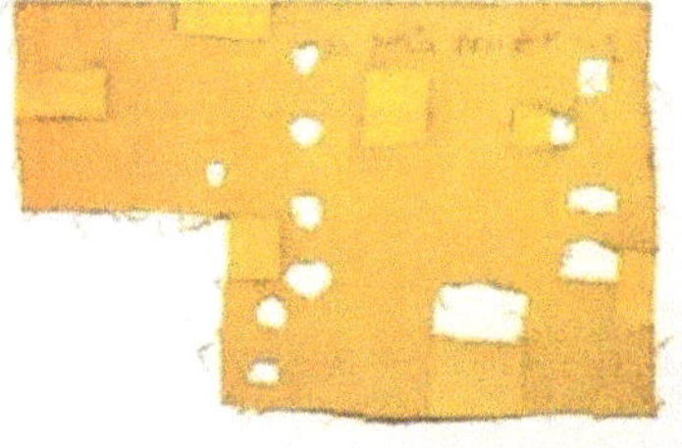

Da Pouca Paciência, 1987

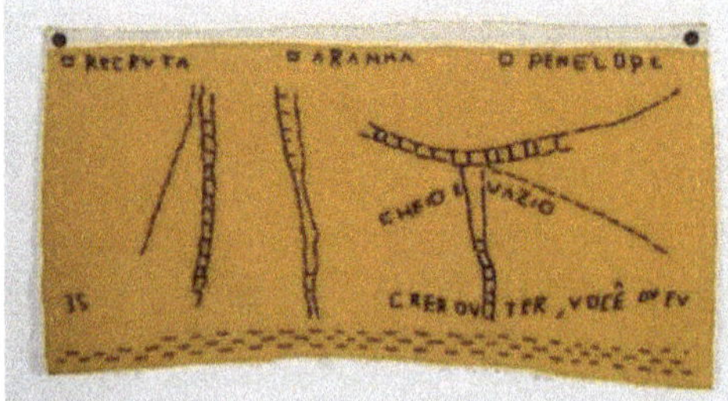

The Penelope, the Sentinel, the Spider, 1992

Penelope is certainly one of the universal representatives of the implied feminine values of dedication, patience and virtue. However, if Leonilson relates to these values, he can occasionally deconstruct them too. In the small, orange-painted canvas, *Da Pouca Paciência* (*About Lack of Patience*), for instance, he signifies the renunciation of patience using rough cuts, resembling holes. Lightly painted holes emphasize the clear cuts, and loose threads left behind are attached to the canvas by layers of paint. Revealing the contradictory feelings attached to longing and waiting, Leonilson presents the tension between hoping and impatience as essential to creative procedures. It appears that the values contained in Bourgeois's and Leonilson's poetic images of emotional places suggest that traditionally-considered womanly tasks are closely related to art making. It also seems that for Bourgeois and Leonilson, art making can provide emotional support to oneself and others by facilitating a resonance between the artists' and the viewers' subjectivity.

Penelope's decision to focus on her weaving marks the importance of a procedure which subverts waiting into action, which helps endure longing as well as the passage of time. In similar ways, Leonilson and Bourgeois recognize their feelings, examine them and, thus, find ways to act creatively, whether through long hours of sewing and stitching, or nervous cutting. In longing, Leonilson, like Bourgeois, suggests that facing profound psychological states can subvert the passive position of waiting into actions which embrace the emotional dimension whilst surpassing it.

Just as Yeats formulated longing and belonging as a tension between past childhood and the present lover's body, Leonilson's and Bourgeois's productions evolve on the tension between salvaging the past while creating in the present. Their represented emotions carry poetic values that rely on the intricate connection and interdependency between the memory of yesterday and the perception of today, as well as on the correlation and balance between absence and embodiment.

Regarding subjectivity, Leonilson's and Bourgeois's poetic images reveal the existence of a gap between what would be a record of past events – or a more literal representation of these – and the contents of their art pieces, an aspect which is reinforced by the intricate relation between verbal and visual elements in their productions. Thus, these artists' creative processes, as related to their emotional lives, must be considered in terms of a critical undertaking towards subjectivity – not only their own, but also one their viewers may relate to.

While longing and belonging can be perceived in Bourgeois's and Leonilson's œuvres in procedures that subtly separate their own lives from their poetic achievements, their creations let one envision a heartfelt image: we pertain to the things we long for as long as those are beyond our reach.

BIBLIOGRAPHY

Arnheim, Rudolf, *Art and Visual Perception*, Berkeley: University of California Press, 1974.

Aumont, Jacques, *A Imagem*, Campinas: Papyrus, 1993.

Bachelard, Gaston, *The Poetics of Space*, Boston: Beacon Press, 1994.

Baumann, Zigmut, *Liquid Modernity*, Cambridge: Polity, 2000.

Beck, Ana Lúcia and Berwanger da Silva, Maria Luiza, "Bleeding words – Louise Bourgeois's and José Leonilson's Love Images", *Primerjalna književnost* (Comparative Literature), 39.1, June 2016, 141-162.

Beck, Ana Lúcia, *Palavras Fora de Lugar – Leonilson e a inserção de Palavras nas Artes Visuais*, Dissertation, Porto Alegre: PPGAV/UFGRS, 2004. http://hdl.handle.net/10183/77868 [accessed 19/01/2018].

Bourgeois, Louise, Marie-Laure Bernadac and Hans Ulrich Obrist, *Louise Bourgeois, Destruction of the Father, Reconstruction of the Father*, Cambridge: MIT Press, 1998.

Calvino, Italo, *Six Memos for the Next Millennium*, Cambridge: Harvard University Press, 1988.

Celant,Germano, *Louise Bourgeois – The Fabric Works*, Milan: Skira, 2010.

Foucault, Michel, *Manet and the Object of Painting*, London: Tate Publishing, 2011.

Harley, Karen (dir.), *Leonilson – Com o oceano inteiro para nadar*, documentary film, 19 min. colored, Brazil: MPC & Associados, 1997.

Itaú Cultural, *Arquivo e memória o legado do artista*, "Projeto Leonilson e a Internacionalização da Obra" Symposium. https://www.youtube. com/watch?v=yMjWfBrFXal [accessed 19/01/2018].

Johnson, Mark, *The Meaning of the Body*, Chicago: The University of Chicago Press, 2008.

Kristeva, Julia, *Tales of Love*, New York: Columbia University Press, 1987.

Lagnado, Lisette, *Leonilson: são tantas as verdades/So Many are the Truths,*, São Paulo: DBA Melhoramentos/Fiesp, 1998.

Lakoff, George and Johnson, Mark, *Philosophy in the Flesh*, New York: Basic Books, 1999. Kindle Edition.

———, *Metaphors We Live By*, Chicago: University of Chicago Press, 1980.

Larratt-Smith, Philip (ed.), *Louise Bourgeois: o retorno do desejo proibido,* São Paulo: Instituto Tomie Ohtake, 2011.

Magalhães, Ana Maria and Peixoto, Charles (dir.), *Sprayjet*, short film, 14 min, coloured, Brazil: Embrafilme, 1985.

Mesquita, Ivo, *Leonilson – use, é lindo, eu garanto*, São Paulo: Cosac&Naify, 1997.

Mitchell, Juliet, "O ciúme sublime de Louise Bourgeois", in Philip Larratt-Smith (ed.), *Louise Bourgeois: o retorno do desejo proibido,* São Paulo: Instituto Tomie Ohtake, 2011, 49-67.

Morris, Frances, *Louise Bourgeois: teciendo el tempo*, Málaga: Centro de Arte Contemporaneo de Málaga, 2004.

Müller-Westermann, Iris (ed.), *Louise Bourgeois: I have been to Hell and back*, Ostfildern: Hatje Cantz, 2014.

Nader, José (dir.), *A paixão de J.L.*, documentary film, 82 min, coloured, Brazil: Estudio Já Filmes, 2014.

Nixon, Mignon, "L.", in Philip Larratt-Smith (ed.), *Louise Bourgeois: o retorno do desejo proibido,* São Paulo: Instituto Tomie Ohtake, 2011, 83-94.

Ostrower Fayga, *Universos da Arte*, Rio de Janeiro: Editora Campus, 1983.

Paz, Octávio, *El Arco y la Lira*, México D.F.: Fondo de Cultura Economica, 1972.

Pedrosa, Adriano (curator), *Leonilson Truth-Fiction*, São Paulo: Pinacoteca do Estado/Cobogo Editora, 2014.

Rivera, Tania, *O Avesso do Imaginário*, São Paulo: Cosac&Naify, 2013.

Ulster, Kulf, *Louise Bourgeois*, Ostfildern: Hatje Kantz Verlag, Kindle Edition.

Waldenfels, Bernhard, "Responsive love", *Primerjalna književnost* (Comparative Literature), 39.1, June 2016, 15-29.

Webb, Timothy, "Introduction", *W.B. Yeats Selected poems,* edited by Timothy Webb, London: Penguin Books, 2000, 10-30.

Yeats, W. B., *Collected Poems,* London: Macmillan London Limited, 1984.

Zima, Peter V., "Love and Longing: Absolute Desire from Romanticism to Modernism", *Primerjalna književnost* (Comparative Literature), 39.1, June 2016, 77-89.

See Appendix on p. 207 for more details.

CHAPTER 12

Total Recall: Longing and Nostalgia in the (Post)Digital Age

Anna Notaro

We live in extraordinary times, the pace of change in all fields of knowledge, social and economic organization is fast, and yet nothing has impacted more on the lives of ordinary individuals than the birth of the Web twenty-five years ago and the so-called "digital revolution".[67] Assessing such impact in its wide ranging ramifications is beyond the scope of this essay, which will concentrate instead on some selected areas of interest under the headings: longing for connection, longing for the past and the post-digital condition, in order to show how behind contemporary popular phenomena like "retromania" lie deeply-held anxieties stirred by an often too simplistic narrative of progress. Thinking about technology à la Silicon Valley, in terms of blindly positive progress and disruptive experience,[68] encourages a technocratic and uncritical approach to thinking about the human good, which in turn incites and validates an analogous uncritical approach to the past. Ultimately, it is only by inquiring about the moral implications and the creative potential of new technologies that we can truly make ours the most satisfying and exciting times to be alive.

LONGING FOR CONNECTION

In a column of *The Guardian* entitled "In this post-digital age, we still thrill to the power of live", author and former chair of the British National Trust Simon Jenkins finds it hugely reassuring to witness the "tyranny of the internet" crumbling. While acknowledging the obvious, that the digital is "an astonishing new means of communication", Jenkins is keen to point out that "it has not satiated the human appetite for moving, meeting and touching".[69] The evidence for such an assertion consists in the 'power of live', as expressed in the popularity of concerts, theatres,

---

[67] The number of Internet users has grown from 16 million in 1995 to 2,937 million in March 2014. "History and Growth of the Internet from 1995 till Today", http://www.internetworld-stats.com/emarketing.htm [accessed 20/03/2015].

[68] A disruptive experience, in this context, refers to the one brought about by a new technology that displaces an established one, often creating a completely new industry. Harvard Business School professor Clayton M. Christensen coined the term disruptive technology in his 1997 best-selling book, *The Innovator's Dilemma,* New York: Harvard Business School Press, 1997.

[69] Simon Jenkins, "In this post-digital age, we still thrill to the power of live", *The Guardian,* 20/06/2014. http://www.theguardian.com/commentisfree/2014/jun/20/post-digital-thrill-power-of-live-antidote-glastonbury [accessed 03/02/ 2015].

lectures, festivals across the world, and in the fact that the way in which we live our lives has not been hugely disrupted after all, no 'telework' has supplanted our commute to work and brick and mortar universities have not been replaced by online ones. Besides, shows like *512 Days* (London, Serpentine Gallery, 11 June–25 August 2014) by renowned performance artist Marina Abramovic demonstrate, in the words of Serpentine Director Hans Ulrich Obrist, that "In the digital age there is a real necessity for a live experience, for physical interaction".[70] Visitors at the show are invited to leave their digital devices at the entrance (although the performance is video-recorded by the artist). Once inside Abramovic takes some by the hand, placing her hand between their shoulder blades to transmit 'energy', before leaving them facing the gallery wall for as long as they like. One might speculate that the thrill for the visitors does not consist entirely in communing in silent mindfulness with their inner selves, rather in touching and being touched by the celebrity artist. What visitors commune with is the *aura* of Marina Abramovic, the connection they long for is with her powerful charisma. In any case, for Jenkins this is another sure sign that the post-digital is all about 'human congregation'.[71]

The post-digital condition will be addressed in the last section of this essay, in the meantime suffice to say that the renewed emphasis on the 'human congregation' is evidence of our complex and evolving relationship to the physical and the digital, as it expresses itself in popular culture, in the manner in which we construct, manipulate and archive our personal and public memories, relate to fellow human beings and to the objects we surround ourselves with. Such a relationship allows for the continuous re-construction of identity and the practices of re-configuring the self typical of our post-digital age.

Narrative, one of the most ancient communication tools, has undergone substantial structural changes in a culture of virtual inter-connectivity and instant information.[72] These changes have had a phenomenal impact on the way we read and write. Digital Apps, iBooks, and other interactive titles have embedded rich media, such as animation, video, and audio into the reading (and writing) experience. Reading is not exclusively the solitary experience we are familiar with, the built-in Wi-Fi and 3G of some e-reading devices allows readers to see what their friends are reading, share highlights and rate books not only in the context of platforms for book lovers like Goodreads, but on Facebook and Twitter also. Empowered by technological advancements, any reader now has the ability to become an author, publishing her ideas in blogs, revising encyclopaedia entries in Wikipedia, creating her own fictional world in virtual communities. Unsurprisingly, digital publishing has grown exponentially from the past twenty years as a result of software production tools, Internet distribution and online publishing services. So, it is hard to understand why e-book sales dropped by 10 percent in the first five months of 2015 or why

---

[70] *Ibid.*
[71] *Ibid.*
[72] As I extensively discuss in my article: Anna Notaro, "How Networked Communication has changed the ways we tell stories", *Between*, 4:8, 2014. http://ojs.unica.it/index.php/between/article/view/1341 [accessed 17/03/2017].

Amazon opened a physical shop in Seattle in November of the same year. [73] In 2007 *Newsweek* covered the launch of the Kindle e-reader by interviewing Jeff Bezos, CEO of Amazon.com, who triumphantly announced: "Books are not Dead, they are just going digital" and "the future of reading is just a click away".[74] It turned out that print books, 'the last bastion of analogue' as Bezos defined them in that interview, have not gone extinct,[75] in fact already in January 2007 at the "Google's Unbound" conference science-fiction author Cory Doctorow spoke of the "deep emotional attachment to the codex" readers felt and that "it might be ok to be pervy for paper".[76] Crucially, most speakers agreed on the necessity to "move beyond the 'death of the book' debate", already heated then, "to a more nuanced understanding of the complementary role of paper and electronic media".[77] Doctorow was very percipient in understanding that the deep attachment to the book form is based on an emotional and sensorial connection. More recently, *New York Times* tech blogger Nick Bilton wrote about wandering into a West Village bookstore on a visit to New York: "I immediately felt a sense of nostalgia that I haven't felt in a long time. The scent of physical books—the paper, the ink, the glue—can conjure up memories of a summer day spent reading on a beach, a fall afternoon in a coffee shop, or an overstuffed chair by a fireplace as rain patters on a windowsill".[78]

However, Bilton leaves the bookstore without buying anything:

> I was reminded of the impracticality of these physical books. While they were beautiful, I remembered that I wouldn't be able to search for specific words in them. Or share passages with friends, simply by copying and pasting, on Twitter and Facebook. Or that I can't stuff 500 different books in my backpack without breaking my back… Yes, I miss physical books. I miss

---

[73] As Anuj Srivas writes: "There has been some speculation that the Amazon bookstore is a mirage, a Trojan, whose only purpose is to serve as general brand awareness, the way Microsoft has opened up several 'experience' stores across the United States". "The Past, Present and Future of the Printed Book", *The Wire,* 08/11/2015. http://thewire.in/2015/11/08/the-past-present-and-future-of-the-printed-book-14947/ [accessed 10/11/ 2018]. On this topic see also Matthew Yglesias, "Why Amazon just opened a physical bookstore", *Vox*, 5/11/ 2015. http://www.vox.com/2015/11/5/9672394/amazon-books-physical-store [accessed 06/11/2017]. For Michael Tamblyn, the CEO of ereading company Kobo, "What we're seeing […] is the healthy recalibration of a truly hybrid industry", Molly Flatt, "The ebook is dead, long live the ebook", *The Memo,* 8/12/ 2015 http://www.thememo.com/2015/12/08/the-ebook-is-dead-long-live-the-ebook/ [accessed 15/12/2018].

[74] Steven Levy, "Amazon: Reinventing the Book", *Newsweek,* 17/11/2007. http://europe.newsweek.com/amazon-reinventing-book-96909?rm=eu [accessed 01/02/ 2018].

[75] Interestingly, a recent study has demonstrated that print books are getting longer, as a "response to clickbait" http://news.nationalpost.com/arts/books-are-getting-longer-confirms-a-new-study [accessed 17/03/2017].

[76] Charles, Watkinson, "Are publishers 'pervy for paper' and other twisted thoughts about Google's 'UnBound'", 21/01/2007. http://charleswatkinson.blogspot.co.uk/2007/01/are-publishers-pervy-for-paper-and.html [accessed 01/02/2018].

[77] *Ibid.*

[78] Nick, Bilton, "An E-Book Fan, Missing the Smell of Paper and Glue", *New York Times,* 18/6/2012. http://bits.blogs.nytimes.com/2012/06/18/caught-between-nostalgia-for-print-and-the-practicality-of-digital/ [accessed 01/02/2018].

> bookstores, too. I miss them a lot. I only hope that someone figures out how to give their digital counterparts a little more feeling.[79]

Luckily, the market has come to the rescue of nostalgic digital readers, who can now recapture that new (or old) book scent thanks to an aerosol e-book enhancer. Readers' choice of aromas includes: 'Classic Musty Scent', which feels a bit like having the collected works of Shakespeare in a can, 'Eau, you have cats', which feels like borrowing a book from grandma's house, and 'Scent of Sensibility', aimed at women readers, which feels like living in a Jane Austen novel.[80]

There is some truth in the 'Madeleine effect', as Proust perceptively understood olfactory memory is an emotionally powerful link to our past.[81] However, it is unlikely that an aerosol could lend digital books that *feeling* Bilton, and others, long for. Also, the reasons why digital books have failed to ignite our imagination (ironically despite the meaning of the word Kindle),[82] and an explanation for the recent drop in sales might lie elsewhere. Author and graphic designer Craig Mod details in a thought-provoking piece his initial enamourment with the Kindle e-reader followed by his recent migration back to print. The main problem for Mod is the closed nature of the digital book ecosystem:

> When we buy a physical book, we can do with it what we want – cut up the pages, burn it for warmth, give it to friends, and so on [...] Contemporary digital publishing stacks are mostly closed. As readers, when we buy an Amazon Kindle or Apple iBooks digital book, we have no control over what software we can use to read it, or what happens to our notes and other meta information culled from our reading data.[83]

Mod notes: "As our hardware has grown more powerful and our screens more capable, our book-reading software has largely stagnated", before concluding: "When media is too locked down, too rigid, when it's too much like a room with most of the air sucked out of it, stale and exhausting, the exploration stops. And for the intersection of books and digital there's still much exploration to be had."[84]

Books are not the only media objects which have survived the digital revolution against the odds; a comparison mindful of medium specificity could be established with vinyl's longevity within the record industry. According to a report released by

---

[79] *Ibid.*

[80] http://smellofbooks.com/. There is also a choice of book-scented candles, http://ebookfriendly.com/book-smell-perfumes-candles/, and page flip sound effects http://www.soundjay.com/page-flip-sounds-1.html [all accessed 17/03/2017].

[81] Recent findings in the science of memory have vindicated Proust, as the British psychologist Charles Fernyhough elegantly explains in his book Pieces of Light, London: Profile Books, 2013.

[82] Kindle means to set alight or start to burn, to arouse or be aroused, to make or become bright. The word's roots are from the Old Norse word kyndill, meaning Candle. http://www.printmag.com/article/who-named-the-kindle-and-why/ [accessed 17/03/2017].

[83] Craig Mod, "Future Reading", AEON, 01/10/ 2015. https://aeon.co/essays/stagnant-and-dull-can-digital-books-ever-replace-print [accessed 10/10/2017].

[84] *Ibid.*

the Recording Industry Association of America (RIAA), vinyl music sales brought in almost $60 million more than ad-supported streaming services during the first half of 2015,[85] while in the UK more than one million vinyl records have been sold in 2015 - the first time such a milestone has been achieved since 1996. Britain's biggest supermarket British supermarket giant Tesco is also cashing in on the comeback of record players by selling LPs for the first time in its history.[86] Vinyl is in high demand among hipsters, the generation that grew up with such a format, but also among youngsters whose reasons for buying vinyl, according to a recent poll, are: chance to own a permanent copy of the record, better sound quality, and the fact that more money ends up in the artist's pocket.[87] For Gennaro Castaldo from music industry body the BPI, "The difference between vinyl and other formats is that it's viewed as an art form [...]- the audio quality, the sleevenotes, the cover art [...]Whilst other formats are being superseded every time technology improves, vinyl doesn't really fit into that category because it's more than that".[88] Indeed, the fact that vinyl culture has experienced a remarkable revival at a time when the digital revolution is far from over might seem a paradox, and yet as Ian Woodward and Dominik Bartmanski explain in their *Vinyl: The Analogue Record in the Digital Age* there are several different dimensions of vinyl that jointly comprise an analogue/material sensory formation: it is a tactile object, with special audio qualities (not necessarily better, but different), it is characterised by a long and relatively stable heritage and tradition; it is a commodity that can be owned and collected (unlike streaming of music) and it is endowed with its own peculiar pragmatics, haptics, poetics and even politics. Lastly, it is a totemic object for different urban scenes that strive for social distinction and authenticity at a time of wholesale virtualization of culture. For Woodward and Bartmanski the revival of the analogue and the physical makes sense in the context of the seeming de-materialization and widespread digitalization of cultural consumption. [89] Such arguments are persuasive enough, however the somewhat dismissive characterization of nostalgia as 'merely a craze' typical of some material studies approaches to contemporary culture is dubious. Vinyl's 'rebirth of its cool' should be viewed also from such a perspective, as we shall see in the next section. In the meantime, suffice it to remember that, as musician and visual artist Brian Eno predicted decades ago, the

---

[85] Jamieson Cox, "Vinyl sales are more valuable than ad-supported streaming in 2015", *The Verge*, 28/09/2015. http://www.theverge.com/2015/9/28/9408233/vinyl-sales-ad-supported-streaming-riaa-2015-report [accessed 31/10/2017].

[86] Sarah Butler, "Tesco to sell LPs for first time in its history", *The Guardian*, 4/12/ 2015. http://www.theguardian.com/business/2015/dec/04/tesco-to-sell-lps-for-first-time-in-its-history?CMP=Share_iOSApp_Other [accessed 10/12/2017].

[87] Patrick Foster, "Vinyl sales boom as young music fans move beyond online streaming", *The Telegraph*, 11/12/2015. http://www.telegraph.co.uk/news/shopping-and-consumer-news/12044846/Return-of-the-record-Tesco-first-supermarket-to-sell-vinyls.html [accessed 12/12/2017].

[88] Dave Lee, "Vinyl record sales hit 18-year high", 27/11/ 2014. http://www.bbc.co.uk/news/technology-30216638 [accessed 28/11/2017].

[89] Dominik Bartmanski and Ian Woodward, *Vinyl: The Analogue Record in the Digital Age*, London: Bloomsbury Publishing, 2015.

key to future (tech)nostalgia, in van der Heijden's definition of the word,[90] lies precisely in the imperfections and limitations of a medium:

> Whatever you now find weird, ugly, uncomfortable and nasty about a new medium will surely become its signature. CD distortion, the jitteriness of digital video, the crap sound of 8-bit - all of these will be cherished and emulated as soon as they can be avoided. It's the sound of failure: so much modern art is the sound of things going out of control, of a medium pushing to its limits and breaking apart. The distorted guitar sound is the sound of something too loud for the medium supposed to carry it. The blues singer with the cracked voice is the sound of an emotional cry too powerful for the throat that releases it. The excitement of grainy film, of bleached-out black and white, is the excitement of witnessing events too momentous for the medium assigned to record them.[91]

What Eno is alluding to is that there is more to the argument of the intrinsic quality or superiority of a medium, behind the fetish of outmoded technology and the re-staging of 'authentic' analogue elements such as 'grainy film, of bleached-out black and white', lies a desire for connection which is emotional, symbolic and sensual. This is particularly significant in the context of our technologically accelerated culture where technology, and in particular social media, is shaping the way that we communicate, interact and think of others and ourselves. Our increased connectivity has blurred many boundaries, the personal and the public, the virtual and the real, avatars act as symbolic selves for their creators thus merging true and idealized selves, while language itself has been abridged to reflect such changes. Critics like Nicholas Carr have noted how the boundaries of space, dimension and depth are also blurred moving us from the three dimensional world to two dimensional screen spaces and "intimate portable worlds that increasingly enclose us".[92] Another critic of the contemporary age of digital connectivity, Sherry Turkle, has discussed in *Reclaiming Conversation: The Power of Talk in the Digital Age* the damaging consequences of never being far from email or text or Twitter or Facebook and the impact it has on family life, on education, on romance and on the possibilities of solitude.[93] In her previous book *Alone Together, Why We Expect More From Technology and Less From Each Other*, Turkle had warned that:

> When online life becomes your game, there are new complications. If lonely, you can find continual connection. But this may leave you more isolated, without real people around you. So you may return to the Internet for another

[90] Tim van der Heijden, "Technostalgia of the present: From technologies of memory to a memory of technologies", *NECSUS*, Autumn 2015. http://www.necsus-ejms.org/technostalgia-present-technologies-memory-memory-technologies/#_edn3 [accessed 03/12/2017].

[91] Brian Eno, *A Year with Swollen Appendices,* London: Faber & Faber, 1996.

[92] Nicholas Carr, "Real Time Kills Real Space", 06/06/2009. http://www.roughtype. com/?p=1233 [accessed 03/05/2017].

[93] Sherry Turkle, *Reclaiming Conversation,* London & New York: Penguin Press, 2015.

> hit of what feels like connection. Again, the Shakespeare paraphrase comes to mind: we are "consumed with that we were nourished by".[94]

Turkle's argument that people are increasingly functioning without face-to-face contact is in sharp contrast to the revival of the 'power of live' discussed at the start of this section, also it has been refuted by several studies which have demonstrated how today public spaces are a more likely source for interacting than they were three decades ago[95] and technology is not driving us apart after all.[96] As sociologist Manuel Castells notes, the rise of the 'Me-centered society', characterised "by an increased focus on individual growth and a decline in community understood in terms of space, work, family, and ascription in general" has not resulted in "the end of community" and "individuation does not mean isolation".[97]

In the end, it is unlikely that we are losing our capacity to relate to each other, how we connect is changing, but our need to connect and relate remains. Considering the role played by nostalgia in these complex social dynamics is crucial to such an understanding.

LONGING FOR THE PAST

How contemporary technologies seem to encourage nostalgia and for what purpose is only one aspect of an intellectually exhilarating, and very complex subject of scholarly inquiry. Succinctly put, nostalgia has different functions, it is used to evoke, influence and activate a range of emotional responses, affecting all areas of contemporary life. Yet, nostalgia is as much about fantasy as it is about memory. Indeed, a certain degree of ingenuity and imagination is inherent in the term itself, which was coined in the 17th century by the young physician Johannes Hofer who joined the two Greek roots, *nostos* meaning 'return home' and *algia* 'longing' to describe the symptoms of homesick Swiss mercenaries.[98]

In the "Nostalgia" episode of her popular *Digital Human* series for BBC Radio 4, academic and broadcaster Aleks Krotoski asks whether the Internet is "a nostalgia machine trapping us in the past".[99] Krotoski's question is fitting if one considers that

---

[94] Sherry Turkle, *Alone Together,* New York: Basic Books, 2013, 227.

[95] Keith N. Hampton. "Change in the Social Life of Urban Public Spaces: The Rise of Mobile Phones and Women, and the Decline of Aloneness over 30 years", Urban Studies, 29/05/2014. http://usj.sagepub.com/content/early/2014/05/28/0042098014534905 [accessed 03/11/2017].

[96] Mark Oppenheimer, "Technology Is Not Driving Us Apart After All", *New York Times*, 17/01/2014. http://www.nytimes.com/2014/01/19/magazine/technology-is-not-driving-us-apart-after-all.html?_r=0 [accessed 02/04/2017].

[97] Manuel Castells, "The Impact of the Internet on Society: A Global Perspective 2014", OpenMind, 2014. https://www.bbvaopenmind.com/en/article/the-impact-of-the-internet-on-society-a-global-perspective/?fullscreen=true [accessed 30/10/2017].

[98] As Svetlana Boym jokingly notes, Hofer also suggested *nosomania* and *philopatridomania* to describe the same symptoms but that "luckily, these failed to enter common parlance" in "Nostalgia and Its Discontents", *Hedgehog Review*, 9:2, Summer/July, 2007, 7-18.

[99] Aleks Krotoski, *Digital Human* "Nostalgia", 02/10/2015. http://www.bbc.co.uk/ programmes/b04n31cr [accessed 01/11/2017].

nostalgia is inscribed in the same language of the Internet, with its endless return to a 'home page', not to mention online trends like Throw Back Thursdays,[100] apps like Timehop, Twitter accounts like Retronaut or Old Pics Archive and the vogue for digital photograph apps such as Hipstamatic and Instagram, which give snapshots the period look associated with an analogue camera. We live in a world where nostalgia for the past permeates every aspect of our digital present. Furthermore, we are perfectly comfortable with feeding the nostalgia machine ourselves, thus becoming willing accomplices of our own entrapment. As Will Self has pointed out: "the preservation of individual memories, once a laborious process, has become increasingly cheaper and ubiquitous, but it wasn't until the last decade that the seamless interconnection of mobile recording devices with the world wide web allowed for the retention of the past almost in its entirety".[101] Thus, we have reached a state of Total recall,[102] in fact "Total recall seems to be the goal", Andreas Huyssen writes, before asking "Is this an archivist's fantasy gone mad?"[103]

Opinions differ as to whether "Social media's function as a conveyor belt of bite-sized nostalgia" allowing anything we have ever entered "to be spat back out on a whim"[104] is a cause of grief or comfort. As Mary Beth Oliver, co-director of the Media Effects Research Laboratory at Penn State puts it: "I don't think nostalgia is necessarily pain free [...] There's a reason we call it bittersweet".[105] The problem is that algorithms are not (yet) capable of discerning the right kind of nostalgia for us, the poignant and useful one, from the one which plunges us into depression.[106] Besides, it might be possible that social media is killing nostalgia, as Charlotte Lytton believes, by making redundant our ability to have nostalgic moments at a time when everything can be archived. Conversely, the ongoing expansion of social media might be bringing nostalgia back to its roots. For Katharina Niemeyer: "The way to keep in touch with your home country is through the mobile phone and social networks" so, she argues: "family members and friends from the past will pass along movies, music, art, everything they're missing while off on their journey. Social media, then, becomes a way to mainline the initial emotion that had doctors scratching their heads back in the 1600s: homesickness. Nostalgia becomes what it used to be".[107]

---

[100] This is a trend among social media sites such as Instagram, Twitter and Facebook wherein users post or repost older photographs with the hashtag #ThrowbackThursday.

[101] Will Self, "A Point of View: Nostalgia - it's not like it used to be", 14/12/2012. http://www.bbc.co.uk/news/magazine-20726824 [accessed 02/02/2018].

[102] *Total Recall* is a 1990 film directed by Paul Verhoeven and inspired by the 1966 short story "We Can Remember it for You Wholesale" by Philip K. Dick. It seemed only fitting to recycle the title for this essay since it effectively captures the paradoxical nature of the relationship between nostalgia and memory.

[103] Quoted in Simon Reynolds, *Retromania: Pop Culture Addiction to Its Own Past,* London: Faber & Faber, 2011, 56.

[104] Rick Paulas, "The WayBack Machine", The Morning News, 07/10/2015. http://www.themorningnews.org/article/the-wayback-machine [accessed 09/11/ 2017].

[105] in Josh Dzieza, "Facebook's new nostalgia feature is already bringing up painful memories", *The Verge*, 2/04/ 2015. http://www.theverge.com/2015/4/2/8315897/facebook-on-this-day-nostalgia-app-bringing-back-painful-memories [accessed 02/05/2017].

[106] See Scott Bryan, "12 Reasons Why Timehop is Guaranteed to Make You Feel Depressed", 03/07/2014. http://www.buzzfeed.com/scottybryan/back-to-the-future#.tnkGzxZaX [accessed 30/10/2017].

[107] In Paulas, "The WayBack Machine".

The above views might not be mutually exclusive; nostalgia is a frustrating field of study, as one of the most influential scholars of the field noted.[108] Perhaps it is exquisitely fitting that some of the most valuable insights into nostalgia have come from the *émigré* Svetlana Boym, photographer, novelist, playwright, Harvard professor and author of *The Future of Nostalgia*.[109] Boym distinguishes between two types of nostalgia: "Restorative nostalgia does not think of itself as nostalgia, but rather as truth and tradition", whereas "Reflective nostalgia dwells on the ambivalences of human longing and belonging and does not shy away from the contradictions of modernity. Restorative nostalgia protects the absolute truth, while reflective nostalgia calls it into doubt".[110]

Such distinctions are not intended as "absolute binaries", Boym warns us, there are in fact some "grey areas" and an inherent paradox in modern nostalgia, in that:

> the universality of its longing can make us more empathetic towards fellow humans, and yet the moment we try to repair that longing with a particular belonging—or the apprehension of loss with a rediscovery of identity and especially of a national community and unique and pure homeland—we often part ways with others and put an end to mutual understanding. *Algia* (or longing) is what we share, yet *nostos* (or the return home) is what divides us.[111]

The above passage is not only persuasive, but exemplary in its understanding of contemporary intolerance towards migrants and related, misguided intentions to build walls, "unreflective nostalgia can breed monsters", Boym writes echoing Goya's motto for his famous etching "The Sleep of reason produces monsters" (1799).[112]

For Boym it is apropos that the "global epidemic of nostalgia" has appeared when we are at most fascinated with cyberspace and the virtual global village. In fact, "there is a yearning for a community with a collective memory, a longing for continuity in a fragmented world". In this sense, nostalgia works as "a defence mechanism in a time of accelerated rhythms of life and historical upheavals".[113] This might explain why, as Simon Reynolds writes in *Retromania* "instead of being the threshold to the future, the first ten years of the twenty-first century turned out to be the 'Re' Decade [...] dominated by the 're-' prefix: revivals, reissues, remakes, re-enactments. Endless retrospection".[114] As for the word 'retro', from its original reference "to a self-conscious fetish for period stylisation (in music, clothing, design) expressed creatively through pastiche and citation" it now has come "to describe pretty much anything that relates to the relatively recent past of popular culture".[115] Thus, retromania is not

---

[108] Boym, "Nostalgia and Its Discontents", 11.
[109] Svetlana Boym, *The Future of Nostalgia,* New York: Basic Books, 2001.
[110] Boym, "Nostalgia and Its Discontents", 13.
[111] *Ibid.*, 9.
[112] *Ibid.*, 10.
[113] *Ibid.*
[114] Simon Reynolds, Retromania: Pop Culture Addiction to Its Own Past, London: Faber & Faber, 2011, xi.
[115] *Ibid.*, xii-xiii.

limited to our rediscovered passion for vinyl or print books, as discussed in the previous section, it includes fashion, video games, photography and television programmes. But what does the success of a retro-television show like *Mad Men* (2007-15), to pick one of the most popular, tell us about our age? Mark Greif believes that:

> *Mad Men* is an unpleasant little entry in the genre of Now We Know Better. We watch and know better about male chauvinism, homophobia, anti-semitism, workplace harassment, housewives' depression, nutrition and smoking. [...] *Mad Men* is currently said to be the best and 'smartest' show on American TV. We're doomed.[116]

Whereas for Richard Williams, "*Mad Men* [...] allows viewers to experience – albeit vicariously – a whole range of pleasures that are now more or less forbidden. These include smoking [...]; drinking [...]; extra-marital sex".[117]

Both perspectives seem viable and complement each other perfectly. Unsurprisingly, the US fashion chain *Banana Republic* following the success of the show launched a "*Mad Men* Limited Edition Collection" with the slogan "you'd be mad not to", where the "not to" alludes simultaneously to acquiring such trendy retro-garments and having sexual liaisons. Reynolds is right when he reminds us that "Rummaging through yesterday's wardrobe closet has been integral to the fashion industry for some time" and that "Fashion is the nexus between late capitalism and culture, where they intermesh".[118] The link between the logic of late capitalism and nostalgia, in its popular expression as retromania is a valid one because it explains how a pre-packaged usable past is industrially produced to function as a marketing device for mass consumption. The cycle of continuous consumption gives rise to a sort of 'newness fatigue' – a frustration with, in Benjamin's words, the 'hellish repetition' of the new as 'always-the-same'.[119] Boym acutely observes that: "The sheer overabundance of nostalgic artefacts marketed by the entertainment industry [...] reflects a fear of untameable longing and non-commodified time".[120] Boym's comments are inspiring, however one could argue that 'the fear of untameable

---

[116] Mark Greif, "You'll Love the Way It Makes You Feel", *London Review of Books*, 30, 20, 23/10/2008, 15-16. http://www.lrb.co.uk/v30/n20/mark-greif/youll-love-the-way-it-makes-you-feel [accessed 03/02/2017].

[117] Richard Williams, "Forbidden Pleasures", 08/11/2013. http://richardjwilliams.net/tag/ breaking-bad/ [accessed 03/10/2017].

[118] Reynolds, *Retromania,* 421. For some images of the Banana Republic *Mad Men* collection see http://tinyurl.com/zm5qr7z [accessed 21/03/2017]

[119] Susan Buck-Morss, *The Dialectics of Seeing: Walter Benjamin and the Arcades Project,* Cambridge: MIT Press, 1989, 108.

[120] Boym, "Nostalgia and Its Discontents", 11.

longing' she refers to underscores the archetypal fear of the Feminine.[121] Longing is a woman's condition, if one is to believe Google.[122]

Furthermore, even TV shows like *The Great British Bakeoff* (2010-) end up (unwillingly?) celebrating the toxic marriage of traditional British values and conventional gender roles, as the 50s styled "Keep Calm and Watch Great British Bakeoff" poster by JMK[123] 'pinned' on social network Pinterest reveals.

One aspect of contemporary retromania omitted so far regards those communities of retrophiles[124] who, in Boym's words on nostalgia above, long "for continuity in a fragmented world". Are such communities also evidence that nostalgia works as "a defence mechanism in a time of accelerated rhythms of life and historical upheavals"? As Fiona Smith and Mary Brown point out, following their examination of retrophilic discourses on Internet sites:

> it is not that people necessarily have a longing for some authentic and original concept of the past itself – it may be, however, the completeness of past experience that they really desire. Ironically, retrophiles are able to have retro-lifestyles successfully because they live in the present, where their experiences are enhanced by the choice afforded to them by both the consumer society and the Internet. It could be said that retrophilia is not possible except in a postmodern society where people can exercise endless choice in the retro-marketplaces.[125]

The next section is going to focus on the ironies of retromania identified by Smith and Brown without following though the established theoretical framework of postmodernism. It is possible in fact that the internet has rendered postmodernism obsolete as an artistic strategy by assimilating its principles and making them accessible to everyone.[126] The ironies still abound, only they should be viewed through the multilayered hybridity lens of the post-digital.

---

[121] Erich Neumann, *The Fear of the Feminine and Other Essays on Feminine Psychology,* Princeton: Princeton University Press, 1994.

[122] A Google.UK image search for 'longing' returns mostly women in various 'longing contexts', see http://tinyurl.com/ha99w3b [accessed 21/03/2017].

[123] See the JMK poster at https://uk.pinterest.com/pin/498914464940875731/ [accessed 21/03/2017]. For a thought-provoking discussion of the "Keep Calm and Carry On" poster as an example of "austerity nostalgia" see Owen Hatherley, "Keep Calm and Carry On – the sinister message behind the slogan that seduced the nation", The Guardian, 08/01/2016. http://www.theguardian.com/books/2016/jan/08/keep-calm-and-carry-on-posters-austerity-ubiquity-sinister-implications?CMP=share_btn_tw [accessed 09/01/2017].

[124] Brown and Smith define the term 'retrophile' as "a wide classification that includes re-enactors (home front re-enactors; 'pin-up' girls; big band singers), lifestyle enthusiasts (people who try to replicate particular styles and who meet with other enthusiasts at 1940s' events), people who like 'old' films (1940s or 1950s Hollywood cinema)". Mary Brown and Fiona Smith, "Negotiating meaning in the consumption of the past", *Journal of Fandom Studies*, 2, 2 October 2014, 147-161.

[125] *Ibid.*, "Negotiating meaning", 158.

[126] Jennifer Allen, "Postmodern Postmortem", Frieze, 133, September 2010. http://www.frieze.com/issue/article/postmodern-postmortem/ [accessed 10/11 2017].

THE POST-DIGITAL CONDITION

Simon Reynolds would certainly agree with the spirit of Emerson's epigraph above. "When we listen back to the early 21st century", he asks, "will we hear anything that defines the epoch? Or will we just find a clutter of reproduction antique sounds and heritage styles?" For Reynolds "We live in the digital future, but we're mesmerised by our analogue past".[127]

Mesmerising is exactly how one might describe the image of the analogue phone reproduced below. There is even a spectral quality to it - a conceptual dimension not at all alien to the study of media[128] – which manifests itself in the rotary dial, in the shadowy, haptic traces of the human fingers which once used it. Is it possible that old media do not die but they just come back to haunt us?[129]

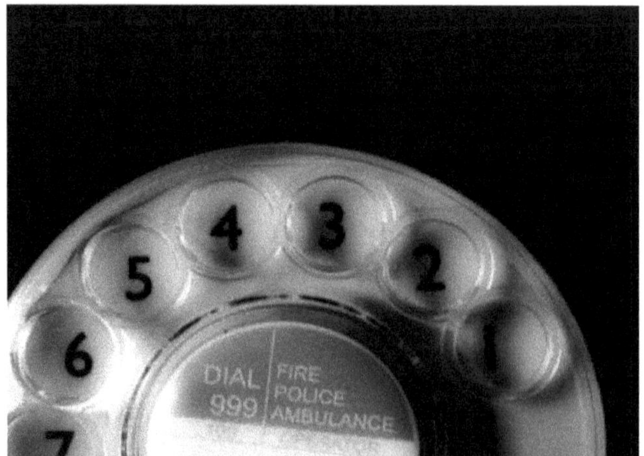

Fig.1. Photo by Ferdinand von Prondzynski (reproduced with permission)

It is more plausible that the photo, taken with an iPhone6 camera and edited with Photoshop, represents the multilayered hybridity that characterizes the post-digital condition. We seem to be caught in a transitional state, torn between our love for the past and the mundane objects of personal memory, and our attraction for the present and the alluring promises of the future. We are seduced by technology's Promethean power and by the illusion of agency it confers us. Manipulating the image of an old analogue phone masquerades our desire to shape our lives across eternal continuity, it

---

[127] Simon Reynolds, "Total recall: why retromania is all the rage", *The Guardian,* 02/06/ 2011. http://www.theguardian.com/music/2011/jun/02/total-recall-retromania-all-rage [accessed 01/02/2018].

[128] Fred Botting and Catherine Spooner, eds., *Monstrous media/spectral subjects: Imaging gothic fictions from the nineteenth century to the present*, Manchester: Manchester University Press, 2015.

[129] "History teaches us that old media never die—and they don't even necessarily fade away. What dies are simply the tools we use to access media content—the 8-track, the Beta tape. These are what media scholars call *delivery technologies"* Henry Jenkins, *Convergence Culture: where old and new media collide*, New York: University Press, 2006, 16.

reassures us that our earthly existence remains *uno tenore*, one uninterrupted breath, as Kierkegaard writes in *Stages on Life's Way*.[130] It is only because we have this capacity to form a narrative of our lives that we can develop a sense of personal identity, that we can master our fears of mortality, that we can pretend to be the gods of our visual and emotional universe. We are not only *what*, but also *how* we remember.

Hybridity as a concept originated in the 1990s with the work of Homi K. Bhabha[131] to describe the ambivalent nature of post-colonial identity, the concept is worth revisiting, following Florian Cramer, to reflect upon the post-digital hybridity of 'old' and 'new' media. Cramer's starting example is the "You're not a real hipster – until you take your typewriter to the park" meme from 2013, that is the image of a young man typing on a mechanical typewriter while sitting on a park bench. The young man's intention was to promote his storytelling services while sitting in the park, the typewriter was pragmatically the technology most suitable for the task. For Cramer, the meme:

> illustrates the post-digital hybridity of 'old' and 'new' media, since the writer advertises (on the sign on his typewriter case) his Twitter account "@rovingtypist", and conversely uses this account to promote his story-writing service. He has effectively repurposed the typewriter from a prepress tool to a personalised small press, thus giving the 'old' technology a new function usually associated with 'new media', by exploiting specific qualities of the 'old' which make up for the limitations of the 'new'.[132]

Crucially, in Cramer's view, "there is a qualitative difference between simply using superficial and stereotypical ready-made effects, and the thorough discipline and study required to make true 'vintage' media work, driven by a desire for non-formulaic aesthetics".[133] This is not the place to dwell on the conceptual intricacies of the term 'vintage' which spans from oenology to media, to quote from the title of Katharina Niemeyer's insightful piece on the topic,[134] it is preferable instead to focus upon the 'qualitative difference' which, for Cramer, makes post-digital practices 'meaningful', that is: "when they do not merely revive older media technologies, but functionally repurpose them in relation to digital media technologies: zines that become anti-blogs or non-blogs, vinyl as anti-CD, cassette tapes as anti-MP3, analogue film as anti-video".[135] This is an interesting adaptation of the concept of

---

[130] Søren Kierkegaard, *Stages on Life's Way*, Princeton: Princeton University Press, 1988, (1845).

[131] Homi K. Bhabha, *The Location of Culture*, London: Routledge, 1994.

[132] Florian, Cramer, "What is 'Post-digital'?" *APRJA*, 3:1, 2014. http://www.aprja.net/? p=1318 [accessed 01/11/2017].

[133] *Ibid.*

[134] Katharina Niemeyer, "A theoretical approach to vintage: From oenology to media", NECSUS, Autumn, 2015. http://www.necsus-ejms.org/a-theoretical-approach-to-vintage-from-oenology-to-media/ [accessed 10/12/2017].

[135] Cramer, "What is 'Post-digital'?"

remediation, as developed by Bolter and Grusin,[136] which describes how new visual media achieve their cultural significance precisely by paying homage to, rivalling, and refashioning old media (and vice versa).

One of the best examples to illustrate what Cramer defines as the need for "thorough discipline and study required to make true 'vintage' media work" is the analogue camera movement and *The Lomography Society International*, in particular. The company founded in 1992 by Austrian students who stumbled upon an old Russian camera while in Prague, now employs some 400 mainly young people and has over three dozen gallery shops around the world. In the words of Bastian Schürholz, Lomography's retail expansion manager, "We're not against digital photography [...] We like to keep the analogue spirit alive".[137] Lomography is more than an old-fashioned analogue technique, it presents itself as a whole lifestyle based on two apparently contradictory mottos: "leave the digital grime behind" and "Live offline but share online", which coexist successfully since "living analogue is sexy, contagious, tantalising", however "a little helping of digital technology is not a crime".[138] Lomography does not forgo the Internet and the techno-economic realities of our time, it proposes a hybrid coexistence by recalibrating technology's functions and purposes.[139] Hybrid recalibrations, albeit of a different sort, are common in the post-digital age, if one considers Kickstarter projects like "Hemingwright", which combines the renowned writer appeal (Hemingway) and the retro look and functionality of a mechanical keyboard with an e-ink display for a 'distraction free' writing experience, all for a retail price of $499.[140] The theme of the old technology able to rescue today's users from the vulnerabilities of the digital one is also behind the reappraisal of the classic typewriter as "unhackable" technology, following Snowden's revelations and the heated debate on issues of surveillance and privacy.[141] Not exactly a rescue, rather a hybrid marriage is the one proposed by artists-musicians Brian Eno and Karl Hyde who released an augmented reality app, Eno • Hyde, as a promo for their 2014 album, "Someday World". As we read in the promotion material, the app "takes the classic medium of vinyl and marries it with image

---

[136] David Bolter and Richard Grusin, *Remediation*, Boston: MIT Press, 1999.

[137] THEME, "Leave the Digital Grime Behind", 28/03/2012. http://www.the.me/lomography-leave-the-digital-grind-behind/#ixzz3rq7C8V49 [accessed 03/09/2017].

[138] http://www.lomography.com/ [accessed 21/03/2017].

[139] This is in contrast to other subcultures which reject 'techo-capitalist value systems' and turn to zine style paper-n-scissors magazines, typewriters, and VHS film as forms of expression and exploration. As an example, see "Follow Me on Dead Media", a videography on an alternative skateboarding scene in Helsinki by Joonas Rokka, Pekka Rousi and Vessi Hämäläinen, https://vimeo.com/104001507 [accessed on 20/03/2017].

[140] Darrell Etherington, "Hemingwrite Modernizes the Typewriter with an E-Ink Screen and Cloud Storage", *Techcrunch*, 10/12/2014. http://techcrunch.com/2014/12/10/hemingwrite/ [accessed 03/03/2017].

[141] Siobhan Lyons, "Typewriters are back, and we have Edward Snowden to thank", The Washington Post, 12/11/2014. https://www.washingtonpost.com/posteverything/wp/ 2014/11/12/typewriters-are-back-and-we-have-edward-snowden-to-thank/ [accessed 15/11/2017]. Small consolation is perhaps the fact that "Privacy is not the only illusion in the new age of data; government secrecy is too. Big Brother might be watching, but he is also being watched" David von Drehle, "The Surveillance Society", *Time*, 1/08/2013. http://nation.time.com/2013/08/01/the-surveillance-society/ [accessed 01/02/2018].

recognition and augmented reality technology, in a melding of analogue and digital worlds".[142]

This essay took its lead from Simon Jenkins' somewhat narrow view that the post-digital age is all about 'human congregation' and the 'power of live', so it might be apt to approach its conclusions by discussing *Portals* (2011), "an evening-length multi-media musical exploration of the human longing for connection in the digital age".[143] The strong production features violinist Tim Fain (also producer and creative director) and interweaves films by Kate Hackett, performances by pianist Nicholas Britell, dance films choreographed and directed by Benjamin Millepied, and the words of Leonard Cohen spoken by Fred Child, with the music of Pulitzer Prize winners William Bolcom and Aaron Jay Kernis. The concert/recital is conceived as "an onstage 'dialogue' between live and multimedia works"[144] with Fain performing live while the other artists are seen on video, projected on a large screen behind him. Fain also makes screen appearances, sometimes playing a second violin line. The inspiration for *Portals* originated from Fain's collaboration with acclaimed musician Philip Glass on the *Book of Longing* (2007), a Song Cycle based on Leonard Cohen's poetry, however Portals is more ambitious, in that it aims to explore "the ways in which we communicate, and, through communication, find meaning in the digital age".[145] Fain is well aware that "In an era when our expressions of love and sorrow, of togetherness and longing—such private emotions—are sometimes displayed so publicly on the web, the potential for artistic communication through digital media is endless".[146] The intention to exploit such endless potential is confirmed when watching *Portals'* official trailer, for pianist Nicholas Britell, *Portals* "breaks the boundaries of what to expect from a concert", while for film director Kate Hackett, the work is about "how we perceive 'live' performance and what our expectations are for what a performance should be".[147] In an interview with Vogue Fain elaborates further on his intentions:

> I've always been fascinated by how visuals make sound more clear [...] I wanted to expand on what a performance can be. Plenty of people use video, but I wanted to make something that really reflected growing up with Skype and Facebook—I mean, I'm addicted to my phone as much as everybody else, but I wanted to use that for something compelling and beautiful".[148]

[142] Synthhead, "Brian Eno & Karl Hyde Release Augmented Reality App", 23/05/ 2014. http://www.synthtopia.com/content/2014/05/23/eno-%E2%80%A2-hyde-ios-app/#more-57115 [accessed 03/04/2015].
[143] http://www.portalsproject.com/ [accessed 21/03/2017].
[144] *Ibid.*
[145] *Ibid.*
[146] *Ibid.*
[147] *Ibid.*
[148] Molly Creeden, "Classical Music Gets a Modern Update in the Hands of Violinist Tim Fain", *Vogue*, 20/09/2011. http://www.vogue.com/873785/classical-music-gets-a-modern-update-in-the-hands-of-violinist-tim-fain/ [accessed 01/02/2018].

Portals has been very successfully received, a reviewer for *The Australian* defined it as poignantly as: "pensive, poetic and mesmerising [...] a superb demonstration of what is possible when sense and sentiment are the drivers of cross-art-form multimedia collaboration, rather than the novelty of new technology and the incessant quest for innovation".[149]

The conclusion to draw from artistic practices like *Portals* is that there is much more to the post-digital condition than a 'crumbling of the internet' before the 'power of live', such power can coexist with other fascinating experimentations, also capable of stirring enthralling human emotions. Technology's capacity to distract us in a vortex of meaningless noise and relentless consumption is paralleled by an endless capacity to create, to turn late modernity into a site for a renewed craft, if only we can turn our digital addictions into "something compelling and beautiful", to quote Fain. Similarly, behind our longing for the past, as expressed in contemporary retromania, lies much more than postmodern vacuity or loss of history. As Jean Baudrillard[150] argued, a nostalgic sensibility is the best mechanism we have to engage with history in the present, to cope with loss and to shape our future.

Bibliography

Allen, Jennifer, "Postmodern Postmortem", *Frieze*, 133, September 2010. http://www.frieze.com/issue/article/postmodern-postmortem/ [accessed 10/11/2017].

Bartmanski, Dominik and Ian Woodward, *Vinyl: The Analogue Record in the Digital Age*, London: Bloomsbury Publishing, 2015.

Baudrillard, Jean, "History: A Retro Scenario" *Simulacra and simulation* Ann Arbor: University of Michigan Press, 1994, 43-8.

Bhabha, Homi, K. *The Location of Culture*, London: Routledge, 1994.

Bilton, Nick, "An E-Book Fan, Missing the Smell of Paper and Glue", *New York Times*, 18/06/2012.

http://bits.blogs.nytimes.com/2012/06/18/caught-between-nostalgia-for-print-and-the-practicality-of-digital/ [accessed 03/11/2017].

Botting Fred and Catherine Spooner, eds, *Monstrous Media/Spectral Subjects: Imaging Gothic Fictions from the Nineteenth Century to the Present*, Manchester: Manchester University Press, 2015.

Boym, Svetlana, *The Future of Nostalgia*, New York: Basic books 2001.

———, "Nostalgia and Its Discontents", *Hedgehog Review*, 9, 2, Summer/July 2007, 7-18.

Brown Mary and Fiona Smith, "Negotiating meaning in the consumption of the past", *Journal of Fandom Studies*, 2, 2 October 2014, 147-161.

Bolter David and Richard Grusin, *Remediation*, Boston: MIT Press, 1999.

Bryan, Scott, "12 Reasons Why Timehop is Guaranteed to Make You Feel Depressed", 3/07/2014. http://www.buzzfeed.com/scottybryan/back-to-the-future#.tnkGzxZaX [accessed 30/10/2017].

Buck-Morss, Susan, *The Dialectics of Seeing: Walter Benjamin and the Arcades Project*, Cambridge: MIT Press, 1989.

---

[149] Eamonn Kelly, "Perfect union of sight and sound", *The Australian* 29/10/2012. http://www.theaustralian.com.au/arts/perfect-union-of-sight-and-sound/story-e6frg8n6-1226504832214 [accessed 01/02/2018].

[150] Jean Baudrillard, "History: A Retro Scenario" *Simulacra and Simulation*, Ann Arbor: University of Michigan Press, 1994, 43-8.

Butler, Sarah, "Tesco to sell LPs for first time in its history", *The Guardian,* 4/12/2015. http://www.theguardian.com/business/2015/dec/04/tesco-to-sell-lps-for-first-time-in-its-history?CMP=Share_iOS App_Other [accessed 10/12/ 2017].

Carr, Nicholas, "Real Time Kills Real Space", 06/06/2009. http://www.roughtype.com/?p=1233 [accessed 03/05/2017].

Castells, Manuel, "The Impact of the Internet on Society: A Global Perspective 2014", *OpenMind* ,2014. https://www.bbva openmind.com/en/article/the-impact-of-the-internet-on-society-a-global-perspective/?fullscreen=true [accessed 30/10/2017].

Christensen, Clayton, *The Innovator's Dilemma,* New York: Harvard Business School Press, 1997.

Cox, Jamieson, "Vinyl sales are more valuable than ad-supported streaming in 2015", *The Verge*, 28/09/2015. http://www.theverge.com/2015/9/28/9408233/vinyl-sales-ad-supported-streaming-riaa-2015-report [accessed 31/10/2017].

Cramer, Florian, "What is 'Post-digital'?" *APRJA*, 3, 1, 2014. http://www.aprja.net/?p=1318 [accessed 01/11/2017].

Creeden, Molly, "Classical Music Gets a Modern Update in the Hands of Violinist Tim Fain", *Vogue*, 20/09/ 2011. http://www.vogue.com/ 873785/classical-music-gets-a-modern-update-in-the-hands-of-violinist-tim-fain/ [accessed 30/09/2017].

von Drehle, David, "The Surveillance Society", *Time,* 01/08/2013. http://nation.time.com/2013/08/01/the-surveillance-society/ [accessed 01/02/2018].

Dzieza, Josh, "Facebook's new nostalgia feature is already bringing up painful memories", *The Verge*, 2/04/ 2015. http://www.theverge.com/2015/4/2/8315897/facebook-on-this-day-nostalgia-app-bringing-back-painful-memories [accessed 02/05/2017].

Eno, Brian, *A Year with Swollen Appendices,* London: Faber & Faber, 1996.

Etherington, Darrell, "Hemingwrite Modernizes the Typewriter with an E-Ink Screen and Cloud Storage", *Techcrunch* 10/12/2014. http://tech crunch.com/2014/12/10/hemingwrite/ [accessed 03/03/2017].

Fernyhough, Charles, *Pieces of Light,* London: Profile Books, 2013.

Flatt, Molly, "The ebook is dead, long live the ebook", *The Memo* 8/12/2015 http://www.thememo.com/2015/12/08/the-ebook-is-dead-long-live-the-ebook/ [accessed 15/12/2017].

Foster, Patrick, "Vinyl sales boom as young music fans move beyond online streaming", *The Telegraph,* 11/12/2015. http://www.telegraph.co.uk/news/shopping-and-consumer-news/12044846/Return-of-the-record-Tesco-first-supermarket-to-sell-vinyls.html [accessed 12/12/2017].

Greif, Mark, "You'll Love the Way It Makes You Feel", *London Review of Books*, 30:20, 23/10/2008, 15-16. http://www.lrb.co.uk/v30/n20/mark-greif/youll-love-the-way-it-makes-you-feel [accessed 03/02/2017].

Hampton, Keith, N. "Change in the social life of urban public spaces: The rise of mobile phones and women, and the decline of aloneness over 30 years", *Urban Studies*, 29/05/2014. http://usj.sagepub.com/content/early/2014/05/28/ 0042098014534905 [accessed 03/11/2017].

Hatherley, Owen, "Keep Calm and Carry On – the sinister message behind the slogan that seduced the nation", *The Guardian,* 8/01/ 2016. http://www.theguardian.com/books/2016/jan/08/keep-calm-and-carry-on-posters-austerity-ubiquity-sinister-implications?CMP=share_btn_tw [accessed 09/01/2016].

Jenkins, Henry, *Convergence Culture: where old and new media collide*, New York: University Press, 2006.

Jenkins, Simon, "In this post-digital age, we still thrill to the power of live", *The Guardian,* 20/06/2014. http://www.theguardian.com/commentisfree/2014/jun/20/post-digital-thrill-power-of-live-antidote-glastonbury [accessed 03/02/ 2017].

Kelly, Eamonn, "Perfect union of sight and sound", *The Australian* 29/10/ 2012. http://www.theaustralian.com.au/arts/perfect-union-of-sight-and-sound/story-e6frg8n6-1226504832214 [accessed 03/10/2017].

Kierkegaard, Søren, *Stages on Life's Way*, Princeton: Princeton University Press, 1988, (1845).

Krotoski, Aleks, *Digital Human* "Nostalgia", 02/10/2015. http://www.bbc.co.uk/programmes/b04n31cr [accessed 01/11/2017].

Lee, Dave, "Vinyl record sales hit 18-year high", 27/11/2014. http://www.bbc.co.uk/news/technology-30216638 [accessed 28/11/2017].

Levy, Steven, "Amazon: Reinventing the Book", *Newsweek*, 17/11/2007. http://europe.newsweek.com/amazon-reinventing-book-96909?rm=eu [accessed 01/02/2018].

Lomography, "Leave the Digital Grind Behind", http://microsites. lomography.com/prophecies/the-10-prophecies [accessed 01/09/2017].

Lyons, Siobhan, "Typewriters are back, and we have Edward Snowden to thank", *Washington Post*, 12/11/2014. https://www.washingtonpost.com/ posteverything/wp/2014/11/12/typewriters-are-back-and-we-have-edward-snowden-to-thank/ [accessed 15/11/2017].

Mod, Craig, "Future Reading", *AEON*, 01/10/2015. https://aeon.co/essays/stagnant-and-dull-can-digital-books-ever-replace-print [accessed 10/10/2017].

Neumann, Erich, *The Fear of the Feminine and Other Essays on Feminine Psychology*, Princeton: Princeton University Press, 1994.

Niemeyer, Katharina, "A theoretical approach to vintage: From oenology to media", *NECSUS*, Autumn, 2015. http://www.necsus-ejms.org/a-theoretical-approach-to-vintage-from-oenology-to-media/ [accessed 10/12/2017].

Notaro, Anna, "How Networked Communication has changed the ways we tell stories", *Between* http://ojs.unica.it/index.php/between/article/view/1341 Vol 4. No 8, 2014 [accessed 21/03/2017].

Oppenheimer, Mark, "Technology Is Not Driving Us Apart After All", *New York Times*, 17/01/2014. http://www.nytimes.com/2014/01/19/magazine/technolo gy-is-not-driving-us-apart-after-all.html?_r=0 [accessed 02/04/2017].

Paulas, Rick, "The WayBack Machine", *The Morning News*, 7/10/2015. http://www.themorningnews.org/article/the-wayback-machine [accessed 09/ 11/ 2017].

Reynolds, Simon, *Retromania: Pop Culture Addiction to Its Own Past*, London: Faber & Faber, 2011.

———, "Total recall: why retromania is all the rage", *The Guardian*, 02/06/2011. http://www. theguardian.com/music/2011/jun/02/total-recall-retromania-all-rage [accessed 03/06/2017].

Self, Will, "A Point of View: Nostalgia - it's not like it used to be", 14/12/2012. http://www.bbc.co.uk/news/magazine-20726824 [accessed 02/12/2017].

Srivas, Anuj, "The Past, Present and Future of the Printed Book", *The Wire*, 08/11/2015. https://thewire.in/14947/the-past-present-and-future-of-the-printed-book/ [accessed 10/11/2018].

Synthhead, "Brian Eno & Karl Hyde Release Augmented Reality App", 23/05/ 2014. http://www.synthtopia.com/content/2014/05/23/eno-%E2%80%A2-hyde-ios-app/#more-57115 [accessed 03/04/2017].

THEME, "Leave the Digital Grime Behind", 28/03/2012. http://www.the. me/lomography-leave-the-digital-grind-behind/#ixzz3rq7C8V49 [accessed 03/09/2017].

Turkle, Sherry, *Alone Together*, New York: Basic Books, 2013.

———, *Reclaiming conversation*, London & New York: Penguin Press, 2015.

van der Heijden, Tim, "Technostalgia of the present: From technologies of memory to a memory of technologies", *NECSUS*, Autumn 2015. http://www.necsus-ejms.org/technostalgia-present-technologies-memory-memory-technologies/#_edn3 [accessed 03/12/2017].

Watkinson, Charles, "Are publishers 'pervy for paper' and other twisted thoughts about Google's 'UnBound'", 21/01/2007. http://charleswatkinson.blogspot.co.uk/2007/01/are-publishers-pervy-for-paper-and.html [accessed 03/07/2017].

Williams, Richard, "Forbidden Pleasures", 08/11/2013. http://richardjwilliams.net/tag/breaking-bad/ [accessed 03/10/2017].

Yglesias, Matthew, "Why Amazon just opened a physical bookstore", *Vox*, 5/11/2015. http://www.vox.com/2015/11/5/9672394/amazon-books-physical-store [accessed 06/11/2017].

Notes on Contributors

Ana Lúcia Beck has a PhD in Comparative Literature (UFRGS/King's College London) and a Master in Art History, Theory and Critique (UFRGS). Her main research interest is the relation between words and images in literature and the visual arts. Her recent publications include: "Silent Landscapes: A Comparative Approach to José Leonilson and Louise Bourgeois", *Canadian Review of Comparative Literature* (2017), and "Bleeding Words: Louise Bourgeois's and José Leonilson's Love Images", *Primerjalna književnost* (2016). She currently teaches art history and theory in the Visual Arts Department at Universidade do Estado de Santa Catarina, Florianópolis, Brazil.

Narvika Bovcon is Associate Professor of Visual Communication design specializing in the computer graphic design, information visualization, and graphical user interface design. As a member of the Computer Vision Lab, she teaches at the Faculty of Computer and Information Science of the University of Ljubljana, Slovenia. In 2009, she published a monograph (in Slovenian) *Art in the World of Smart Machines*. Since 2016, she has been the editor of the journal *Likovne besede* (Art Words). Narvika Bovcon and Aleš Vaupotič have co-authored numerous new-media art projects, and are active new-media art producers and curators.

Claudia Cao (Phd) recently completed her Post-Doc Fellowship at the University of Cagliari. Her recent publications include *Le riscritture di Great Expectations. Sei letture del classico dickensiano* (Mimesis Edizioni, 2016), a book on the rewritings of Charles Dickens' *Great Expectations*, and a co-edited volume on sisters and sisterhood in literature and the arts (*Sorelle e sorellanza nella letteratura e nelle arti*, Franco Cesati Editore, 2017). She also co-edited a special issue on "Maschere del tragico" in *Between*, the Italian open-access journal of Comparative Literature (http://ojs.unica.it/index.php/between/issue/ view/93), of whose editorial board she is also a member.

Massimo Fusillo is Professor of Literary Criticism and Comparative Literature at the University of L'Aquila, Italy, where he is Coordinator of the PhD Program on Literary Genres and Vice Chancelor for cultural activities. He is also member of the Executive Council of the International Association of Comparative Literature (ICLA), and of the Academia Europaea. His latest book was translated in 2017 by Bloomsbury: *The Fetish. Literature, Cinema, Visual Art* (https://www.bloomsbury.com/us/the-fetish-9781501312359/). He co-edited, together with Stefano Ercolino, Mirko Lino and Luca Zenobi, *Imaginary Films in Literature* (Brill|Rodopi, 2016).

Colm Kenny is a teacher of English and mathematics at second level. He has taught courses in Literature, Comparative Literature and Philosophy of Education at undergraduate and postgraduate levels, and continues to tutor and teach part-time at

Dublin City University' Institute of Education. He recently completed his doctoral studies written on ethics, education and narrative fiction under the supervision of Brigitte Le Juez and Francesca Lorenzi. His latest work deals with "The Port and Promise of Comparative Literature for Ethics Education: A Comparative Study of Jean-Pierre and Luc Dardenne's *La Promesse* and Aki Kaurismäki's *Le Havre*".

Brigitte Le Juez is a retired Associate Professor of Comparative Literature, Dublin City University, Ireland. She is the current chief editor of the *Journal of the European Society of Comparative Literature* (https://escl-selc.eu/). Her research interests include literary cinema, film adaptation, ekphrasis, imagology and reception theory. She co-edited, with Olga Springer, a volume of essays, *Shipwreck and Island Motifs in Literature and the Arts* (Brill, 2015). Among her 2017 publications, two special issues as guest editor on "Longing and Belonging", one with *The Wenshan Review*, and the other with *Between*. More on https://dcu.academia.edu/BrigitteLeJuez.

Panayiota Mini is Associate Professor in Film History at the Department of Philology of the University of Crete, Greece. Her PhD dissertation (UW-Madison, 2002) concerned Pudovkin's silent cinema. She has published essays on Greek cinema and Soviet cinema, including a chapter on Soviet cinema in *The Routledge Companion to Cinema and Politics* (ed. Yannis Tzioumakis and Claire Molloy, 2016). Her monograph (in Greek) on *The Filmic Form of Pain and of Aching Recollection: Takis Kanellopoulos' Modernism* is in print from the National Bank of Greece Cultural Foundation. http://www.philology.uoc.gr/staff/mini/.

Anna Notaro is Senior Lecturer in Contemporary Media Theory at Duncan of Jordanstone College of Art & Design, University of Dundee, UK. Recent publications include: "The many futures of the book", *PKn* (2012, https://ojs.zrc-sazu.si/primerjalna_knjizevnost/ issue/download/578/215), and "How Networked Communication has changed the ways we tell stories", *Between* (2014, http://ojs.unica.it/ index.php/between/article/view/1341). Work in progress: "Knocking on Europe's door: how narratives of fear, insecurity and nostalgia shape collective perceptions of immigration". Personal homepage: www.notarofam.com/annawork. Twitter: @Notanna1.

Carlinda Nuñez is Associate Professor at Rio de Janeiro State University, Brazil. She holds a PhD (1991) in Comparative Literature from Rio de Janeiro Federal University. Her main research interest is the reception of Classics. Her present project, "Under the sign of Atlas: Survival of the Ancient in Theories and Fictions of the 20th and early 21st centuries", focuses on the intercultural manifestations of classical culture in contemporary literature, arts, media and cultural life, as do her publications, such as "Ismene, Princess of Thebes, and the Postmodern Pathos" (*Soletras Revista*, 2016, http://www.e-publicacoes.uerj.br/index.php/ soletras/ article/view/28930).

Maria Cristina Ribas is Associate Professor at Rio de Janeiro State University, Brazil. She holds a PhD (1998) in Literary Theory from Rio de Janeiro Federal University. Her current research focuses on Intermediality and the project

"Discussions and Literary Re-readings in Contemporary Times: the Media Transposition". Recently published works in Brazilian academic journals include: "Literature and Cinema: a Brief Theoretical Walk in the Adaptation Woods"; "Chatwin and Herzog, Book and Film: Intertwined Lives in Brazilian Backlands"; "A Singular Dialogue between Chan-Wook's Film *Handmaiden* and Waters' Novel *Fingersmith*" (forthcoming).

Nina Shiel received her PhD from Dublin City University, Ireland, in 2015 for her Irish Research Council-funded project on ekphrasis of virtual worlds in contemporary science fiction. She has examined the concept of ekphrasis in digital contexts in the collections *Internet Research, Theory and Practice: Perspectives from Ireland* (ed. Cathy Fowley, Claire English & Sylvie Thouësny, Research-publishing.net, 2013) and *Metamorphoses of (New) Media* (ed. Julia Genz and Ulrike Kuehle, Cambridge Scholars Publishing, 2015). She has a strong interest in interdisciplinary research and is currently based in Lancaster University.

Aleš Vaupotič is Dean of the School of Humanities and Head of the Research Centre for Humanities at the University of Nova Gorica, Slovenia. As Associate Professor, he teaches literary theory, world literature and digital humanities. In his work he combines artistic and scholarly approaches. His areas of research include semiotics, digital humanities, theory of new media and theory of literary realism. Narvika Bovcon and Aleš Vaupotič have co-authored numerous new-media art projects, and are active new-media art producers and curators.

Beata Waligorska-Olejniczak is Associate Professor and Head of the Department of Comparative Studies in Literature and Culture at the Institute of Russian and Ukrainian Philology of Adam Mickiewicz University in Poznan, Poland. She is the (co)author of three monographs (in Polish): *New Russian Cinema and the Literary and Film Tradition* (2017), *Sacrum on the Way: Venedict Erofeev's* Moscow-Petushki, *Quentin Tarantino's* Pulp Fiction *and Montage Reading* (2013) and *Theatrical Gesture in Chekhov's* The Seagull *and Free Dance: the Aesthetic Context of the Great Theatre Reform* (2009). https://amu.academia.edu/WaligorskaOlejniczak.

Mark Wallace was awarded his PhD from Dublin City University, Ireland, in 2016 for the thesis *The Unspeakable Victorian: Thomas Carlyle, Ideology and Adaptation*. He then worked in DCU's Higher Education Research Centre and recently co-edited the *Guide for Universities Engaging in Social Responsibility* (UNIBILITY, 2017) with Dr Katharina Resch of the University of Vienna. His work on recent adaptations of Sherlock Holmes will appear in the collection *Adaptation as a Collaborative Art: Process and Practice* (ed. Bernadette Cronin, Rachel MagShamhráin and Nikolai Preuschoff, Palgrave Macmillan, 2018 [forthcoming]).

Index

D

E

F

G

H

I

J

K

L

M

N

O

P

R

S

Appendix

Images and details of work(s) in Chapter 11:

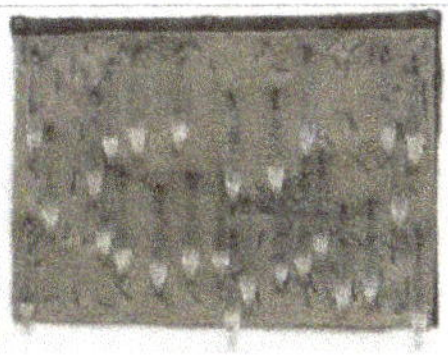

PL.1296.0/00
Voilá mon Coeur, c. 1989
Crystals, thread, felt, and metallic paint on unstretched canvas 22 x 30 x 2 cm
Photo: Edouard Fraipont / ©Projeto Leonilson

Voilá mon Coeur [reverse]
Thread on unstretched canvas
22 x 30
©Projeto Leonilson

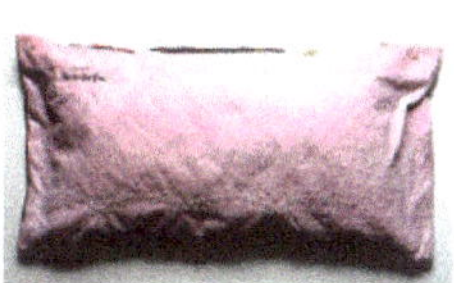

PL.0847.0/00
Ninguém, 1992
Thread on embroidered cotton pillowcase, chequered cotton fabric, and pillow
23,5 x 46 x 5 cm
Photo: Edouard Fraipont / ©Projeto Leonilson

PL.0820.0/00
Para o meu vizinho de sonhos, c. 1991
Thread on felt
90 x 38 cm
Photo: Rubens Chiri / © Projeto Leonilson

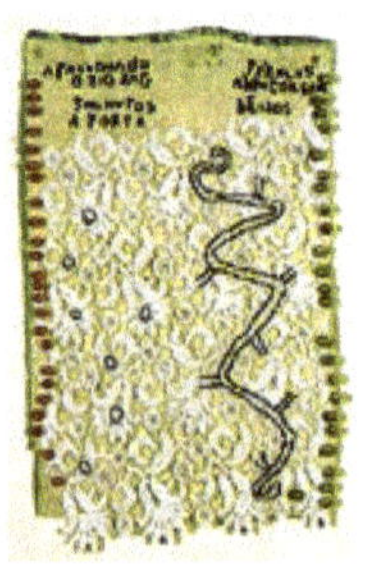

PL.1455.0/00
O apaixonado o zig zag 5 minutos, 1991
Guipure lace, thread, and beads on unstretched canvas 33 x 20,5 cm
Photo: Rubens Chiri / © Projeto Leonilson

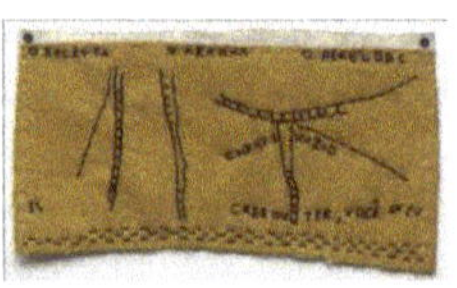

PL.1149.0/00
O recruta; o aranha; o Penélope, 1992 Thread on felt and unstretched canvas
18 x 35 cm
Photo: Edouard Fraipont / ©Projeto Leonilson

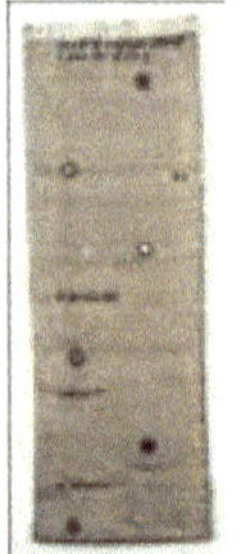

PL.1355.0/00
O Penélope, o recruta, o aranha, c. 1992 Thread and sequins on voile and unstretched canvas 50,5 x 18 cm
Photo: Vicente de Mello / ©Projeto Leonilson

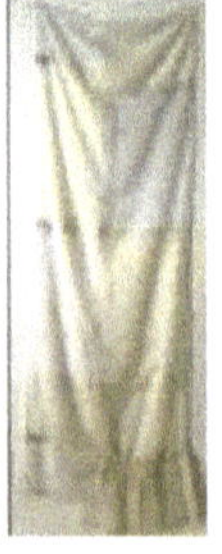

PL.1531.0/00
O Penélope, 1993 Thread on voile 229 x 80 cm
©Projeto Leonilson

PL.1354.0/00
Da pouca paciência, c. 1987
Acrylic paint and cutting on cut unstretched canvas 26 x 41 cm
Photo: Vicente de Mello / ©Projeto Leonilson

www.ingramcontent.com/pod-product-compliance
Lightning Source LLC
LaVergne TN
LVHW052352100826
845147LV00013B/821

* 9 7 8 1 6 1 2 2 9 9 9 2 1 *